Siegel's
CRIMINAL LAW

Essay and Multiple-Choice Questions and Answers

Brian N. Siegel
J.D., Columbia Law School

and

Lazar Emanuel
J.D., Harvard Law School

and

Jason Tannenbaum
J.D., University of Pennsylvania Law School

ΛSPEN

PUBLISHERS

1185 Avenue of the Americas, New York, NY 10036
www.aspenpublishers.com

Aspen Publishers is proud to welcome Emanuel Publishing Corporation's highly successful study aids to its list of law school publications. As part of the Aspen family, Steve and Lazar Emanuel will continue their work on these popular titles, widely purchased by students for more than a quarter century. With the addition of the Emanuel titles, Aspen now offers the most comprehensive selection of outstanding publications for the discerning law student.

About the Authors

Professor Brian N. Siegel received his *Juris Doctorate* from Columbia Law School, where he was designated a Harlan Fiske Stone Scholar for academic excellence. He is the author of *How to Succeed in Law School* and numerous works pertaining to preparation for the California Bar examination. Professor Siegel has taught as a member of the adjunct faculty at Pepperdine School of Law and Whittier College School of Law, as well as for the UCLA Extension Program.

Lazar Emanuel is a graduate of Harvard Law School. In 1950, he became a founding partner of the New York firm now known as Cowan, Liebowitz & Latman. From 1960 through 1971, he was president of Communications Industries Corp., multiple licensee of radio and television stations in the Northeast. Since 1987, he has served as Executive Vice President and General Counsel of Emanuel Publishing Corp. He has edited many of the publications in the Professor Series of study aids and in the Siegel's series of Essay and Multiple-Choice Question & Answer books.

Jason Tannenbaum graduated from Brandeis University in 1984 and received his J.D. from the University of Pennsylvania Law School in 1987. After three years with the firm of Nutter, McClennen & Fish in Boston, he served as Assistant U.S. Attorney for New Jersey from 1990 to 1993. He is presently studying for a Ph.D. in Political Science at Northwestern University.

Acknowledgment

The authors gratefully acknowledge the assistance of the California Committee of Bar Examiners which provided access to questions upon which many of the questions in this book are based.

Introduction

Although your grades are a significant factor in obtaining a summer internship or permanent position at a law firm, no formalized preparation for finals is offered at most law schools. Students, for the most part, are expected to fend for themselves in learning the exam-taking process. Ironically, law school exams ordinarily bear little correspondence to the teaching methods used by professors during the school year. They require you to spend most of your time briefing cases. Although many claim this is "great preparation" for issue-spotting on exams, it really isn't. Because you focus on one principle of law at a time, you don't get practice in relating one issue to another or in developing a picture of the entire course. When exams finally come, you're forced to make an abrupt 180-degree turn. Suddenly, you are asked to recognize, define and discuss a variety of issues buried within a single multi-issue fact pattern. In most schools, you are then asked to select among a number of possible answers, all of which look inviting but only one of which is right.

The comprehensive course outline you've created so diligently and with such pain, means little if you're unable to apply its contents on your final exams. There is a vast difference between reading opinions in which the legal principles are clearly stated, and applying those same principles to hypothetical exams and multiple choice questions.

The purpose of this book is to help you bridge the gap between memorizing a rule of law and **understanding how to use it** in the context of an exam. After an initial overview describing the exam writing process, you will be presented with a large number of hypotheticals which test your ability to write analytical essays and to pick the right answers to multiple-choice questions. **Do them — all of them!** Then review the suggested answers which follow. You'll find that the key to superior grades lies in applying your knowledge through questions and answers, not rote memory.

In the sample answers (both to the essays and to the multiple choice), you will notice occasional references to *Emanuel* on *Criminal Law*. The reference tells you where in the outline to find the relevant discussion. Thus, a reference to "Ch. 5–III(A)(5)(d)" means Chapter 5, section (Roman numeral) III, capital letter A within that section, number 5, paragraph d. This notation is perhaps less convenient than page numbers, but it helps us keep the reference constant from one edition of a book to the next.

GOOD LUCK !

Table of Contents

Essay Answers

Multiple Choice Questions

Answers to Multiple Choice Questions

Tables and Index

Preparing Effectively for Essay Examinations[1]

To achieve superior scores on essay exams, a student must (i) learn and understand "blackletter" principles and rules of law for each subject, and (ii) analyze how those principles of law arise within a test fact pattern. One of the most common misconceptions about law school is that you must memorize each word on every page of your casebooks or outlines to do well on exams. The reality is that you can commit an entire casebook to memory and still do poorly on an exam. Reviewing hundreds of student answers has shown us that most students can recite the rules. The ones who do **best** on exams understand how problems (issues) stem from the rules which they have memorized and how to communicate their analysis of these issues to the grader. The following pages cover what you need to know to achieve superior scores on your law school essay exams.

The "ERC" Process

To study effectively for law school exams you must be able to **"ERC"** (**E**lementize, **R**ecognize, and **C**onceptualize) each legal principle listed in the table of contents of your casebooks and course outlines. **Elementizing** means reducing the legal theories and rules you learn, down to a concise, straightforward statement of their essential elements. Without a knowledge of these precise elements, it is not possible to anticipate all of the potential issues which can arise under them.

For example, if you are asked, "what is self-defense?", it is **not** sufficient to say, "self-defense is permitted when, if someone is about to hit you, you can prevent him from doing it." This layperson description would leave a grader wondering if you had actually attended law school. An accurate elementization of the self-defense principle would be something like this: "Where one reasonably believes she is in imminent danger of an offensive touching, she may assert whatever force she reasonably believes necessary under the circumstances to prevent the offensive touching from occurring." This formulation correctly shows that there are four separate, distinct elements which must be satisfied for this defense to be successfully asserted: (i) the actor must have a **reasonable belief** that (ii) the touching which he seeks to prevent is **offensive**, (iii) the offensive touching is **imminent**, and (iv) the actor must use no greater force than she **reasonably believes is necessary under the circumstances** to prevent the offensive touching from occurring.

---

1. To illustrate the principles of effective exam preparation, we have used examples from Torts and Constitutional Law. However, these principles apply to all subjects. One of the most difficult tasks faced by law students is learning how to apply principles from one area of the law to another. We leave it to you, the reader, to think of comparable examples for the subject-matter of this book.

Recognizing means perceiving or anticipating which words within a legal principle are likely to be the source of issues, and how those issues are likely to arise within a hypothetical fact pattern. With respect to the self-defense concept, there are four *potential* issues. Did the actor reasonably believe that the person against whom the defense is being asserted was about to make an offensive contact upon her? Was the contact imminent? Would the contact have been offensive? Did the actor use only such force as she reasonably believed was necessary to prevent the imminent, offensive touching?

Conceptualizing means imagining situations in which each of the elements of a rule of law have given rise to factual issues. *Unless a student can illustrate to herself an application of each element of a rule of law, she does not truly understand the legal principles behind the rule!* In our opinion, the inability to conjure up hypothetical problems involving particular rules of law foretells a likelihood that issues involving those rules will be missed on an exam. It is therefore *crucial* to (i) *recognize* that issues result from the interaction of facts with the appropriate words defining a rule of law; and ii) develop the ability to *conceptualize* fact patterns involving each of the words contained in the rule

For example, an illustration of the "reasonable belief" portion of the self-defense principle in tort law might be the following:

> One evening, A and B had an argument at a bar. A screamed at B, "I'm going to get a knife and stab you!" A then ran out of the bar. B, who was armed with a concealed pistol, left the bar about 15 minutes later. As B was walking home, he suddenly heard running footsteps coming up from behind him. B drew his pistol, turned and shot the person advancing toward him (who was only about ten feet away when the shooting occurred). When B walked over to his victim, he recognized that the person he had killed was not A (but was instead another individual who had simply decided to take an evening jog). There would certainly be an issue whether B had a reasonable belief that the person who was running behind him was A. In the subsequent wrongful-death action, the victim's estate would certainly contend that the earlier threat by A was not enough to give B a reasonable belief that the person running behind him was A. B could certainly contend in rebuttal that given the prior altercation at the bar, A's threat, the darkness, and the fact that the incident occurred within a time frame soon after A's threat, his belief that A was about to attack him was "reasonable."

An illustration of how use of the word "imminent" might generate an issue is the following:

> X and Y had been feuding for some time. One afternoon, X suddenly attacked Y with a hunting knife. However, Y was able to wrest the knife away From X. At that point X retreated about four feet away from Y and screamed: "You were lucky this time, but next time I'll have a gun and you'll be finished." Y, having good reason to believe that X would subsequently carry out his threats (after all,

X had just attempted to kill Y), immediately thrust the knife into X's chest, killing him. While Y certainly had a reasonable belief that X would attempt to kill him the **next time** the two met, Y would probably **not** be able to successfully assert the self-defense privilege since the "imminency" element was absent.

A fact pattern illustrating the actor's right to use only that force which is reasonably necessary under the circumstances might be following:

D rolled up a newspaper and was about to strike E on the shoulder with it. As D pulled back his arm for the purpose of delivering the blow, E drew a knife and plunged it into D's chest. While E had every reason to believe that D was about to deliver an offensive impact on him, E probably could not successfully assert the self-defense privilege because the force he utilized in response was greater than reasonably necessary under the circumstances to prevent the impact. E could simply have deflected D's prospective blow or punched D away. The use of a knife constituted a degree of force by E which was **not** reasonable, given the minor injury which he would have suffered from the newspaper's impact.

"Mental gymnastics" such as these must be played with every element of every rule you learn.

Issue-Spotting

One of the keys to doing well on an essay examination is issue-spotting. In fact, issue spotting is **the** most important skill you will learn in law school. If you recognize all of the legal issues, you can always find an applicable rule of law (if there is any) by researching the issues. However, if you fail to perceive an issue, you may very well misadvise your client about the likelihood of success or failure. It is important to remember that (1) an issue is a question to be decided by the judge or jury; and (2) a question is "in issue" when it can be disputed or argued about at trial. The bottom line is that if **you don't spot an issue, you can't discuss it**.

The key to issue-spotting is to approach a problem in the same way as an attorney would. Let's assume you're a lawyer and someone enters your office with a legal problem. He will recite the facts to you and give you any documents that may be pertinent. He will then want to know if he can sue (or be sued, if your client seeks to avoid liability). To answer your client's question intelligently, you will have to decide the following: (1) what theories can possibly be asserted by your client; (2) what defense or defenses can possibly be raised to these theories; (3) what issues may arise if these theories and defenses are asserted; (4) what arguments can each side make to persuade the factfinder to resolve the issue in his favor; and (5) finally, what will the **likely** outcome of each issue be. **All the issues which can possibly arise at trial should be discussed in your answer.**

How to Discuss an Issue

Keep in mind that *rules of law are the guides to issues* (i.e., an issue arises where there is a question whether the facts do, or do not, satisfy an element of a rule); a rule of law *cannot dispose of an issue* unless the rule can reasonably be *applied to the facts.*

A good way to learn how to discuss an issue is to start with the following mini-hypothetical and the two student responses which follow it.

Mini-Hypothetical

A and B were involved in making a movie which was being filmed at a bar. The script called for A to appear to throw a bottle (which was actually a rubber prop) at B. The fluorescent lighting at the bar had been altered, the subdued blue lights being replaced with rather bright white lights. The cameraperson had stationed herself just to the left of the swinging doors which served as the main entrance to the bar. As the scene was unfolding, C, a regular patron of the bar, unwittingly walked into it. The guard who was stationed immediately out-side the bar, had momentarily left his post to visit the restroom. As C pushed the barroom doors inward, the left door panel knocked the camera to the ground with a resounding crash. The first (and only) thing which C saw, how-ever, was A (who was about 5 feet from C) getting ready to throw the bottle at B, who was at the other end of the bar (about 15 feet from A). Without hesita-tion, C pushed A to the ground and punched him in the face. Plastic surgery was required to restore A's profile to its Hollywood-handsome pre-altercation form.

Discuss A's right against C.

Pertinent Principles of Law:

1. Under the rule defining the prevention-of-crime privilege, if one sees that someone is about to commit what she reasonably believes to be a felony or misdemeanor involving a breach of the peace, she may exercise whatever degree of force is reasonably necessary under the circumstances to prevent that person from committing the crime.

2. Under the defense-of-others privilege, where one reasonably believes that someone is about to cause an offensive contact upon a third party, she may use whatever force is reasonably necessary under the circumstances to prevent the contact. Some jurisdictions, however, limit this privilege to situations in which the actor and the third party are related.

First Student Answer

"Did C commit an assault and battery upon A?

"An assault occurs where the defendant intentionally causes the plaintiff to be reasonably in apprehension of an imminent, offensive touching. The facts state that C punched A to the ground. Thus, a battery would have occurred at this point. We are also told that C punched A in the face. It is reasonable to assume that A saw the punch being thrown at him, and therefore A felt in imminent danger of an offensive touching. Based upon the facts, C is liable for an assault and battery upon A.

"Were C's actions justifiable under the defense-of-others privilege?

"C could successfully assert the defense of others and prevention of crime privileges. When C opened the bar doors, A appeared to be throwing the bottle at B. Although the "bottle" was actually a prop, C had no way of knowing this fact. Also, it was necessary for C to punch A in the face to assure that A could not get back up, retrieve the bottle, and again throw it at B. While the plastic surgery required by A is unfortunate, C could not be successfully charged with assault and battery."

Second Student Answer

"Assault and Battery:

"C committed an assault (causing A to be reasonably in apprehension of an imminent, offensive contact) when A saw C's punch about to hit him, and battery (causing an offensive contact upon A) when he (i) C knocked A to the ground, and (ii) C punched A.

"Defense-of-Others/Prevention-of-Crime Defenses:

"C would undoubtedly assert the privileges of defense-of-others (where defendant reasonably believed the plaintiff was about to make an offensive contact upon a third party, he was entitled to use whatever force was reasonably necessary to prevent the contact); and prevention-of-crime defense (where one reasonably believes another is about to commit a felony or misdemeanor involving a breach of the peace, he may exercise whatever force is reasonably necessary to prevent that person from committing a crime).

"A could contend that C was not reasonable in believing that A was about to cause harm to B because the enhanced lighting at the bar and camera crash should have indicated to C, a regular customer, that a movie was being filmed. However, C could probably successfully contend in rebuttal that his belief was reasonable in light of the facts that (i) he had not seen the camera when he attacked A, and (ii) instantaneous action was required (he did not have time to notice the enhanced lighting around the bar).

"A might also contend that the justification was forfeited because the degree of force used by C was not reasonable, since C did not have to punch A in the face after A had already been pushed to the ground (i.e., the danger to B was no longer present). However, C could argue in rebuttal that it was necessary to knockout A (an individual with apparently violent propensities) while the opportunity existed, rather than risk a drawn-out scuffle in which A might prevail. The facts do not indicate how big A and C were; but assuming C was not significantly larger than A, C's contention will probably be successful. If, however, C was significantly larger than A, the punch may have been excessive (since C could presumably have simply held A down)."

Critique

Let's examine the First Student Answer first. It mistakenly phrases as an "issue" the assault and battery committed by C upon A. While the actions creating these torts must be mentioned in the facts to provide a foundation for a discussion of the applicable privileges, there was no need to discuss them further because they were not the issue the examiners were testing for.

The structure of the initial paragraph of First Student Answer is also incorrect. After an assault is defined in the first sentence, the second sentence abruptly describes the facts necessary to constitute the commission of a battery. The third sentence then sets forth the elements of a battery. The fourth sentence completes the discussion of assault by describing the facts pertaining to that tort. The two-sentence break between the original mention of assault and the facts which constitute this tort is confusing; the facts which call for the application of a rule should be mentioned *immediately* after the rule is stated.

A more serious error, however, occurs in the second paragraph of the First Student Answer. While there is an allusion to the correct principle of law (prevention of crime), the *rule is not defined*. As a consequence, the grader can only guess why the student thinks the facts set forth in the subsequent sentences are significant. A grader reading this answer could not be certain that the student recognized that the issues revolved around the *reasonable belief* and *necessary force* elements of the prevention-of-crime privilege. Superior exam-writing requires that the pertinent facts be *tied* directly and clearly to the operative rule.

The Second Student Answer is very much better than the First Answer. It disposes of C's assault and battery upon A in a few words (yet tells the grader that the writer knows these torts are present). More importantly, the grader can easily see the issues which would arise if the prevention-of crime-privilege were asserted (i.e., "whether C's belief that A was about to commit a crime against B was reasonable" and "whether C used unnecessary force in punching A after A had been knocked to the ground"). Finally, it also utilizes all the facts by indicating how each attorney would assert those facts which are most advantageous to her client.

Structuring Your Answer

Graders will give high marks to a clearly-written, well-structured answer. Each issue you discuss should follow a specific and consistent structure which a grader can easily follow.

The Second Student Answer above basically utilizes the *I-R-A-A-O format* with respect to each issue. In this format, the *I* stands for the word *Issue*, the *R* for *Rule of law*, the initial *A* for the words *one side's Argument*, the second *A* for *the other party's rebuttal Argument*, and the *O* for your *Opinion as to how the issue would be resolved.* The *I-R-A-A-O* format emphasizes the importance of (1) discussing *both* sides of an issue, and (2) communicating to the grader that where an issue arises, an attorney can only advise her client as to the *probable* decision on that issue.

A somewhat different format for analyzing each issue is the *I-R-A-C format.* The *"I"* stands for *"Issue;"* the *"R"* for *"Rule of law;"* the *"A"* for *"Application of the facts to the rule of law;"* and the *"C"* for *"Conclusion."* I-R-A-C is a legitimate approach to the discussion of a particular issue, within the time constraints imposed by the question. The *I-R-A-C format* must be applied to each issue; it is not the solution to an entire exam answer. If there are six issues in a question, for example, you should offer six separate, independent *I-R-A-C* analyses.

We believe that the *I-R-A-C* approach is preferable to the *I-R-A-A-O* formula. However, either can be used to analyze and organize essay exam answers. Whatever format you choose, however, you should be consistent throughout the exam and remember the following rules:

First, *analyze all of the relevant facts.* Facts have significance in a particular case *only as they come under the applicable rules of law.* The facts presented must be analyzed and examined to see if they do or do not satisfy one element or another of the applicable rules, and the essential facts and rules must be stated and argued in your analysis.

Second, you must communicate to the grader the *precise rule of law* controlling the facts. In their eagerness to commence their arguments, students sometimes fail to state the applicable rule of law first. Remember, the *"R"* in either format stands for "Rule of Law." Defining the rule of law *before* an analysis of the facts is essential in order to allow the grader to follow your reasoning.

Third, it is important to treat *each side of an issue with equal detail.* If a hypothetical describes how an elderly man was killed when he ventured upon the land of a huge power company to obtain a better view of a nuclear reactor, your sympathies might understandably fall on the side of the old man. The grader will nevertheless expect you to see and make every possible argument for the other side. Don't permit your personal viewpoint to affect your answer! A good lawyer never does! When discussing an issue, always state the arguments for each side.

Finally, don't forget to *state your opinion or conclusion* on each issue. Keep in mind, however, that your opinion or conclusion is probably the *least* important part of an exam answer. Why? Because your professor knows that no attorney can tell her client exactly how a judge or jury will decide a particular issue. By definition, an issue is a legal dispute which can go either way. An attorney, therefore, can offer her client only her best opinion about the likelihood of victory or defeat on an issue. Since the decision on any issue lies with the judge or jury, no attorney can ever be absolutely certain of the resolution.

Discuss All Possible Issues

As we've noted, a student should draw *some* type of conclusion or opinion for each issue raised. Whatever your conclusion on a particular issue, it is essential to anticipate and discuss *all of the issues* which would arise if the question were actually tried in court.

Let's assume that a negligence hypothetical involves issues pertaining to duty, breach of duty, proximate causation and contributory negligence. If the defendant prevails on any one of these issues, he will avoid liability. Nevertheless, even if you feel strongly that the defendant owed no duty to the plaintiff, you *must* go on to discuss all of the other potential issues as well (breach of duty, proximate causation and contributory negligence). If you were to terminate your answer after a discussion of the duty problem only, you'd receive an inferior grade.

Why should you have to discuss every possible potential issue if you are relatively certain that the outcome of a particular issue would be dispositive of the entire case? Because at the commencement of litigation, neither party can be *absolutely positive* about which issues he will win at trial. We can state with confidence that every attorney with some degree of experience has won issues he thought he would lose, and has lost issues on which he thought victory was assured. Since one can never be absolutely certain how a factual issue will be resolved by the factfinder, a good attorney (and exam-writer) will consider *all* possible issues.

To understand the importance of discussing all of the potential issues, you should reflect on what you will do during the actual practice of law. If you represent the defendant, for example, it is your job to raise every possible defense. If there are five potential defenses, and your pleadings only rely on three of them (because you're sure you will win on all three), and the plaintiff is somehow successful on all three issues, your client may well sue you for malpractice. Your client's contention would be that you should be liable because if you had only raised the two additional issues, you might have prevailed on at least one of them, and therefore liability would have been avoided. It is an attorney's duty to raise *all* legitimate issues. A similar philosophy should be followed when taking essay exams.

What exactly do you say when you've resolved the initial issue in favor of the defendant, and discussion of any additional issues would seem to be moot? The answer is simple. You simply begin the discussion of the next potential issue with something like, "Assuming, however, the plaintiff prevailed on the foregoing issue, the next issue would be…" The grader will understand and appreciate what you have done.

The corollary to the importance of raising all potential issues is that you should avoid discussion of obvious non-issues. Raising non-issues is detrimental in three ways: first, you waste a lot of precious time; second, you usually receive absolutely no points for discussing a point which the grader deems extraneous; third, it suggests to the grader that you lack the ability to distinguish the significant from the irrelevant. The best guideline for avoiding the discussion of a non-issue is to ask yourself, "would I, as an attorney, feel comfortable about raising that particular issue or objection in front of a judge"?

Delineate the Transition From One Issue to the Next

It's a good idea to make it easy for the grader to see the issues which you've found. One way to accomplish this is to cover no more than one issue per paragraph. Another way is to underline each issue statement. Provided time permits, both techniques are recommended. The essay answers in this book contain numerous illustrations of these suggestions.

One frequent student error is to write a two-paragraph answer in which all of the arguments for one side are made in the initial paragraph, and all of the rebuttal arguments by the other side are made in the next paragraph. This is *a bad idea*. It obliges the grader to reconstruct the exam answer in his mind several times to determine whether all possible issues have been discussed by both sides. It will also cause you to state the same rule of law more than once. A better-organized answer presents a given argument by one side and follows that immediately in the same paragraph with the other side's rebuttal to that argument.

Understanding the "Call" of a Question

The statements *at the end of* an essay question or of the fact pattern in a multiple-choice question is sometimes referred to as the "call" of the question. It usually asks you to do something specific like "discuss," "discuss the rights of the parties," "what are X's rights?" "advise X," "the best grounds on which to find the statute unconstitutional are:," "D can be convicted of:," "how should the estate be distributed," etc. The call of the question should be read carefully because it tells you exactly what you're expected to do. If a question asks, "what are X's rights against Y?" or "X is liable to Y for:..." you don't have to spend a lot of time on Y's rights against Z. You will usually receive absolutely no credit for discussing facts that are not required by the question. On the other hand, if the call of an essay question is simply "discuss" or "discuss the rights of the parties" then *all* foreseeable issues must be covered by your answer.

Students are often led astray by an essay question's call. For example, if you are asked for "X's rights against Y" or to "advise X", you may think you may limit yourself to X's viewpoint with respect to the issues. This is *not correct*! You cannot resolve one party's rights against another party without considering the issues which might arise (and the arguments which the other side would assert) if litigation occurred. In short, although the call of the question may appear to focus on one of the parties to the litigation, a superior answer will cover all the issues and arguments which that person might *encounter* (not just the arguments she would *make*) in attempting to pursue her rights against the other side.

The Importance of Analyzing the Question Carefully Before Writing

The overriding *time pressure* of an essay exam is probably a major reason why many students fail to analyze a question carefully before writing. Five minutes into the allocated time for a particular question, you may notice that the person next to you is writing furiously. This thought then flashes through your mind, "Oh, my goodness, he's putting down more words on the paper than I am, and therefore he's bound to get a better grade." It can be stated *unequivocally* that there is no necessary correlation between the number of words on your exam paper and the grade you'll receive. Students who begin their answer after only five minutes of analysis have probably seen only the most obvious issues, and missed many, if not most, of the subtle ones. They are also likely to be less well organized.

Opinions differ as to how much time you should spend analyzing and outlining a question before you actually write the answer. We believe that you should spend at least 12-18 minutes analyzing, organizing, and outlining a one-hour question before writing your answer. This will usually provide sufficient time to analyze and organize the question thoroughly *and* enough time to write a relatively complete answer. Remember that each word of the question must be scrutinized to determine if it (i) suggests an issue under the operative rules of law, or (ii) can be used in making an argument for the resolution of an issue. Since you can't receive points for an issue you don't spot, it is usually wise to read a question *twice* before starting your outline.

When to Make an Assumption

The instructions on an exam may tell you to *"assume"* facts which are necessary to the answer. Even where these instructions are *not* specifically given, you may be obliged to make certain assumptions with respect to missing facts in order to write a thorough answer. Assumptions should be made when you, as the attorney for one of the parties described in the question, would be obliged to solicit additional information from your client. On the other hand, assumptions should *never be used to change or alter the question.* Don't ever write something like "if the facts in the question were ..., instead of ..., then ... would result." If you do this, you are wasting time on facts which are extraneous to the problem before you. Professors want you to deal with *their* fact patterns, not your own.

Students sometimes try to "write around" information they think is missing. They assume that their professor has failed to include every piece of data necessary for a thorough answer. This is generally *wrong*. The professor may have omitted some facts deliberately to see if the student *can figure out what to do* under the circumstances. In some instances, the professor may have omitted them inadvertently (even law professors are sometimes human).

The way to deal with the omission of essential information is to describe (i) what fact (or facts) are missing, and (ii) why that information is important. As an example, go back to the "movie shoot" hypothetical we discussed above. In that fact pattern, there was no mention of the relative strength of A and C. This fact could be extremely important. If C weighed 240 pounds and was built like a professional football linebacker, while A tipped the scales at a mere 160 pounds, punching A in the face after he had been pushed to the ground would probably constitute unnecessary force (thereby causing C to forfeit the prevention-of-crime privilege). If the physiques of the parties were reversed, however, C's punch to A's face would probably constitute reasonable behavior. Under the facts, C had to deal the *"knockout"* blow while the opportunity presented itself. The last sentences of the Second Student Answer above show that the student understood these subtleties and correctly stated the essential missing facts and assumptions.

Assumptions should be made in a manner which keeps the other issues open (i.e., necessitates discussion of all other possible issues). Don't assume facts which would virtually dispose of the entire hypothetical in a few sentences. For example, suppose that A called B a "convicted felon" (a statement which is inherently defamatory, *i.e.,* a defamatory statement is one which tends to subject the plaintiff to hatred, contempt or ridicule). If A's statement is true, he has a complete defense to B's action for defamation. If the facts don't tell whether A's statement was true or not, it would *not* be wise to write something like, "We'll assume that A's statement about B is accurate, and therefore B cannot successfully sue A for defamation." So facile an approach would rarely be appreciated by the grader. The proper way to handle this situation would be to state, "if we assume that A's statement about B is not correct, A can not raise the defense of truth." You've communicated to the grader that you recognize the need to assume an essential fact and that you've assumed it in such a way as to enable you to proceed to discuss all other potential issues.

Case Names

A law student is ordinarily *not* expected to recall case names on an exam. The professor knows that you have read several hundred cases for each course, and that you would have to be a memory expert to have all of the names at your fingertips. If you confront a fact pattern which seems similar to a case which you have reviewed (but you cannot recall the name of it), just write something like, "One case held that ..." or "It has been held that ..." In this manner, you have informed the grader that you are relying on a case which contained a fact pattern similar to the question at issue.

The only exception to this rule is in the case of a landmark decision. Landmark opinions are usually those which change or alter established law.[2] These cases are usually easy to identify, because you will probably have spent an entire class period discussing each of them. *Palsgraf v. Long Island Rail Road* is a prime example of a landmark case in Torts. In these special cases, you may be expected to remember the case by name, as well the proposition of law which it stands for. However, this represents a very limited exception to the general rule which counsels against wasting precious time trying to memorize case names.

---

2. The only subject to which this does not apply is Constitutional Law, since here virtually every case you study satisfies this definition. Students studying Constitutional Law should try to associate case names with holdings and reproduce them in their exam answers.

How To Handle Time Pressures

What do you do when there are five minutes left in the exam and you have only written down two-thirds of your answer? One thing *not* to do is write something like, "No time left!" or "Not enough time!" This gets you nothing but the satisfaction of knowing you have communicated your personal frustrations to the grader. Another thing *not* to do is insert the outline you may have made on scrap paper into the exam booklet. Professors rarely will look at these items.

First of all, it is not necessarily a bad thing to be pressed for time. The person who finishes five minutes early has very possibly missed some important issues. The more proficient you become in knowing what is expected of you on an exam, the greater the difficulty you may experience in staying within the time limits. Second, remember that (at least to some extent) you're graded against your classmates' answers and they're under exactly the same time pressure as you. In short, don't panic if you can't write the "perfect" answer in the allotted time. Nobody does!

The best hedge against misuse of time is to *review as many old exams as possible*. These exercises will give you a familiarity with the process of organizing and writing an exam answer, which, in turn, should result in an enhanced ability to stay within the time boundaries. If you nevertheless find that you have about 15 minutes of writing to do and five minutes to do it in, write a paragraph which summarizes the remaining issues or arguments you would discuss if time permitted. As long as you've indicated that you're aware of the remaining legal issues, you'll probably receive some credit for them. Your analytical and argumentative skills will already be apparent to the grader by virtue of the issues that you have previously discussed.

Write Legibly

Make sure your answer is legible. Students should *not* assume that their professors will be willing to take their papers to the local pharmacist to have them deciphered. Remember, your professor may have 75-150 separate exam answers to grade. If your answer is difficult to read, you will rarely be given the benefit of the doubt. On the other hand, a legible, well-organized paper creates a very positive mental impact upon the grader.

Many schools allow students to type their exams. If you're an adequate typist, you may want to seriously consider typing. Typing has two major advantages. First, it should help assure that your words will be readable (unless, of course, there are numerous typos). Second, it should enable you to put a lot more words onto the paper than if your answer had been handwritten. Most professors prefer a typed answer to a written one.

There are, however, a few disadvantages to typing. For one thing, all the typists are usually in a single room. If the clatter of other typewriters will make it difficult for you to concentrate, typing is probably *not* wise. To offset this problem, some students wear earplugs during the exam. Secondly, typing sometimes makes it difficult to change or add to an earlier portion of your answer. You may have to withdraw your paper from the carriage and insert another. Try typing out a few practice exams before you decide to type your exam. If you do type, be sure to leave at least one blank line between typewritten lines, so that handwritten changes and insertions in your answers can be made easily.

If you decide against typing, your answer will probably be written in a "bluebook" (a booklet of plain, lined, white paper which has a light blue cover and back). It is usually a good idea to write only on the odd numbered pages (i.e., 1, 3, 5, etc.). You may also want to leave a blank line between each written line. Doing these things will usually make the answer easier to read. If you discover that you have left out a word or phrase, you can insert it into the proper place by means of a caret sign ("∧"). If you feel that you've omitted an entire issue, you can write it on the facing blank page. A symbol reference can be used to indicate where the additional portion of the answer should be inserted. While it's not ideal to have your answer take on the appearance of a road map, a symbol reference to an adjoining page is much better than trying to squeeze six lines into one, and will help the grader to discover where the same symbol appears in another part of your answer.

The Importance of Reviewing Prior Exams

As we've mentioned, it is *extremely important to review old exams.* The transition from blackletter law to essay exam can be a difficult experience if the process has not been practiced. Although this book provides a large number of essay and multiple-choice questions, *don't stop here*! Most law schools have recent tests on file in the library, by course. We strongly suggest that you make a copy of every old exam you can obtain (especially those given by your professors) at the beginning of each semester. The demand for these documents usually increases dramatically as "finals time" draws closer.

The exams for each course should be scrutinized *throughout the semester.* They should be reviewed as you complete each chapter in your casebook. Generally, the order of exam questions follows the sequence of the materials in your casebook. Thus, the first question on a law school test may involve the initial three chapters of the casebook; the second question may pertain to the fourth and fifth chapters, etc. In any event, *don't wait* until the semester is nearly over to begin reviewing old exams.

Keep in mind that no one is born with the ability to analyze questions and write superior answers to law school exams. Like any skill, it is developed and perfected only through application. If you don't take the time to analyze numerous examinations from prior years, this evolutionary process just won't occur. Don't just *think about* the answers to past exam questions; take the time to *write the answers down*. It's also wise to look back at an answer a day or two after you've written it. You will invariably see (i) ways in which the organization could have been improved, and (ii) arguments you missed.

As you practice spotting issues on past exams, you will see how rules of law become the sources of issues on finals. As we've already noted, if you don't *understand* how rules of law translate into issues, you won't be able to achieve superior grades on your exams. Reviewing exams from prior years should also reveal that certain issues tend to be lumped together in the same question. For instance, where a fact pattern involves a false statement made by one person about another, three potential theories of liability are often present — defamation, invasion of privacy (false, public light) and intentional infliction of severe emotional distress. You will need to see if any or all of these apply to the facts.

Finally, one of the best means of evaluating if you understand a course (or a particular area within a subject) is to attempt to create a hypothetical exam for that topic. Your exam should contain as many issues as possible. If you can write an issue-packed exam, you probably know that particular area of law. If you can't, then you probably haven't yet acquired an adequate understanding of how the principles of law in that subject can spawn issues.

As Always, a Caveat

The suggestions and advice offered in this book represent the product of many years of experience in the field of legal education. We are confident that the techniques and concepts described in these pages will help you prepare for, and succeed, at your exams. Nevertheless, particular professors sometimes have a preference for exam-writing techniques which are not stressed in this work. Some instructors expect at least a nominal reference to the *prima facie* elements of all pertinent legal theories (even though one or more of those principles is *not* placed into issue). Other professors want their students to emphasize public policy considerations in the arguments they make on a particular issue. Because this book is intended for nationwide consumption, these individualized preferences have *not* been stressed. The best way to find out whether your professor has a penchant for a particular writing approach is to ask her to provide you with a model answer to a previous exam. If an item is not available, speak to upperclass students who received a superior grade in that professor's class.

One final point. While the rules of law stated in the answers to the questions in this book have been drawn from commonly used sources (i.e., casebooks, hornbooks, etc.), it is still conceivable that they may be slightly at odds with those taught by your professor. In instances where a conflict exists between our formulation of a legal principle and the one which is taught by your professor, *follow the latter!* Since your grades are determined by your professors, their views should always supersede the views contained in this book.

Essay Exam Questions

Question 1

David broke into the home of Arnold. No one was at home. After taking several expensive items, David attempted to escape from Arnold's house. Arnold, however, arrived home from a hunting trip just as David was climbing out a side window. Arnold yelled at David to stop, but David began to run down the street. Arnold grabbed his hunting rifle and attempted to shoot David in the leg. The bullet missed David, but fatally shot Bill, who was driving a car down David's street. Edith, Bill's wife, was also in the car and suffered a stroke after seeing her husband shot. The car rolled into a tree and came to a stop. Fred, a passerby, opened the driver's door with the intention of assisting the occupants. However, when he saw the bullet wound in Bill's chest, Fred decided there was nothing he could do. Fred noticed that Bill wore an expensive watch and began to remove it. Bill opened one eye and faintly motioned Fred away. Fred, however, took the watch off Bill's hand, saying, "You won't need this where you're going, my friend." Moments later, Bill died. Subsequently, Arnold, David and Fred were apprehended by the police.

What crimes were committed and by whom?

Question 2

Able, a police undercover agent, invited Baker and Charley, whom Able suspected of having committed a series of recent crimes, to her home for a few drinks. Able mentioned to them how impressed she was with the daring and skill of the persons responsible for the recent crimes. Baker then suggested that a nearby drugstore would be a "pushover" to rob. Able decided to join in the robbery, in hopes of obtaining evidence of Baker's and Charley's past crimes.

All three drove to the store, which was operated by Dogge. While Baker waited in the car, Charley mingled with several customers in the part of the store nearest the entrance. Able approached Dogge, drew her gun, and handed Dogge a note that read, "I am a police undercover agent. Pretend to be frightened. Give me the money in the cash register." Dogge complied with Able's direction. Able turned to leave and, as she neared Charley, Dogge drew a gun from beneath the counter and fired at Able. The shot missed Able but struck Easey, a customer who was standing in the line of fire. Charley then drew his gun and shot Dogge. Immediately after the shooting, Able replaced the money in the cash register and went to the aid of Dogge. Baker and Charley fled, but were later apprehended.

Dogge recovered from his wounds. Easey initially showed improvement toward recovery of her wounds, but she subsequently contracted a virus while still in the hospital and died.

Discuss the possible criminal culpability of all parties.

Question 3

Bob, age 13, and Hal, age 16, bored by the prospect of another long summer afternoon, set out on their favorite pastime—rummaging through the garages and toolsheds of neighbors. In the past they had sometimes stayed and used the tools found there, but other times they had taken small items. For the first time, Hal's younger brother Mike, age 6, tagged along.

The boys entered Smith's garage, which was attached to the rear of her home, through the closed but unlocked garage door. Bob and Hal rummaged through the tool boxes and practiced cutting wood on the table saw. Mike, alone near a corner shelf in the garage, saw a gold watch that had been left there inadvertently by Smith. Mike picked up the watch, put it in his pocket, and without a word left for home.

After about an hour in the garage, Bob and Hal also left and continued to Jones's toolshed for the stated purpose of taking a large screwdriver that had, on a prior occasion, caught Bob's fancy. Jones's shed was detached and sat about 50 yards from his house, but within a three foot high picket fence that surrounded the shed and house. Although the door was always locked, the boys had never had difficulty in prying open the door, and on this occasion they again broke the lock.

As Hal pushed the door open and stepped into the shed, he was shot in the head, suffering a fatal wound. On the prior evening, Jones had mounted a loaded pistol in the shed, aimed at the door and connected so that the pistol would discharge automatically if the door were pushed open. Jones told the police he mounted the gun to protect his property from thieves, but that he intended only to scare them away and never intended to kill anyone. No statute prohibited the use of spring guns.

1. Bob and Mike are charged with burglary of Smith's garage and larceny of Smith's watch.

2. Bob is charged with burglary of Jones's toolshed.

3. Jones is charged with the murder of Hal.

Discuss the results of each charge.

Question 4

E, an employee of M. Co., knew that his friend A owned a large quantity of obsolete tires. E telephoned A and it was agreed that if E obtained a purchaser for the tires, A would pay E one-half of the selling price as a "finder's fee." The next day, E asked his old friend, X, to have lunch with him. After a few drinks paid for by E, X (an unemployed attorney with numerous unpaid creditors), at E's suggestion, telephoned M. Co. and offered to purchase a large quantity of the type of tires owned by A. After the call, X asked E what they were going to do with the tires. E replied jokingly, "I'll help you sell them, and then we'll drink the proceeds." This answer appeared to satisfy the slightly inebriated X.

That afternoon, after E returned to work, J, the manager of M. Co., told E about the telephone call that she had received from X, and asked E if he knew where that type of tire could be procured. E advised J that he had heard that A owned a large quantity of them. J then called A who offered to sell her tires for $2,000. Since the retail price for the quantity of tires requested by X on the telephone was $3,500, J paid A the $2,000. J then verbally instructed T, the M. Co. delivery person, to transport the tires from A's premises to the location specified by X. J also instructed the delivery person to obtain a certified check before giving the tires to X. When T arrived and began unloading the tires, X was extremely embarrassed (having almost forgotten his earlier call to M. Co.). X reluctantly began to advise T that he wasn't sure he had sufficient funds to buy the tires. However, when T glowered at X and advised him that he didn't want to go through the task of loading the tires back on his truck, X sheepishly wrote out an uncertified check for $3,500. Although T remembered J's instruction to obtain a certified check, it was already late in the afternoon and he didn't want to work overtime. Therefore, T conveniently decided to forget J's verbal instruction. Of course, X's check was returned for "insufficient funds."

J called A and A admitted that she knew E was employed by the M. Co. X contends that he had no knowledge that E was employed by the M. Co. or of any transaction between M. Co., A, and E. X has also advised M. Co. that he will be happy to return the tires if they decline to press criminal charges against him.

Discuss what crime(s), if any, have been committed, and by whom.

Question 5

Dan was in despair over the state of his business because of unfair business practices by Joe, who had opened a store in direct competition with Dan, right across the street. It appeared that Dan would soon be forced out of business. Dan confided in his good friend, Sam, about his gloomy future, telling him, in a half-jesting fashion, that if he were a real friend he would "take care" of Joe and save him from bankruptcy.

The next day Sam, having thought on the plight of his friend Dan, decided to help Dan. To do this he planned to have his court-placed ward, Ace, a 27-year old, mentally handicapped man, break into Joe's store and pour syrup over Joe's merchandise. He explained to Ace that he must put on a skeleton costume and when it was dark he should go into the store Sam would point out and pour the can of syrup all over everything.

The next day Sam told Dan about his plan. Dan replied, "Sounds great, but don't ask me to do anything to help." Sam replied, "All you have to do is sit back and let it happen."

Late the next evening, Sam took Ace to the block where Joe's store was located. Sam pointed out Joe's store and Ace proceeded towards it. Before getting to Joe's, however, he heard a loud scream that frightened him. Disoriented, Ace broke into a business place adjoining Joe's, whereupon he simply hurled the unopened can of syrup towards the rear of the store. Unfortunately, the can of syrup hit a gas line causing an explosion that killed Joe who was in his store taking his end-of-month inventory. The blast also knocked out Ace.

The police arrested Ace. After the police read Ace his *Miranda* rights, Ace told the police why and what he was doing there.

Discuss fully with what crimes Sam and Dan could be charged and with what results.

Question 6

Adams and Barlow frequented the same pool hall. Adams told Barlow that Adams needed help in testing the faithfulness of his girlfriend, Kitty, and, if she proved unfaithful, killing her. The plan was for Adams to bring a box of chocolates laced with LSD to Barlow, who was to offer the chocolates to Kitty. If Kitty accepted the chocolates from Barlow, (a stranger to her), this would satisfy Adams that she was unfaithful to him and deserved to die.

Barlow had always entertained excessive and irrational suspicion and distrust of others. For this reason, and because he feared what Adams would do to him if he refused, he was afraid to refuse to join in the plan.

Adams brought the chocolates to the pool hall, laid the box beside his coat on a bench, and went off to shoot pool. However, Adams had not laced the chocolates with enough LSD to kill a human being. Cox, the proprietor, opened the box and sampled the candy. He soon became unconscious. Adams, discovering Cox and thinking he was dead, put him in a car, drove to a secluded spot across the state line, and left him there. Shortly thereafter Cox died from exposure without regaining consciousness.

Discuss the crime(s) for which Adams and Barlow may be successfully prosecuted.

Question 7

In early November, A, an author, met her friend B, an employee of a publishing company located in a nearby office building. Their discussion focused upon the company's soon-to-be published biographical manuscript about an eccentric billionaire, and upon the amount of money magazines would probably pay to print excerpts of the manuscript. B gave A a drawing of the office, showing exactly where a copy of the manuscript would probably be kept. After carefully reviewing the sketch, A left for the company's building, agreeing to meet B later that night at C's (a mutual friend) apartment with the manuscript. A entered the office through a side door marked on the sketch, took the manuscript, and went to C's apartment (where B was waiting). A, unknowingly, had tripped a silent alarm and the police were able to follow her to the building in which C lived.

Not knowing which apartment the suspect had entered, the police began knocking on every door. Hearing the police search, A and B told C what had happened and A and B hid in the closet. When the police came to C's apartment, C told the officers that he was alone and the police left.

A and B then drove to a local tavern for a few drinks. B went to a table while A walked to the bar and struck up a conversation with the bartender. Sometime later, D, a tavern patron, accidentally brushed against the table, spilling B's drink. A loud argument erupted, and soon B and D were fighting. D was quickly joined by some friends. A entered the fight, drew a knife, and fatally stabbed D. Panicked, A left the tavern and sped away in her car.

A few blocks away, P, a police officer, observed A's vehicle going through a stop sign and began to chase her. Mistakenly believing she was being apprehended for the tavern incident, A increased her speed until it reached 80 mph. P felt she had to take more drastic action to stop the vehicle and began to fire at A's tires. When P finally succeeded in shooting a tire A lost control of her car. The car jumped the curb and struck W, a woman who was waiting for a bus. W died later at the hospital as a result of injuries sustained in the accident.

1. What is the criminal responsibility, if any, of A, B, and C for the office building incident?

2. What is the criminal responsibility, if any, of A and B for D's death?

3. What is the criminal responsibility, if any, of A and P for W's death?

Question 8

In the early afternoon, after several hours of drinking, Ames, Brody, and Cole drove to a local market to purchase more liquor. Ames, the driver, waited in the car while Brody and Cole went in the store.

Just before entering, Brody and Cole realized they had no money. When the clerk placed the requested bottle of whiskey on the counter, Cole picked it up. As the clerk waited for payment, Brody drew a revolver and pointed it at the clerk who gasped and stepped back. The two men ran from the market, Cole waving the bottle and Brody still holding the gun. As they jumped into the waiting car, Brody said to Ames, "Step on it, before the cops get here." Ames drove off at a high speed.

Alerted by radio, officers in a patrol car pursued the fleeing trio and pulled alongside their car when it halted at a stop sign. Brody jumped out and fired at police officers Smith and Jones, killing Smith. A gun battle followed and Cole, who was also armed, joined in the shooting. Brody was then shot and killed by Officer Jones. Officer Jones then apprehended Cole. Ames fled the scene when the gun battle began and was not apprehended until several days later. The jurisdiction has the following murder statute:

1. *Murder.* Murder is the unlawful killing of a human being with malice afore-thought.

2. *Express and Implied Malice.* Such malice may be express or implied. It is express when there is manifested a deliberate unlawful intent to take the life of a fellow human being. It is implied when no reasonable provocation appears or when the circumstances attending the killing show an abandoned and malignant heart.

3. *Murder of First or Second Degree.* All murder that is perpetrated by any kind of willful, deliberate, and premeditated killing or that is committed in the perpetration of, or in an attempt to perpetrate, a robbery or burglary, is murder of the first degree; all other kinds of murder are of the second degree.

Discuss whether Cole and Ames committed: (a) burglary or robbery; and (b) murder and, if so, the degree of murder. Include in your discussion all defenses that each may have.

Question 9

Dave suffered from paranoid schizophrenia that became acute whenever he drank an excessive amount of alcoholic beverages. Dave's closest friend was Vince. Valerie, Vince's girlfriend, lived in a room behind the Pothouse (a local pub). Victoria worked there as a waitress.

One afternoon Dave met Vince at the Pothouse. Vince got drunk, while Dave had five large glasses of beer. Vince ordered sandwiches and told Dave to eat one. When Dave refused, Vince picked up a sandwich and said, "Eat it, you stupid bastard!" Everyone in the Pothouse laughed at Dave. Dave became enraged. He stood up, shook his fist at Vince, and said, "I'll be back and you'll be dead." Dave stomped out and began walking toward his house. En route he passed his friend Homer's house. Dave remembered that Homer had a gun, and felt that Homer would lend it to him if Dave asked. It was dark outside and there were no lights on in the house.

Dave decided to go into Homer's house through the back. He walked around to the back of the house, where he found a sliding glass door that had not been closed, and went inside. Looking for Homer's .357 Magnum revolver, Dave opened a closet door and looked inside. Just then, Dave remembered that Homer kept the gun in a nearby desk. Dave walked over to the desk and took the pistol. Dave walked out the front door of Homer's house, locking it behind him, and began thinking about how he would kill Vince.

Dave went back to the Pothouse where he quickly drank two strong drinks of bourbon and water. He then pulled out the Magnum, walked outside, and kicked open the door to Valerie's room. Vince, Valerie and Victoria were talking in the room. Dave pointed the gun at Vince who was seated right next to Valerie. Valerie screamed. Dave fired one shot killing Vince. The bullet went through Vince, ricocheted, and hit Victoria in the leg. She was not killed.

Discuss Dave's criminal liability, if any.

Question 10

Dr. Erasmus Jones is one of the world's foremost heart surgeons. On April 10, the State Department called him at his home in Connecticut and requested that he perform a heart operation on "a very important figure in world affairs" (they did not tell him the patient's identity). The operation was to be performed on April 12 at Walter Reed Hospital, in Washington, D.C., they said. Jones was further informed that while the operation was a delicate one and that the patient would die without it, it would be a routine one for Jones, who had invented and perfected the technique required. Jones explained that he had just received news that his son had been killed in a traffic accident and he felt entirely too nervous and upset to perform the operation. He was firmly pressed by the State Department and he reluctantly agreed to meet a special Air Force plane at the Hartford airport the morning of April 11 and perform the operation on the 12th.

After the call on the evening of the 10th, several friends visited the doctor to comfort him in his grief. He told them about the call as they began drinking. As the evening progressed and the group became intoxicated, one of the visitors said he had heard that an ill Russian general had just defected to the United States. The group concluded that this was probably the important person in question and urged Jones not to help him. One friend suggested that Jones call the State Department and tell them to go to Hell, but Jones said, "I don't owe them anything. Let 'em find another man if they can. Frankly, I hope the bastard dies." They then all drove up to a remote part of Vermont for a three day fishing trip.

When Jones did not show up at the airport, the State Department tried to locate him, to no avail. The patient, the 75-year-old wife of the Prime Minister of Canada, died of heart failure late in the evening on April 12.

Discuss what crime(s) Jones and his friends could be charged with, and the defenses, if any, they could raise against those charges.

Question 11

A dialed B's number on the telephone. B's phone was answered by C, B's brother, who sounded much like B. A said, "Hey, B, this is A. Your pal T is going to break into X's jewelry store tonight. Let's wait outside the store and grab what he steals. I'll be over at ten o'clock." C hung up the telephone without replying.

A arrived at B's apartment at ten o'clock. C had left earlier without telling B of A's phone call. A explained the reason for his presence to B, and the two hurriedly drove toward the jewelry store. As they neared it, B said, "I've changed my mind. You go ahead if you want, but stop the car and let me out." A did so, then continued onto the store. B paused at a phone booth intending to report A to the police, but changed his mind and walked directly home.

When A arrived at the store, he discovered C already there, watching the front door. In a few minutes, as A also watched, T cautiously approached the store, entered with a master key, and emerged shortly carrying a bag of stolen jewelry. C ran toward T, snatched at the bag but missed it. However, A leaped on T from behind and held his arms while C took the bag from him. A and C then ran toward A's car to escape. The police arrived at this moment, responding to a burglar alarm that T had set off in the store. T surrendered without resistance, but A and C continued to flee. C pulled a pistol and attempted to fire at a pursuing policeman. The gun was defective, however, and exploded when C pulled the trigger, killing him instantly.

Discuss the crimes, if any, of which A, B, and T are guilty.

Question 12

Axe, wanting to get rich the easy way, decided to "pull a job." His plans, however, required the assistance of two others. Therefore, he contacted Boss and Chum and explained his plan to steal Lady Carot's diamonds from her house. Both Boss and Chum agreed to help Axe, and Chum volunteered to "borrow" a car from a friend. Both Axe and Boss were aware that Chum had twice been arrested for car theft. Unknown to Axe and Boss, Chum did not borrow a car, but took Mr. Wheel's car without his permission.

Late that night, Axe, Boss and Chum drove to a spot near Lady Carot's house and quietly approached the rear of the house. As Axe began to open a rear window, Chum thought she heard Lady Carot drive up to the front of the house. Chum was so frightened that she stated she did not want to go through with the plan, and then quickly returned the car to Mr. Wheel's house. As she started to walk away from the car, Chum was arrested.

Meanwhile, Axe and Boss decided to proceed without Chum and entered the house through a rear window. Axe searched upstairs while Boss searched downstairs. Unable to find the diamonds downstairs, Boss advised Axe, "This gig is a bummer; count me out," left the house, and returned home. Axe, also unable to find the diamonds, began to leave when he was confronted by Lady Carot, who was pointing a gun at him. Although she exclaimed, "Freeze or I'll shoot," Axe pushed the gun away and struck her, leaving her unconscious.

Axe and Boss are later arrested.

Discuss.

Question 13

Don, in need of funds, approached his friend Oscar, who sold stereo equipment. Oscar told Don he had no cash to give him, but that he owned thousands of dollars worth of readily saleable and fully insured stereo equipment stored in his own warehouse nearby. Don replied that under the circumstances, Oscar would not lose any money if some of the equipment "disappeared," and Don sold it. Oscar then said he would give Don a duplicate key to the warehouse so that Don, with Don's brother Allen, could remove the equipment, on condition that Don reimburse him for any loss which he could not recover from his insurance company. Don said, "That's great," and left with the key.

Don told Allen about the plan and Allen agreed to help him. Don and Allen entered the warehouse with the key, and the two men loaded Don's truck with $50,000 worth of equipment. After the items were removed and the warehouse locked, it was agreed that Allen would immediately drive the truck and equipment to Mexico, to be joined later by Don. It was also agreed that Don should go home by means of an automobile the two had seen in an enclosed parking area to the rear of the warehouse.

Allen drove away and Don reentered the warehouse to reach the parking area. He took the automobile, drove it through the closed and locked gate of the fence that enclosed the parking area and went to his apartment.

Allen was driving in excess of the speed limit when a highway patrol car attempted to stop him. Allen, believing the theft had been discovered, attempted to escape by driving over 100 mph. In the ensuing chase the highway patrol officer lost control of her patrol car and was killed when the car overturned.

A. Discuss whether Don committed burglary (1) in the removal of the stereo equipment and (2) in the theft of the vehicle.

B. Discuss whether Don is guilty of either murder or manslaughter in the death of the highway patrol officer.

C. Discuss whether Oscar is criminally liable for any crime(s) for which Don is culpable.

Question 14

Dave had arranged with the Fine Arts Gallery to inspect, after its night-time closing, the hanging of Old Masters paintings he had loaned the gallery. While en route to the gallery for such purpose Dave saw Amos, a rival art collector. Dave suspected that Amos had in some way obtained from Dave's office his only memorandum of the address of an obscure art dealer who possessed a painting both Dave and Amos coveted. Dave stepped up behind Amos, struck his pipe in Amos' back, and said, "Don't move or I'll shoot." As Amos raised his arms, Dave took Amos' billfold from his pocket and ran off. Dave took only the memorandum from the billfold and then threw the billfold with the other contents intact, under a street light where he expected Amos to find it.

Dave proceeded to the Fine Arts Gallery where he found the door broken open and the guard, who resided there, bleeding and unconscious from a head wound. Dave grabbed a lance from an exhibit and dashed into the room where his paintings were hanging. There he saw Bob slashing the paintings. Dave was too stunned to react for a moment, but he recovered quickly and threw the lance just as Bob slashed another painting. The lance killed Bob.

Discuss with what crimes Dave can reasonably be charged, and what defenses he may reasonably raise.

Question 15

Clyde was the shipping manager at a plant owned by the Acme Distillery Company. Clyde heard that Bob was in the business of purchasing stolen whiskey and asked Bob if he would be interested in purchasing a truckload. Bob said that he would. Clyde then told Bob to be at Bob's garage around 4:00 p.m. the next day.

The next day, Clyde approached Tank, a truck driver, and offered her $1,000 to drive the truck. Clyde said that he would arrange to have the truck loaded and would alter the shipping records so that the load wouldn't be missed. Clyde also told Tank that he would tell her which truck would be used and where to deliver the whiskey just before Tank left the loading area. Tank replied, "What an unbelievable idea!" Sam, the plant manager, overheard that conversation and contacted the police. The police advised Sam to allow Tank to drive the truck out of the plant and they would follow it to the delivery point. Clyde altered the shipping records so that a truck would be filled with cases of Acme whiskey. Shortly before the truck was completely loaded, however, Tank started to walk towards a telephone to call the police. When Sam and a police officer confronted Tank, she acknowledged that she had "lost her nerve." They instructed her to go through with the plot and not say anything. Tank did this. While Tank and Bob were unloading the truck at Bob's garage, the police arrested Clyde, Tank and Bob.

Discuss the potential criminal culpability of Clyde, Tank, and Bob.

Question 16

Dan proposed to his friend Paul that the two rob the First National Bank (Bank). Paul, thinking that Dan was joking, replied, "Sure, why not?" Dan then produced three pistols and three stocking masks and said, "Okay, let's go." Paul thought that it would be dangerous to back out at that point. He therefore took a pistol, but he secretly resolved to try to thwart the robbery.

On the way to Bank, Dan announced, "We need someone else." Dan then approached a passerby, Mike, pointed a pistol at Mike, and said, "We are going to rob Bank, and you are going to help us or we will kill you." Mike gulped, accepted a mask and an unloaded pistol, and proceeded with Dan and Paul to Bank, doing so only because he reasonably believed the threat was real.

When the three arrived at Bank, Dan assigned Paul to act as lookout. Dan instructed Mike to approach the teller with the pistol and to demand all the teller's cash. Dan then stood back to cover everyone in Bank, including Mike. Dan whispered to Paul, "We will kill anybody who gives us trouble." Paul said nothing.

Immediately thereafter Fred, a stranger to Dan, Paul, and Mike, entered Bank. Dan thereupon shot and severely wounded Fred, who was a federal bank examiner conducting an audit of Bank's accounts.

Based on properly admitted evidence that established the above facts, Dan and Paul were convicted in a federal court of violation of, and conspiracy to violate, a federal statute providing: "Whoever assaults with a deadly weapon any federal officer engaged in the performance of his duties is guilty of a felony." Dan and Paul have appealed, arguing that the evidence does not support convictions either for violation of the federal assault statute or for conspiracy to violate that statute.

Eight months after the robbery attempt, Fred died of his wounds. Dan, Paul and Mike were tried in a state court on charges of assault with a deadly weapon on, and murder of, Fred.

Evidence identical to that admitted in the federal court was then received in the state court trial. Mike filed a timely motion for a directed verdict of acquittal on the ground that the evidence established duress as a matter of law.

1. Discuss how the federal appeals court should rule on Dan and Paul's appeal.

2. Discuss how the state trial court should rule on Mike's motion for a directed verdict.

Question 17

The ABC Corporation was engaged in buying and selling used cars. Adams, Black and Cooper held all of the stock and, except for an office assistant, were its only officers and employees.

Adams, while demonstrating a used Oldsmobile to Riley, a prospective customer, in a grossly negligent manner, injured Stanley, a pedestrian, who later died. Adams sold the auto to Riley for $1,500 with terms of $100 down and the balance due at the end of the month, at which time delivery would be made. When Riley tendered the balance of the purchase price at the end of the month, he discovered that Adams had knowingly resold the car to Williams. Riley forcibly repossessed the vehicle from Williams.

Black sold a used Chevrolet to Hand for $1,000 whereupon Hand gave Black a certified check payable to Black. Somehow, Hand had procured the check beforehand and had forged the name "U.R. Stuck" as the bank officer who certified the check. Black gave Hand a certificate of title to the automobile.

Cooper, without knowledge and consent of either Adams or Black, borrowed $500 as a personal loan from a local finance company and for security delivered a certificate of title on a used Ford, owned by ABC. Cooper intended to repay the loan within three days.

Discuss all possible bases of criminal liability involved.

Question 18

X's new wristwatch stopped running and she took it to J's jewelry store to be repaired. J gave X a claim ticket when J accepted the watch. Deeply in debt to numerous bookies, J repaired the watch quickly and placed it in the store window in an effort to sell it. X returned a week later and presented her ticket to redeem the watch. J told her it was not ready yet. Shortly thereafter, J sold the watch to Y.

Later that same evening, at her weekly bowling league, X noticed her watch on Y's wrist, as Y sat at the scoring table on a nearby alley. X rushed up to her and angrily demanded the watch. Concerned because of a previous argument with X, Y began to fumble through her pants pockets for the receipt to prove that she had purchased the watch. X, thinking that Y was reaching for a weapon, struck her on the head with a heavy metal ashtray, causing a serious injury.

D, a police detective assigned to investigate the situation, went to J's store the following morning and offered J $50 for one of the watches he was repairing. J refused, indicating that the watch had been left for repairs and was not for sale. Before leaving the store, D raised his offer to $100 and J accepted. J gave the watch to D and took the $100.

The same evening of the incident with Y, X's husband, Q, in X's absence, contacted L, their landlord, for the sixth time in two days, stating that the heating system was not functioning properly. L, as he had done continually in the past, refused to take any action. In the early morning hours, the furnace exploded, causing a fire. After leaving the building, Q realized that his youngest child was still asleep inside. Upon reentering to rescue the baby, he was badly burned and died the following day as a result.

Discuss what crimes, if any, were committed and what defenses, if any, you would expect to be raised.

Question 19

Alex had received, as a gift from his father, a solid gold wristwatch engraved with Alex's initials. One day, beset with hard times, Alex pawned the watch at Ben's pawnshop. A month later Alex returned from work to find that his father had paid him a surprise visit. When Alex's father asked to see the watch, Alex told him it was being cleaned. Fearing that his father might disinherit him if his father learned that he had pawned the watch, Alex rushed down to Ben's after work the next day to redeem it. As a result of rush hour traffic, however, Alex got there at 6:11 p.m. to find the pawnshop was closed. Looking inside, Alex could see his watch lying on a counter next to a window. Alex decided to try to get his watch out of the pawnshop so that his father would not become suspicious about its absence.

The window of the pawnshop was slightly ajar, enabling Alex to push it up and extend a pole, which he used to pull the watch toward the window. Alex had just begun to pull the watch out through the window when a grating noise startled Ben, who was eating dinner upstairs with his family. Ben grabbed his gun and rushed downstairs, where he saw the figure of a man crouching just outside the open window. Thinking Alex's pole might be a rifle, Ben fired a shot towards Alex. The bullet ricocheted, just missing Alex. Startled, Alex dropped the pole and ran home, not realizing that his watch had fallen to the ground just beneath the pawn shop window.

Later that evening, Cliff was walking by the pawnshop when he noticed Alex's watch lying on the ground. Cliff decided to take the watch home in an effort to locate the owner. But once Cliff got home, he realized the watch was quite valuable, so he decided to keep it. However, Cliff soon became nervous and gave the watch to his friend Don, telling him, "Here, you can have this watch, but be careful, it's hot." Don kept the watch.

1. Alex is charged with:

    a. Burglary;

    b. Larceny;

    c. Attempted burglary; and

    d. Attempted larceny.

2. Ben is charged with assault with a deadly weapon.

3. Cliff is charged with larceny.

4. Don is charged with:

    a. Receiving stolen property; and

    b. Attempting to receive stolen property.

Discuss the issues raised by these charges.

Question 20

Carlo operated a gambling casino in a state where gambling is a misdemeanor. One night Tom, Mac, Fred and Sam went to the casino shortly before closing time. The four hid in the men's room until the casino closed, then they emerged brandishing guns.

While Tom, Mac, and Sam held the employees at gunpoint, Fred prepared to blow open the safe with nitroglycerin. The safe was in Carlo's office, just off the main gambling room. It was eight feet tall and four feet square, and was large enough to walk into. It sat on the floor in the corner and was not attached to the building, although it was too heavy to move without special equipment. The nitroglycerin went off prematurely and blew the safe open, killing Fred. Tom, Mac and Sam grabbed three sacks of money from the safe, each containing $10,000, all of which came from the gambling tables.

As the trio was leaving the casino with the money, they encountered Eb on the front steps. Eb shouted, "Death to gamblers," shot and killed Mac, and then turned the gun on Sam. Sam shot and wounded Eb, who survived. Tom and Sam jumped into their car with the loot and fled. As they were fleeing, Carlo came out of the casino with a rifle and fired a shot at the departing car. The shot killed Tom. Eb told police that he had thought Mac was one of the casino operators; Eb was trying to eliminate the casino because he had lost all his money there, wrecking his life. Eb was unaware that anything unusual was going on at the casino.

Discuss the criminal liabilities, if any, of Sam, Eb, and Carlo.

Essay Exam Answers

Answer to Question 1

CRIMES OF ARNOLD ("A")

Murder

The State ("State") could charge Arnold with murder for Bill's ("B") death.

A murder occurs when the defendant has committed a homicide (the killing of one human being by another) with malice aforethought (the intent to kill or cause serious bodily harm). Although A would argue he was attempting only to shoot David ("D") in the leg, an intent to cause serious bodily harm could be inferred from A's use of a hunting rifle. Even though A may not have been aware of B, under the transferred intent doctrine (when a person intends to commit a particular crime against one individual, but inadvertently commits the same or a similar crime against another person, that person's intent is deemed transferred from the intended to the actual victim), A's desire to shoot D would be transferred to B. *See* ELO Ch. 2-IV(A).

State could assert that A is guilty of second-degree murder since he evidenced a wanton *mens rea* (i.e., consciously engaged in conduct that he knew, or should have known, posed a high probability of death or serious injury to other human beings) by shooting at D while other persons were in the vicinity. It is unclear from the facts whether A should have recognized the likelihood of hitting someone other than D (this determination would depend upon facts such as: how good a marksman A was, how far D was from A, how obvious B's presence was to A, etc.). *See* ELO Ch. 8-II(D).

State could also contend that A at least acted recklessly (engaged in conduct that posed a substantial risk of death or serious bodily injury to other human beings) by shooting at D while other individuals were in the vicinity, and therefore is culpable of involuntary manslaughter. *See* ELO Ch. 8-II(E).

In response, A could contend that the shooting was privileged under the "fleeing felon" justification. Traditionally, a private citizen can use force capable of causing death or serious injury to prevent a felon's escape. Today, however, many jurisdictions require that the felon must have been engaged in a "dangerous" felony (one that involved a risk or likelihood of serious physical harm to others) for this privilege to apply. Assuming D's conduct constituted a felony (discussed below), under the traditional view, A's shooting would be privileged. Even under the emerging view, A could still contend that burglary is arguably a "dangerous" felony, since there is always the risk that the occupant of the home that was invaded would return and a physical confrontation could then result. However, State could argue in rebuttal that A was aware that D's conduct had not posed a risk of serious harm to others since the house was vacant during D's larceny and any "confrontation" was brought on by A, because D was running away.

Assuming the modern view is followed, the "fleeing felon" justification would probably ***not*** be available to A. *See* ELO Ch. 4-VII(B)(4)(d).

[The defense-of-property privilege is not applicable, since one can never exercise force capable of causing death or serious bodily harm to protect property.] *See* ELO Ch. 4-VI(B).

A would assert alternatively that, even if the "fleeing felon" privilege was unavailable, the charge should be reduced from murder to voluntary manslaughter. A would argue that this is a situation in which an otherwise complete defense of justification does not exist because of the defendant's unreasonable mistake (thinking that he could use deadly force to prevent the felon from escaping). A would probably prevail in getting the charge reduced to manslaughter assuming that the jurisdiction does not allow deadly force to be used to prevent such felonies. *See* ELO Ch. 4-V(E).

[Adequate provocation probably is ***not*** applicable, since a reasonable person would not think of killing another merely because the latter had stolen the former's property.]

Attempted Murder/Assault as to D

A probably also could be prosecuted for the attempted murder of D (the crime of attempt occurs when the defendant has taken a substantial step toward completing the target crime with the intent to commit that crime). A's shooting at D with his hunting rifle arguably constitutes attempted murder, since A should have recognized there was a substantial certainty that if his bullet struck D, D could die or be seriously injured. *See* ELO Ch. 5-II(A)(2).

Alternatively, A could be charged with attempted battery and assault of D, since A presumably placed D in fear of imminent injury when he heard A's original shot. (It is unclear from the facts whether D saw A pointing the rifle at him.)

Assault/Battery as to E

State could conceivably charge A with battery for the stroke suffered by Edith ("E"). A battery is usually defined as intentionally or recklessly causing bodily injury to, or offensive touching of, another individual. Even assuming that (1) A's intent toward D could be transferred to E (which is unlikely, since the harm suffered by E was dissimilar to that which A desired to cause D), or (2) A's conduct could be characterized as reckless, there was no physical contact with E. Therefore, A probably could not be convicted of battery against E. *See* ELO Ch. 8-VII(A).

An assault occurs where the defendant intentionally places the victim in fear of imminent injury. E probably feared for her own life when she saw that B was suddenly shot. Here, the transferred intent doctrine might apply since the harm suffered by E (fear of imminent injury) would be the same or similar to that suffered by D. However, if the transferred intent doctrine is found not to apply, an assault conviction cannot be sustained since reckless conduct will not suffice to support a conviction for assault. *See* ELO Ch. 8-VII(B).

CRIMES OF D

Murder/Manslaughter

State could charge D with second-degree murder under the felony-murder rule (according to which the defendant is deemed to have the *mens rea* for murder, even though he did not intend or desire the victim's death, when during or as a consequence of the defendant's perpetration of an independent, inherently dangerous felony, a homicide occurs). *See* ELO Ch. 8-III(A).

State also could charge D with burglary (the trespassory breaking and entering into the dwelling of another, at night, with the specific intention of committing a felony or, in some states, a theft crime such as larceny, therein), and with larceny (the trespassory taking and carrying away of the personal property of another with the intent to permanently deprive the victim thereof). Since the facts are silent, State will succeed only if David's burglary occurred at night or if this jurisdiction has abandoned the requirement that burglary occur at night. *See* ELO Ch. 9-II(A)-(F) and VII(A)-(F).

State could contend that D is guilty of second-degree murder under the felony-murder rule ("FMR"), arguing that B's death occurred as a consequence of D's burglary. D, however, could assert in rebuttal that (1) A's wanton intervening conduct extinguished the causal connection between the burglary and B's death, and (2) under these facts D was not engaged in an inherently "dangerous" felony since he was exiting a previously unoccupied home with several items. State could respond that (1) the causal connection was not broken by A's conduct, since it is reasonably foreseeable that the occupants of a burglarized dwelling might return before the intruder had left, and (2) if this occurs, there is always the possibility of a violent confrontation between a burglar and the returning occupant. Although these are close issues, State would probably prevail. *See* ELO Ch. 2-V(D).

If D's burglary is **not** deemed to be a "dangerous" felony, State could contend that D is culpable of involuntary manslaughter under the misdemeanor-manslaughter rule (according to which the defendant is deemed to have the *mens rea* for involuntary manslaughter when a homicide occurs as a consequence of, and in the course of, the defendant's perpetration of a felony that is not inherently dangerous, or of a misdemeanor or other unlawful act). While D again would contend that there was not a sufficient causal connection between his conduct and B's death, a conviction probably would result if this doctrine was applied. *See* ELO Ch. 8-VI(B).

Finally, given the facts, it is assumed that D would be prosecuted for burglary. If State cannot show all the elements of burglary, D could be successfully prosecuted for larceny.

CRIMES OF FRED ("F")

Robbery

Robbery occurs when the defendant commits a larceny by taking property from the person or presence of the owner using force or fear. Since B protested the removal of his watch, F probably would be deemed to have obtained the item by force. Although B's protestations were faint, given the circumstances, they were adequate to demonstrate that he was not surrendering the watch freely. Thus, F could be convicted of robbery. *See* ELO Ch. 9-VIII.

Answer to Question 2

CRIMES OF CHARLEY ("C")

Conspiracy

A conspiracy occurs where there is an agreement between two or more persons to commit a crime. Although there does not appear to have been an explicit agreement to rob Dogge's ("D") store, a tacit understanding could be inferred from the following facts: (1) all three drove to D's premises immediately after Baker's ("B") solicitation (discussed below), and (2) C and B conducted themselves in a manner that manifested a jointness of action (i.e., C, while armed, positioned himself to cover Able's ("A") retreat; B drove the getaway car). Thus, C is culpable of conspiracy. A's participation in the crime would be discounted since her "agreement" was feigned. However, this is not significant because the understanding between B and C would suffice to establish a conspiracy. *See* ELO Ch. 6-I(A).

Second Degree Murder

Under the felony-murder rule ("FMR"), if a homicide occurs during and as a result of the defendant's perpetration of an independent, inherently dangerous felony, the defendant is deemed to have the *mens rea* for second-degree murder (regardless of whether the defendant intended or desired the victim's death). The prosecution could contend that Easey's ("E") death was a consequence of C's robbing D's store. C could argue in rebuttal, however, that the FMR is inapplicable in this instance because (1) E's death was not the result of C's conduct, but rather was caused by A's behavior, which in turn caused D to shoot E, (2) the virus that E contracted at the hospital was the actual and proximate cause of E's death (not the wound sustained in the underlying felony of attempted robbery), and (3) in some jurisdictions, the FMR is not extended to situations where the victim's death was caused by someone other than a felon. It will be assumed that this state does not require that a felon actually cause the homicide. The prosecution probably could overcome C's causation argument (discussed below under crimes of D). With respect to C's first assertion, the prosecution could argue that since A was acting in a manner anticipated by C (i.e., drawing a gun and demanding money from the cashier), A was, in effect, acting as C's agent or instrumentality. However, since A was under no direct compulsion to feign a robbery, this argument might fail. Thus, the FMR is probably ***not*** applicable. *See* ELO Ch. 8-III(B)(2).

Attempted Murder

An attempt occurs where the defendant has deliberately engaged in conduct for the specific purpose of committing a crime (i.e., the target offense), and such conduct represents a substantial step towards culmination of it. Although C could contend that he did not intend to kill D (only to compel him to stop shooting at A), the prosecution probably could argue successfully in rebuttal that C must, or should, have recognized there was a substantial possibility that his bullet could have killed D. *See* ELO Ch. 5-II(A).

In the unlikely event that A were not convicted of attempted murder, he would be culpable of aggravated battery (an intentional or reckless application of force upon another causing serious bodily harm or involving a deadly weapon even if serious bodily harm does not result), since he presumably intended to hit D when he fired his gun. *See* ELO Ch. 8-VII(A)(4).

Robbery/Larceny

A robbery occurs when the defendant, by force or the threat of force, in the victim's presence, commits a larceny (i.e., the trespassory taking and carrying away of another's personal property with the intent to permanently deprive the latter thereof). C could not be guilty of robbery. The only party who took money from D using force was A, and A never intended to permanently deprive D of the cash which D tendered. *See* ELO Ch. 9-VIII.

Attempted Robbery

The prosecution could contend that an attempted robbery occurred when C entered D's store and positioned himself by the door to (presumably) cover A's getaway. While C could argue in rebuttal that no attempt could occur until D was accosted by B or C (which never happened), C did commit an overt act that would probably suffice under the modern trend toward broader liability. *See* ELO Ch. 5-III(D).

DEFENSES OF C

Entrapment

C could contend that he was entrapped into the foregoing crimes. This defense exists where a law enforcement official (here, A) induces the defendant to commit a crime that the defendant was not predisposed to commit. Entrapment arguably occurred when A invited B and C to her home and spoke in glowing terms about the recent series of robberies. However, A probably would **not** be deemed to have instigated the crime since A never suggested actually undertaking illegal conduct. *See* ELO Ch. 4-X(A)(2).

CRIMES OF BAKER ("B")

Solicitation/Conspiracy

A solicitation occurs where the defendant requests or encourages another to join in the commission of a crime, with the intent to induce the latter to perform the crime. When B suggested to A and C that the drugstore would be a "pushover" (which seems to have been recognized by A and C as meaning it would be easy to rob), a solicitation occurred. However, since A and C indicated their agreement, this crime would probably be merged into the conspiracy (discussed above). *See* ELO Ch. 7-IX(A).

Attempted Robbery/Attempted Murder

A co-conspirator is vicariously culpable for the crimes committed by other co-conspirators, provided such crimes were in furtherance of the conspiracy or were a reasonably foreseeable consequence. Assuming an attempted robbery occurred, it would certainly appear to be within the scope of the conspiracy. The facts are silent as to whether B was aware that C was armed when the latter entered the drugstore, but it would not be unreasonable to assume that B knew C carried some type of weapon given the nature of the crime. Thus, B probably would also be found guilty of the attempted murder of D. *See* ELO Ch. 6-II(B).

CRIMES OF DOGGE ("D")

Attempted Murder/Murder

The prosecution could contend that D is guilty of the attempted murder of A and the murder of E. D's intent to harm A would probably be applied to E under the transferred intent doctrine (when the defendant intended to commit a criminal act against a particular individual, and as a consequence thereof a different person is harmed, the defendant's intention will be transferred to the person harmed; provided the harm the person suffered is the same or similar to that which the defendant intended to cause to the original individual). *See* ELO Ch. 2-IV(A).

As to the murder charge, D would initially contend that no homicide (the killing of one human being by another) occurred since the actual cause of E's death was the virus (i.e., E's health was improving until she contracted the virus). However, the prosecution probably successfully would contend in rebuttal that "but for" D shooting E, E would not have been in the hospital in a weakened condition (which presumably made her more susceptible to the virus). *See* ELO Ch. 2-II(A).

While D also could argue that the shooting was not the proximate cause of E's death (the virus was an unforeseeable, intervening condition that contributed to E's demise), the prosecution again could contend successfully in rebuttal that one who has been hospitalized for a serious gunshot wound could foreseeably contract a virus that could result in death. (Viruses exist in every hospital.) *See* ELO Ch. 2-III(A).

D could assert the "fleeing felon" privilege (if a citizen reasonably believes that an individual has committed a dangerous felony, and such individual has in fact just committed such offense, the citizen may exercise whatever force he reasonably believes is necessary, under the circumstances, to effectuate the offender's arrest) in response to the prosecution's charges. In response, the prosecution could contend that this defense is not available since (1) D's belief that a felony was occurring might not have been reasonable in light of the fact that A's note advised him that A was an undercover agent, and (2) no felony actually occurred since A had not intended to deprive D of his cash. However, D could argue in rebuttal that he reasonably believed that A's note was simply part of a scheme to illegally obtain the store's money, since A drew a gun as she approached D (D did not know that a second person, also involved in the crime was watching A) and A took the money from D. While D's belief that a felony was occurring was probably reasonable, since A did not (in fact) commit a robbery, this justification might not be persuasive. *See* ELO Ch. 4-V(E).

The murder charge against D would probably be reduced to voluntary manslaughter since D's mistaken belief that A committed a felony was reasonable.

CRIMES OF A

An undercover police officer is ordinarily not culpable for acts which she commits as a feigned accomplice, since such conduct was undertaken for the purpose of obtaining evidence against, and capturing, those who engaged in illegal activity. *See* ELO Ch. 7-III(B)(3)(b).

Answer to Question 3

Are Bob ("B") and Mike ("M") guilty of burglary of Smith's ("S") garage?

Burglary is the trespassory breaking and entering into, at night, the dwelling of another with the intent to commit a felony (which, in many states, includes theft offenses). Presently, many jurisdictions have eliminated the "night-time" element, and have broadened the "dwelling" element to include any structures on a parcel with living quarters. B would contend that burglary is not appropriate because (1) the door that they opened was unlocked, (2) they entered only a garage not a home, and (3) B and M had *not* formed the specific intention of taking anything when they entered S's garage (the facts indicate that B and H only *sometimes* took tools). As to the "breaking," the State probably could contend successfully that this element ordinarily is satisfied by any forced movement of the structure; the door did not need to be locked. Second, State would argue that under the broadened definition, since the garage was "attached" to the home, it should be considered a part of the dwelling. With respect to B, if State could show that B had taken items in the past, State might argue that he entered the garage with the intention of taking something if it interested him and, thus, the "intention" element is satisfied. The success of this argument is questionable. M has an even stronger argument in that he did not possess the specific intention of committing a larceny at the time he entered the garage (even though he arguably did commit one subsequently), since he was tagging along with the older boys for the first time and presumably was only curious to see what they were doing. *See* ELO Ch. 9-VII.

B and M could assert the defense of infancy. At common law, it was conclusively presumed that children under the age of seven did not have the capacity to commit a crime. With respect to children between seven and 14 years of age, there was a presumption that they did not have the capacity to commit a crime, but this could be rebutted by showing malice or an awareness that the conduct was wrong. Assuming this is a common law jurisdiction, M could not be prosecuted for burglary and B could be successfully prosecuted for burglary only if the prosecution rebutted the presumption that B did not understand his actions were wrongful (which is possible). *See* ELO Ch. 3-V(A).

Are B and M guilty of the larceny of S's watch?

Larceny is the trespassory taking and carrying away of another's personal property with the intent to permanently deprive the owner of his property. Even though M's taking of S's watch was trespassory (he wrongfully took the watch from S's possession) and M carried away the watch (by taking it home with him), the intent element is not satisfied. M could again assert the defense of infancy (see above) and, therefore, could not be convicted of larceny. *See* ELO Ch. 9-II(F).

There appears to be no factual basis (conspiracy or accomplice culpability) for holding B responsible for M's actions, even if M were deemed to be guilty of larceny.

Is B guilty of burglary of Jones's toolshed?

Burglary is the trespassory breaking and entering into a structure with the intent to commit a felony or theft offense. While the facts indicate that the requisite "breaking" took place, the facts do not indicate whether B ever actually entered Jones's toolshed. Assuming H stepped into the toolshed first, it is doubtful that B would have any reason to continue in after H was shot. The prosecution could make the argument that H's acts should be imputed to B under a theory of conspiracy between H and B (the agreement between two or more persons to commit an unlawful act) with H's step inside the toolshed constituting the overt act, if this is a jurisdiction that requires one. While the intent to commit the theft offense is clearer here than with S's garage (the facts state that the boys went to Jones's toolshed for the stated purpose of taking a large screwdriver that had previously caught B's eye), the prosecution would again encounter the same defense of infancy. B could be successfully prosecuted for burglary of Jones's toolshed only if the prosecution rebuts the presumption that B did not understand his actions were wrong. *See* ELO Ch. 9-VII.

Is Jones ("J") guilty of Hal's ("H") murder?

A defendant is guilty of first-degree murder where he commits a homicide (the killing of one human being by another) with the intention of causing the victim's death or serious bodily harm, and such killing was premeditated and deliberate. While J probably will contend that he wanted only to scare away potential intruders, one ordinarily is presumed to have intended the natural consequences of one's actions. Rigging a pistol to discharge when a door is opened certainly has the potential to kill or seriously injure anyone who opens the door. The fact that the homicide was accomplished by a pre-set instrument is irrelevant, since one is responsible for setting forces in motion that cause a victim's death. *See* ELO Ch. 8-II(C) and (D).

J could assert two defenses. First, some states allow the use of deadly force to prevent another from invading one's home. Since the toolshed was within the curtilage of J's house, such structure was arguably part of J's "home." Second, J could contend that he was preventing the felony of burglary (discussed above). State could argue in rebuttal, however, that while separate structures on the parcel might constitute part of a dwelling for purposes of the crime of burglary, this is *not* applicable to excuse the use of deadly force in a structure that is not one's actual abode. Second, while one may sometimes kill to prevent a felony, one cannot do so where a lesser degree of force could have accomplished the intended purpose. If J had been in the toolshed, J could have prevented the felony by simply restraining H. Thus, the use of the firearm probably constituted excessive force, and J's defenses should fail. *See* ELO Ch. 4-VI(B).

Answer to Question 4

CRIMES OF E

Solicitation

The crime of solicitation occurs where the defendant requests or encourages another to perform a criminal act (presently, many statutes require that the crime be a felony, but assume that no such requirement exists in this state) with the intent to induce the latter to perform the crime. The prosecution could contend that a solicitation to commit false pretenses (discussed below) occurred when E persuaded X to order tires at a time when E recognized that X probably would be unable to pay for them (i.e., E knew that X was unemployed). It is unclear from the facts whether E knew that X had numerous unpaid creditors, but E realized that X would not have the funds to pay for the tires that M. Co. would deliver to him.

E could argue in rebuttal, however, that he (1) never actually urged or encouraged X to commit a crime (i.e., take possession of the tires without paying for them), and (2) never intended to commit a crime as evidenced by the facts that (a) he had been drinking at the time he spoke to X, and (b) X, being an attorney, would recognize the potential criminal culpability of accepting items without sufficient funds to pay for them. Since E probably expected X to reject the tires when they were actually delivered, E probably lacked the specific intention of inducing criminal behavior by X. Thus, no solicitation occurred. *See* ELO Ch. 7-IX(D).

Conspiracy

The crime of conspiracy occurs where there is an agreement between two or more persons to commit a crime. The prosecution could contend that since X was insolvent and therefore could not lawfully obtain title to the tires, X and E's agreement to resell the tires for the purpose of raising funds constituted a conspiracy to obtain property from the M. Co. by false pretenses (discussed below).

E could argue in rebuttal, however, that (1) the contentions he made with respect to the solicitation charge (i.e., that no specific illegal activity was discussed and there was no intention that X would actually engage in any criminal activity) again apply, and (2) X was too intoxicated to form the specific intention to commit criminal behavior (as evidenced by the fact that he easily accepted E's explanation of what they would do with the tires when the items were actually delivered to X).

The prosecution could contend in rebuttal that (1) despite their slight intoxication, E and X seemed to be cognizant of what they were doing (and therefore could have formed the specific intention to commit a crime), and (2) given the improbability of X's paying for the tires, E and X must have intended to defraud M. Co. The combination of X's inebriated condition and the relative vagueness of understanding between E and X, however would probably result in a finding that X did not have the specific intention to engage in criminal behavior. E (or X), therefore, probably could not be successfully prosecuted for conspiracy. *See* ELO Ch. 6-III(B)(1).

False Pretenses

The crime of false pretenses occurs when the defendant obtains title to another's property by means of a misrepresentation of a material fact, knowing the representation to be false and intending to defraud the owner. The prosecution could contend that this crime was committed when E arranged to receive one-half of the $2,000 payment that M. Co. made to A (after M. Co. had been led to believe that X wanted to purchase those tires). In response, B could argue that (1) no fraudulent misrepresentation was made to M. Co. by him, and (2) the money he received was delivered to him by A, not by M. Co. The prosecution could probably overcome these contentions by asserting that (1) as an employee of M. Co., E had the affirmative obligation to disclose that he had instigated X's order and that X probably would be unable to pay for the tires, and (2) the money that E was to receive from A is easily traceable to that which M. Co. paid for the obsolete tires. While E could respond that he had no affirmative duty to warn his employer about X's financial instability, this assertion will probably fail. *See* ELO Ch. 9-IV.

In the event that E prevailed in his assertion that he had no obligation to disclose X's financial situating to M. Co., the prosecution could contend that (given X's inebriated condition), X was innocently acting as E's instrumentality. Since E knew, or should have known, that X would be unable to pay for the tires, the order that constituted the fraudulent misrepresentation necessary for false pretenses was attributed directly to E. While E undoubtedly will contend that X was **not** sufficiently intoxicated to be deemed to be acting directly under E's influence, the prosecution could probably prevail on this alternative theory, too. *See* ELO Ch. 9-IV(H)(1).

Does E have culpability for X's crime?

A party who has solicited an offense is culpable for that crime if the crime actually is committed by the second party, and is culpable for any other crimes that were a foreseeable outgrowth of the target offense. The prosecution could assert that when E persuaded X to order the tires from M. Co., with knowledge that X probably did not have the funds to pay for them, it was foreseeable that X would give T a bad check when the tires arrived. However, E probably could contend successfully in rebuttal that it was not foreseeable that X would tender an invalid check to T. While the facts are not clear as to what E thought X would do when the tires arrived, two scenarios are possible: (1) E intended to help X sell the tires "and drink the proceeds" or (2) E assumed X simply would refuse delivery from M. Co. In fact, E could contend that X did try to refuse delivery (X told T that he did not have enough money to buy the tires), but T refused to listen and instead told X that he didn't want to reload the tires back on his truck. X's protestations support E's contentions and E probably would *not* be culpable for X's crime. *See* ELO Ch. 7-IX(A).

[No larceny would have occurred because the M. Co. also intended to part with both *ownership* (title) and possession of the items in issue.]

CRIMES OF X

False pretenses

The prosecution could contend that when, in exchange for the tires, X gave T a check for which he knew (or should have known) he did not have sufficient funds, he committed the crime of false pretenses; the check would represent a fraudulent misrepresentation by X. However, in some jurisdictions this argument does not always prevail. The court may hold that title to the tires does not pass until the check is cashed. Thus, if it never clears, there would not be any false pretenses (presumably M. Co. would simply repossess the tires). In other jurisdictions, states have passed explicit bad check statutes that make it a crime to write a check with the knowledge that one does not have sufficient funds to cover it. Most of these bad check statutes also provide that, if the check is returned for insufficient funds and the person who wrote the check does not make good on it within a short period of time, the law presumes the intent to defraud. Consequently, the outcome of this charge by the prosecution against X would depend on the laws of the jurisdiction. *See* ELO Ch. 9-IV(I)(1).

X could contend that (1) he acted under duress (this defense exists where, as a consequence of threats to cause the defendant serious bodily harm, the defendant committed the crime with which he is charged, provided that defendant actually and reasonably believed that such other person would immediately undertake the threatened act) because T glowered at him, or (2) M. Co. assumed the risk or was negligent (via its employee, T) in accepting a non-certified check from X. With respect to the duress claim, the prosecution probably could contend successfully in rebuttal that, despite any menacing looks, T never threatened X with physical harm. In addition, the negligence or assumption of a risk by a victim is no defense to the commission of a crime (the rationale being that the function of criminal law is to assure proper behavior by its citizenry, and thus a victim's contributory negligence does not negate the perpetrator's conduct). *See* ELO Ch. 4-II(F).

Even though M. Co. might not prosecute X in return for the tires, forgiveness by the victim of a crime ordinarily does not absolve the perpetrator from culpability (the rationale being that the commission of a crime is considered to be a wrong against society as a whole, rather than against only the individual victim).

Therefore, X probably could be prosecuted successfully for false pretenses.

CRIMES OF A

A does not appear to be culpable of any criminal offense. Nothing in the facts indicates that at the time A agreed to pay E a finder's fee she knew (or should have known) that E would resort to illegal conduct. Therefore, A could not be prosecuted successfully for false pretenses or any other crime.

Answer to Question 5

CRIMES OF SAM ("S")

The prosecution could charge S with solicitation, conspiracy, burglary, malicious mischief, and murder.

Solicitation

A solicitation occurs when the defendant requests or encourages another to commit a crime with the intent to induce the latter to perform the crime. When S asked Ace ("A") to break into Joe's ("J") premises and pour syrup on J's merchandise, a solicitation probably occurred (assuming that the requested acts constituted a crime). Since the crime of solicitation is complete once the defendant makes his request, S will probably be convicted of solicitation. *See* ELO Ch. 7-IX(B).

Conspiracy

The crime of conspiracy occurs where there is an agreement between two or more persons to commit a crime. The prosecution could contend that since S and A agreed that A would invade J's premises and pour syrup over J's goods, S is guilty of conspiracy to commit malicious mischief (the intentional or reckless injury to or destruction of the property of another). However, S could contend in rebuttal that since A was mentally handicapped, he did not know the nature and quality of his actions nor did he know what he was doing was wrong, and, therefore, is legally insane. The fact that A put on a skeleton outfit, which would tend to make him easier to detect than if he were wearing regular clothing, indicates that A did not sufficiently appreciate that he was helping S in the commission of a crime. Since conspiracy requires the participants to share the specific goal of criminal conduct, it is unlikely that S could be convicted of conspiracy. The prosecution could argue that under the Model Penal Code's "unilateral" theory of conspiracy, S is solely liable even without A being a conspirator, since under this theory only one party's intent is necessary to find the conspiracy. However, the unilateral approach of conspiracy applies to the *scope* of the conspiracy, not the fact of it, and this argument will probably fail. *See* ELO Ch. 6-V(B)(3)(b).

Burglary

Where one who causes innocent or irresponsible persons to engage in conduct constituting the *actus reas* portion of a crime, the innocent or irresponsible party is looked upon as an instrumentality of the defendant. Since A was S's court-placed ward, and A appeared to be incapable of handling his own affairs, A would be considered the instrumentality of S, and A's conduct would be attributed to S.

Traditionally, a burglary is the trespassory breaking and entering into the dwelling of another, at night, with the intent to commit a felony. Under more modern law, however, the structure need not always be a dwelling, and the intent required is to commit a crime, not necessarily a felony (although some states require it to be a theft crime). Assuming A's actions constitute the "breaking and entering" portions of burglary and assuming this jurisdiction extends this crime to all structures (not just dwellings), A's conviction depends on whether malicious mischief (discussed above) constitutes the requisite crime. If the jurisdiction considers malicious mischief to be a crime, then a burglary conviction depends on whether the jurisdiction requires an intent to commit a theft crime or an intent to commit any crime. *See* ELO Ch. 9-VII(A)-(F).

Second degree murder

Arson traditionally is the malicious (meaning intentional or reckless) burning of the dwelling of another. Today, however, many jurisdictions extend this crime to any structure. Assuming this state adheres to the modern view, the prosecution could contend that A committed arson by causing the explosion (an explosion ordinarily suffices to satisfy the "burning" element of arson) in the premises he invaded. In addition, under the felony-murder rule ("FMR"), where a homicide occurs as a consequence of the defendant's perpetration of an independent, inherently dangerous felony, he is guilty of second-degree murder, even though the defendant did not intend or desire to cause the victim's death. Thus, the prosecution could contend that S is guilty of second-degree murder because J's death resulted from the explosion [arson] caused by A.

However, S could raise several counter-arguments. First, he would contend that the explosion (even if attributed to him) was the result of negligent, not reckless, conduct (i.e., throwing an unopened can of syrup at the darkened portion of a business premises could not be characterized as conduct that created a high probability of causing an explosion or fire). Therefore, the malice element for arson is lacking and no conviction could result. Likewise, the underlying independent, inherently dangerous felony necessary for application of the FMR is absent. Moreover, one ordinarily is not liable for the unintended or unforeseeable conduct of an innocent or irresponsible party. Since S only instructed A to pour syrup over J's merchandise, A hurling the can could not have been anticipated by S (and, therefore, S is not culpable for this aspect of A's conduct). Finally, S could assert that the proximate cause between the alleged felony and J's death is lacking (i.e., it was not reasonably foreseeable that throwing an unopened can of syrup towards the rear of an unoccupied business premises would strike a gas line and cause an explosion resulting in the death of an unknown person next door). S probably **would not** be convicted of second-degree murder. *See* ELO Ch. 8-III(C)(3).

Involuntary manslaughter

The prosecution might assert that S is guilty of involuntary manslaughter by directly causing J's death through possessing a reckless *mens rea* (undertaking conduct that posed a substantial risk of death or serious injury to others). The prosecution would claim that since there is always the possibility that a low-grade moron will behave in a manner that creates a life-endangering situation to others, S acted recklessly by choosing A to commit malicious mischief. In rebuttal, S could contend that, assuming A had no prior history of violent conduct, S did not act recklessly in assuming that A would refrain from engaging in life threatening behavior. Thus, S probably would **not** be convicted of involuntary manslaughter simply because he selected a low-grade moron to ruin J's merchandise. *See* ELO Ch. 8-VI(A)(1)(a).

The prosecution could alternatively contend that S could be convicted of involuntary manslaughter under the misdemeanor-manslaughter rule ("MMR") (according to which the defendant is deemed to have the *mens rea* for involuntary manslaughter, even though the defendant did not desire or intend the victim's death, if the death occurs accidentally in the course and as a consequence of the defendant's perpetration of a misdemeanor). With respect to the existence of a misdemeanor, A probably is guilty of attempting to commit malicious mischief to J's merchandise. However, S could contend that the necessary proximate cause between A's attempted misdemeanor (breaking into a store, albeit the wrong store, for the purpose of putting syrup on J's merchandise) and J's ensuing death is lacking. Thus, no conviction under the MMR appears likely. *See* ELO Ch. 8-VI(B).

CRIMES OF DAN ("D")

The prosecution could charge D with solicitation and conspiracy. It could contend that D's suggestion to S that someone should "take care" of J constituted a solicitation. However, D probably could argue successfully in rebuttal that (1) no specific illegal conduct was requested (the phrase "take care of" is sufficiently vague to also include legal conduct, such as a purchase of J's business), and (2) assuming S had no prior history of criminal behavior, D probably did not expect S to undertake illegal activity based upon his casual statement (especially since the facts indicate that D's statement was made in a half-jesting manner). *See* ELO Ch. 7-IX(A).

D has a much harder case to make in response to the charge of conspiracy (an agreement between two or more persons to commit a crime). The facts indicate that the day after D's first conversation with S (in which he "half-jested" that S "take care" of J), S told D about his plan to have A break into J's store and pour syrup over J's merchandise. D's response was, "Sounds great, but don't ask me to do anything to help." S replied, "All you have to do is sit back and let it happen."

In a conspiracy, it is sufficient if each party, by her actions alone, makes it clear to the other(s) that they will pursue a common goal. The prosecution probably could argue successfully that once D learned of the plan, his words, "Sounds great," coupled with his decision to "let [the plan] happen" indicated D that D and S did share a common goal—ruining J's business. *See* ELO Ch. 6-II(A)(1).

If this case arose in a jurisdiction that required not only that an agreement be made, but also the commission of an overt act, D could argue that he committed no overt act. While S's solicitation of A to commit the crime certainly could be considered an overt act, that took place before D's agreement had been secured. However, the prosecution probably would argue successfully that D's conscious decision to let the plan move forward together with the facts that S pointed out J's building to A and A moved ahead with the plan (albeit not in the manner anticipated), constituted the necessary overt act. *Any* act committed in furtherance of the conspiracy will suffice as the overt act, and the courts do not require each conspirator to commit an overt act. Rather, the overt act of any individual conspirator will be deemed an act by all conspirators. Last, the prosecutors could argue that if D had not intended for S to ruin J's merchandise, he would have made his objections clear and stopped any further steps in that direction. *See* ELO Ch. 6-IV(B).

CRIMES OF ACE ("A")

A may be considered legally insane under the doctrine of diminished responsibility, since he was mentally handicapped. A would argue that this mental impairment rendered him unable to form the requisite intent for any of these crimes. Therefore, A would be guilty of no crimes in the events described, despite his actions, since the court will probably determine he lacked the mental capacity necessary to form the requisite *mens rea*. *See* ELO Ch. 3-II(B).

Answer to Question 6

CRIMES OF ADAM ("A")

Solicitation

The crime of solicitation occurs when the defendant requests or encourages another to join in committing a crime, with the intent to induce the latter to perform the crime. The prosecution probably could contend successfully that when A asked Barlow ("B") to assist him by offering the LSD-laced chocolates to Kitty, this crime occurred. However, solicitation ordinarily merges into a conspiracy if the solicitee agrees to perform the criminal act (discussed below). *See* ELO Ch. 7-IX(A).

Conspiracy

A conspiracy occurs where there is an agreement between two or more persons to commit a crime. The prosecution could assert that a conspiracy to commit murder occurred when B agreed to cooperate with A in a plan that might have resulted in Kitty's ("K") death. The fact that K's death would occur only under certain circumstances (i.e., she would actually have to accept and eat the candy) would be of no legal significance, since K's death was intended by A and B if certain conditions were present. A could argue, however, that since B might have a successful defense to a conspiracy charge (either duress or insanity), A cannot be successfully prosecuted for this crime without B. However, duress probably could *not* be successfully asserted by B since (1) the defendant's fear of harm from the coercing party must be reasonable and the facts indicate that B's belief was irrational, and (2) this defense is not applicable to the crime of murder. In addition, insanity is probably inapplicable as a defense because there is no indication that B failed to (1) recognize that his behavior was wrong, or (2) understand the nature of his conduct. Thus, while B's fear of A appears to have been excessive and irrational, he still should have realized that the police would have protected him if he had disclosed A's plot to them. Thus, A would probably be convicted of conspiracy. *See* ELO Ch. 6-III(B).

Attempted murder of K

An attempt occurs when the defendant has taken a substantial step toward completing the target crime with the intent to commit that crime. The prosecution could contend that A's conduct in bringing the LSD-filled chocolates to the pool hall constituted a substantial step toward completion of the target crime (the murder of K). A possessed materials to be used in the commission of a crime that were specially created for that use and served no lawful purpose. In response, A could argue that until the chocolates were actually offered to K, the target crime was merely in the preparatory stage, but the prosecution probably will prevail. *See* ELO Ch. 5-III(D).

If an attempt to murder was found to have occurred, A could argue that no conviction for this crime may occur because the target crime was factually impossible to commit (i.e., due to the inadequate quantity of LSD, K's death could not have resulted from eating the chocolates). However, the prosecution could contend successfully in rebuttal that factual impossibility is no defense where, had the circumstances been as the defendant thought them to be, there would have been a crime. *See* ELO Ch. 5-IV(B)(1).

Murder of Cox ("C")

A could be charged with first-degree murder with respect to the death of C. A murder occurs where the defendant has committed a homicide (the killing of one human being by another) with malice aforethought (the intent to kill or cause the victim serious bodily harm). Where the defendant has acted with premeditation and deliberation, the homicide is characterized as first-degree murder. *See* ELO Ch. 8-IV(C).

While A might initially contend that he was not the actual cause of C's death (C died of exposure to the elements), the prosecution could successfully argue in rebutt... [...] ...king C to a secluded spot and abandoning him there, C wou[ld]...

A cou... [...] ...ximate cause of C's death (i.e., ... [...] (1) C unexpectedly ate some... [...] ...ng dead when he left C in a seclu... [...] ...ld argue successfully in rebut... [...] ...e else in the bowling alley migh... [...] ...tes, and (2) A's intervening negli... [...] ...l is not so unforeseeable as to br... [...] ...mmitted a homicide. *See* ELO...

A al... [...] ...seriously injure C. Hov... [...] ...re the defendant intended to c... [...] ...individual, and as a con... [...] ...in a manner similar to that inte... [...] ...rred to the latter. The pro... [...] ...kill K is transferred to C. Wh... [...] ...ied, A did not intend to cau... [...] ...s body, not to kill him), the pro... [...] ...to kill someone in a similar ma... [...] ...riginal crime. Thus, A is pro... [...] ...2-IV(A)(1).

Ev... [...] ...o kill C was lacking at the tin... [...] ...ld contend that A is guilty of second-degree murder because his conduct was wanton (he consciously engaged in conduct which he knew, or should have known, posed a high probability of death or serious injury to other human beings) at the time he committed the homicide. This mental state is evidenced by the fact that (1) A left chocolates unattended in the pool hall, and (2) despite his lack of medical expertise, A disregarded the possibility that C might only be unconscious at the time A moved C to an isolated area. A could argue in rebuttal either that (1) his conduct was merely negligent, and therefore his conduct was not criminal, or (2) his actions can be characterized only as reckless (he engaged in conduct that created a substantial risk of death or serious injury to other human beings), and, therefore, he can be convicted only of involuntary manslaughter. However, the prosecution probably would prevail since A should have realized that C might not have been dead. Thus, if a first-degree murder conviction were avoided, A probably would be guilty of second-degree murder. *See* ELO Ch. 8-II(D).

Possession of a controlled substance

In most jurisdictions, it is illegal to knowingly possess LSD. If this state has this law, A would also be convicted of this crime.

CRIMES OF BARLOW ("B")

Conspiracy

As discussed above (involving the conspiracy charge against A), B is probably culpable of conspiracy to commit murder.

B's culpability for the crimes of A

A co-conspirator is culpable for crimes committed by other co-conspirators, provided the latter's crimes were within the scope of the conspiracy or a foreseeable outgrowth thereof. Therefore, B also would be convicted of both attempted murder and possession of a controlled substance if A is convicted of these crimes. *See* ELO Ch. 6-IV(D).

With respect to C's murder, however, B would contend that (1) there was no agreement to kill C, (2) it was not foreseeable that A would carelessly leave the chocolates unattended where an unanticipated person could eat one, and (3) it was not foreseeable that A would transport C to a secluded area without ascertaining whether C was unconscious or dead. While the prosecution could argue in rebuttal that it was foreseeable that another person would accidently eat one of the chocolates and that A would fail to seek proper medical help, B should prevail. Thus, B would probably not be convicted for C's murder.

Answer to Question 7

(1) CRIMINAL RESPONSIBILITY OF A, B AND C FOR THE OFFICE BUILDING INCIDENT

Conspiracy

The prosecution could charge A and B with conspiracy to commit burglary and larceny. The crime of conspiracy occurs where there is an agreement between two or more persons to commit a crime. A and B might contend that, while B advised A where a copy of the manuscript was located, they never specifically agreed to take it (i.e., perhaps B simply informed A where the manuscript could be found as a means of expressing his astonishment about the lack of security involving an important manuscript). However, the prosecution probably could argue in rebuttal that the facts that (1) A and B had discussed how lucrative the sale of excerpts from the manuscript would be, (2) the detail in which B described the manuscript's location, (3) B's apparent lack of surprise when A returned to C's apartment with a copy of the manuscript, and (4) B (together with A) hid when the police arrived at C's apartment, is sufficient evidence for a jury to infer that a tacit understanding existed between A and B to remove the copy of the manuscript from B's office building. *See* ELO Ch. 6-II(A)(2).

Burglary/Larceny

At common law, the crime of burglary occurred where the defendant, in a trespassory manner, broke and entered into the dwelling of another, at night, for the purpose of committing a felony therein. Presently, however, many states have deleted the night-time element and have extended the crime to (1) any structure, and (2) situations where a theft offense (not necessarily a felony) was intended within the building. Assuming this to be such a state, the prosecution could contend that a breaking occurred when A moved the side door and that he intended to commit a larceny when he entered the structure (as evidenced by the fact that he removed a copy of the manuscript). *See* ELO Ch. 9-VII(E)(1) and (F).

Larceny is the trespassory taking and carrying away of the tangible personal property of another with the intent to permanently deprive the owner thereof. A and B could contend that while they intended to take the manuscript, they did not intend to commit a larceny because (1) no "tangible" personal property was involved, and (2) there was no "deprivation" of property (i.e., the manuscript) since presumably the publishing entity still had the original manuscript or other copies. The prosecution could argue in rebuttal that (1) the manuscript, itself, is tangible personal property, as is the copyright owned in the manuscript's contents, and (2) A and B intended to permanently deprive the publishing company of that copy of the manuscript. Additionally, since A and B probably intended to sell excerpts of it to other publishing entities, there was an intent to appropriate much of the manuscript's value. Although a close question, A and B could probably be successfully prosecuted for both burglary and larceny. *See* ELO Ch. 9-II(D) and (F).

Culpability of C

Under the traditional common law party rules, an accessory after the fact (one who knowingly assists a felon in avoiding arrest or prosecution with the intent or desire to do so) was culpable for the crimes committed by the felon. Today, however, most jurisdictions instead recognize a distinct and separate crime for this type of conduct (usually called accessory after the fact or obstructing justice). Since the elements of this offense appear to be satisfied (A and B had advised C what they had done, and C obviously desired that they avoid arrest as evidenced by his untruthful statement to the police that no one else was with him), C could probably be successfully prosecuted for being an accessory after the fact. *See* ELO Ch. 7-VIII(A).

(2) CRIMINAL RESPONSIBILITY OF A AND B FOR D'S DEATH

Crimes of B

B would probably have no responsibility for D's death, since A's decision to stab D seems to have been undertaken independently. Furthermore, there is nothing to suggest that A's action was in anyway a foreseeable consequence of the conspiracy to steal the manuscript. Thus B would not be subject to liability as a co-conspirator under these facts. *See* ELO Ch. 6-IV(D).

Crimes of A

A, however, could be charged with murder. A murder occurs where the defendant has committed a homicide (the killing of one human being by another) with malice aforethought (the intent to cause the victim serious bodily harm or death). The facts are unclear as to whether A had become intoxicated prior to the stabbing incident (the facts state only that A had struck up a conversation with the bartender). It will be assumed that A was not intoxicated, and, therefore, she cannot successfully contend that she lacked the ability to form the specific intent to kill or seriously injure D. Since A appears to have acted spontaneously when she saw several persons attack her friend B, A did not seem to premeditate and deliberate the stabbing. Thus, A would probably be charged with second-degree murder. *See* ELO Ch. 8-IV(D).

A could contend in rebuttal, however, that her actions were justified under the privilege of defense of others (where one reasonably believes that another is about to cause death or serious injury to a third party, she can exercise force capable of causing death or serious bodily injury to the aggressor). Whether A's actions would come within this privilege would depend upon whether she reasonably believed that D and his friends were about to kill or seriously injure

B. The facts are silent as to the relative physical sizes of all those involved, whether D and his friends significantly outnumbered A and B, and precisely what D and his friends were doing to B when A stabbed D. (Were they kicking and punching B, or merely pushing or slapping him?) Assuming, however, that A reasonably believed that D and his friends were about to seriously injure or kill B, that the degree of force was reasonably necessary to prevent the harm, and that B would have the right to use the same amount of force in his own defense, A would probably have a valid defense to the murder charge. *See* ELO Ch. 4-V(C).

In the event, however, that A's conduct was not justifiable under the circumstances, her homicide charge probably would be reduced to voluntary manslaughter because she acted in the heat of passion in response to sufficient provocation (i.e., provocation sufficient to cause a reasonable person to lose self-control). A could argue that watching several persons attack her best friend was sufficient provocation. Thus, if the assertion of the privilege described above were **not** successful, A probably would be convicted of voluntary manslaughter only. *See* ELO Ch. 8-V(C) and (D).

(3) CRIMINAL RESPONSIBILITY OF A AND P FOR W'S DEATH

(a) Criminal responsibility of A

The prosecution could contend that A is guilty of second-degree murder of W, if one assumes that A's stabbing of D was **not** privileged, under the felony-murder rule ("FMR") (where a homicide occurs in the course and as a consequence of the defendant's participation in an independent, inherently dangerous felony, the defendant is deemed to have the *mens rea* for second-degree murder, even though she did not intend or desire the victim's death). In the alternative, A could be charged with second-degree murder for causing W's homicide with a wanton *mens rea*. (While a few jurisdictions do not apply the felony-murder rule to situations where someone other than the felon directly committed the homicide, we'll assume that this state is **not** among them.) *See* ELO Ch. 8-IV(D).

A could contend that the FMR is not applicable because (1) he was not in the process of committing a felony (D's murder had occurred before the incident that caused W's death), and (2) P's reckless conduct in shooting A's tire was an unforeseeable, intervening act that extinguished the proximate causation between A's felonious behavior in the tavern and W's death. The prosecution probably could argue successfully in rebuttal that (1) immediate flight—here, attempting a high-speed escape—is within the commission of the felony, and (2) P's conduct was not "unforeseeable" since a person driving at 80 mph to escape a police officer should recognize that the officer might attempt to use deadly force in overtaking her. Thus, *if* A's murder of D was not privileged (i.e., A was engaged in a felony), she would probably be culpable of second-degree murder under the FMR. *See* ELO Ch. 8-III(E)(2).

Even if A's conduct with respect to D was justified, the prosecution could still contend that A acted with a wanton *mens rea* (consciously disregarded a risk that posed a high probability of death or serious bodily injury to others) by driving at 80 mph when P sought to stop her. A again would argue in rebuttal that (1) her conduct was not the proximate cause of W's death, and alternatively (2) her conduct was at most reckless. (i.e., she engaged in conduct that created a substantial and unjustifiable risk of death or serious bodily injury.) Therefore, she could be found culpable of no offense greater than involuntary manslaughter. The prosecution again would contend in rebuttal that (1) P's conduct was not a superseding cause of W's death, and (2) traveling at 80 mph through (presumably) city streets (where the speed limit is usually 35 mph) created a substantial and unjustifiable risk that her car could spin out of control and kill an innocent bystander. Since A's conduct would probably be characterized as wanton, a second-degree murder conviction appears appropriate. *See* ELO Ch. 8-IV(D)(3).

(b) Criminal responsibility of P

Officer P could be charged with (1) second-degree murder for acting wantonly in shooting at A's tires while engaged in a high-speed chase on (presumably) city streets, or alternatively (2) involuntary manslaughter if her conduct could be characterized as reckless. *See* ELO Ch. 8-IV(D)(3) and VI(A)(5).

P might argue in rebuttal that if someone is engaged in a dangerous felony, an officer ordinarily is privileged to exercise whatever force (including that capable of causing death or serious bodily injury) she reasonably believes is necessary to effectuate an arrest. Perhaps P would argue that traveling at 80 mph on city streets constitutes a type of dangerous felonious activity (i.e., reckless endangerment, etc.). But the prosecution would respond that deadly force cannot be used against a person who is fleeing arrest for a misdemeanor. Here, P did not know anything about the tavern incident; she began chasing A for ignoring a stop sign, (at that point, A was not driving 80 mph on city streets). Thus, P could not successfully assert the law officer's arrest privilege and would be liable for manslaughter. *See* ELO Ch. 4-VII(D).

Assuming P's assertion of the foregoing privilege was not successful, she could contend that, at most, her conduct was negligent (i.e., she failed to act reasonably under the circumstances) since she had to weigh the risk of the escape of a potentially dangerous individual (one who would speed away from a police officer at 80 mph) against the possibility that her efforts to stop the speeding vehicle could result in death or serious injury to innocent bystanders. It is doubtful that P's argument will be persuasive, and therefore, a successful criminal prosecution against P is likely.

Answer to Question 8

Did Cole ("C") commit a burglary?

At common law, a burglary was the trespassory breaking and entering into the dwelling of another, at night, with the intent to commit a felony therein. Assume though, that this jurisdiction has extended the crime to (1) cover any structure, (2) include theft offenses within the structure that are not felonies, and (3) not require the incident to have occurred at night. The State might charge C with burglary by entering the market and committing a larceny (the trespassory taking and carrying away of another's tangible personal property with the intent to permanently deprive the latter of such property) therein by departing from the store with whiskey C did not pay for.

C could contend, however, that the entrance into the store was not "trespassory" because it was open to the public. In addition, C might contend that he did not have the intent to commit a larceny when he entered the store since (1) as a consequence of having been drinking for several hours, he did not have the ability to form such an intent, and (2) the thought of taking the bottle without paying for it did not occur to him until Brody ("B") unexpectedly drew the revolver. State probably would argue in rebuttal that (1) the entrance into the store was "trespassory" because the owner's consent did not extend to persons entering the structure for the purpose of stealing items, (2) C's actions were not those of an intoxicated person and, therefore, drunkenness did not prevent C from forming the intent required for burglary, and (3) since C entered the store knowing that neither he or B had any money, he must have formed the intent to steal the liquor prior to actually entering the building. However, even assuming the entrance was "trespassory," mere presence is not enough and State would have a difficult time proving that C intended to commit a larceny within the structure. C could, of course, assert that he presumed that B, alone, would steal the liquor. It is therefore unlikely that C could be successfully prosecuted for burglary. *See* ELO Ch. 9-VII.

Vicarious culpability

Assuming State could successfully prosecute B for burglary, it could assert that C was vicariously culpable as (1) an aider and abettor, or (2) a co-conspirator.

State might contend that C aided and abetted B in the commission of the burglary by accompanying B into the market with the intent to assist in the larceny of the whiskey. However, absent a belief by B that C would actually assist him in stealing the liquor if necessary, this assertion would probably *not* be successful. Thus, C is *not* vicariously capable for B's burglary (if in fact B committed burglary). *See* ELO Ch. 6-II(B) and 7-III(C)(3).

A conspiracy arises where there is an agreement between two or more persons to commit a crime. C could contend that no agreement was ever formed with B to steal the whiskey. State could argue in rebuttal that since B and C entered the store without money, there must have been at least an implicit understanding that they would steal the liquor. However, without additional evidence of an understanding between B and C, this assertion by State probably would **not** be successful. *See* ELO Ch. 6-II(A).

Is C culpable for robbery?

A robbery occurs where the defendant by force, or the threat of force, and in the presence of the victim, commits a larceny. Since an aider and abettor is culpable for the crimes of the original perpetrator, State could contend that C aided and abetted B's robbery by running from the market with the whiskey bottle. C might contend that the "trespassory taking" element of larceny is absent since C had, with the clerk's acquiescence, already picked up the whiskey bottle when B suddenly drew the gun. However, State probably would contend successfully in rebuttal that a "trespassory taking" did occur since the clerk obviously assumed that the whiskey would be paid for prior to being removed from the store. *See* ELO Ch. 9-VIII.

While C also would argue that he could not form the specific intention necessary to be an aider and abettor because of his prior drinking, his ability to function effectively after the bottle had been taken (engaging in a gun battle with the police) would probably result in State being successful with respect to this issue, too. Thus, C probably could be convicted of Robbery.

Is Ames ("A") culpable for any crimes of B and C?

Since there is nothing to indicate that A entered into any type of agreement with B and C to steal the whiskey, or that A knew that neither B nor C had any money when they entered the market, it is unlikely that A could be culpable for B's and C's crimes as a co-conspirator. *See* ELO Ch. 6-II(A).

However, State could assert that since a crime is not deemed to be complete until the perpetrators have reached a "safe haven," A is culpable for B and C's robbery as an aider and abettor. State would argue that A assisted B and C in the commission of the robbery by driving the getaway car with the intent to help B and C reach safety.

A could argue in rebuttal, however, that he was not an aider and abettor since (1) he was too intoxicated to formulate the intent to assist B and C in their robbery, (2) not having witnessed or been specifically told by B or C that they committed a robbery, A was not even aware that B and C had actually engaged in criminal conduct, and (3) he was intimidated into helping B and C because B (who was holding a gun) ordered A to drive away. Although A probably did realize that B and C had committed a robbery, it is *not* likely that State could prove beyond a reasonable doubt that A actually desired to assist B and C in their getaway. Thus, A would probably *not* be culpable for the robbery. *See* ELO Ch. 7-III(A).

Is C vicariously culpable for Officer S's murder?

The discussion about C's culpability must begin with an analysis of whether B could have been successfully prosecuted for first-degree murder had he lived.

Did B commit a murder?

State could probably contend that B acted with malice aforethought since he (1) deliberately intended to take Smith's ("S") life (B shot at S, and a party may be taken to have intended the natural consequences of his actions), or (2) B was engaged in an independent, inherently dangerous felony (robbery). A and C could argue in rebuttal that due to B's earlier drinking, (1) B could not have formed the "deliberate intent" to take another's life, and (2) B did not possess the intent required for robbery. According to the murder statute in the jurisdiction, malice aforethought is present "when there is manifested a deliberate unlawful intent to take the life of a fellow human being." State's argument, that when B shot at Officers S and J, killing S, he manifested the requisite deliberate intent to take S's life, probably would prevail because of the presence of mind inherent in B's actions. *See* ELO Ch. 8-II(B)(3).

The claim that B was too intoxicated to form the specific intent required for robbery probably would be answered by State in a similar fashion. Nothing in B's conduct indicated that he was unable to function coherently, (i.e., after realizing that neither B nor C had any money, B pointed a gun at the liquor store clerk, and ran out the door with the bottle). Thus, State would probably be successful on the felony-murder charge even if it did not prevail on the malice aforethought issue. *See* ELO Ch. 3-IV(B)(2).

Did B commit first-degree murder?

The statute in the jurisdiction defines first-degree murder as "all murder that is perpetrated by any kind of willful, deliberate and premeditated killing or that is committed in the perpetration of, or in attempt to perpetrate, robbery or burglary ... " Even though State could argue willfulness and deliberate intent, it does not appear from the facts that B premeditated killing S, since he was involved in a spontaneous gun battle. Consequently, State would argue that the killing was committed in the perpetration of the robbery. Since a crime is not considered "ended" until the perpetrators have reached safety, it appears that State would prevail on this issue, too, and B would have been successfully prosecuted for first-degree murder. Although C did not actually shoot anyone during the gun battle, shooting at the officers probably would constitute assistance to B. Since an aider and abettor is culpable for the perpetration of the crime in which he assisted and for any crimes that were a reasonably foreseeable outgrowth of the one in which he assisted, State could probably also successfully prosecute C for first-degree murder. *See* ELO Ch. 8-IV(C).

Is A vicariously culpable for Officer S's murder?

In the unlikely event that A was deemed to be an aider and abettor of B and C, A could argue that he withdrew his assistance prior to Officer S's murder. However, for a withdrawal to be effective it must ordinarily be done voluntarily and communicated to all of the other participants. Because A's purported withdrawal was not voluntary (A presumably fled to avoid arrest), and no effort was made to communicate his withdrawal to B and C, A's assertion of this theory would probably *not* be successful. *See* ELO Ch. 6-VII(B)(2).

Answer to Question 9

Did Dave ("D") commit first degree murder?

The prosecution probably would charge D with first-degree murder. This crime occurs where the defendant has committed a homicide (the killing of one human being by another) and such homicide was preceded by premeditation and deliberation. The prosecution could contend that the intent to kill is shown by the facts that (1) D had threatened to kill Vince ("V"), and (2) one is deemed to have intended the natural consequences of his conduct (i.e., death is a natural consequence of shooting V with a Magnum). Premeditation and deliberation are demonstrated by the fact that D went to Homer's home to obtain the Magnum and then returned to the pub with it. *See* ELO Ch. 8-IV(C)(1) and (2).

In rebuttal, D could argue that (1) he was too drunk to form the intent necessary for first-degree murder (he had consumed five beers earlier and two bourbons just before the incident), and (2) his paranoid schizophrenic condition was activated by excessive drinking. Therefore, (a) he was legally insane at the time he killed V (i.e., he did not know that his actions were wrong, since he felt threatened by V), or alternatively (assuming the theory was recognized in this jurisdiction) (b) he had an irresistible impulse (i.e., he lacked the substantial capacity to conform his actions to the law) to kill V. *See* ELO Ch. 8-IV(C)(3).

In rebuttal, the prosecution could argue that (1) D's drinking had no effect upon his reasoning (D had the presence of mind to walk to a friend's home, obtain a weapon, and then return to the pub), and (2) just as voluntary intoxication is ordinarily not a defense to a crime, insanity or an irresistible impulse that is self-induced by excessive drinking should not constitute a defense to criminal behavior. D might respond by contending that (1) his mental condition was *involuntarily* induced in the sense that he had no reason to suspect that five beers over a period of several hours (the facts indicate that D and V had gone to the pub in the afternoon and that the shooting occurred in the evening) would be sufficient to activate his paranoid schizophrenia, and (2) the two bourbons imbibed subsequently at the pub were of no legal consequence since D had already unexpectedly lapsed into a paranoid schizophrenic condition. However, the prosecution probably could contend successfully in rebuttal that D's behavior did not emanate from his drinking, but rather from the public embarrassment he suffered when V loudly called him a "dumb bastard." Prior to that time, there was no indication that the five beers had transformed him into a paranoid schizophrenic. Thus, the prosecution should prevail in its contention that D committed first-degree murder. *See* ELO Ch. 3-IV(C)(1)(d).

Assuming the prosecution was successful with respect to the foregoing issues, D might next contend that (1) there was adequate provocation to reduce the charge to voluntary manslaughter, or (2) if followed in this jurisdiction, the diminished capacity doctrine applies. (i.e., evidence of a mental impairment not rising to the level of insanity is admissible to reduce a charge of first-degree murder to second-degree murder or voluntary manslaughter.) However, the prosecution would argue in rebuttal that (1) the provocation was **not** adequate (i.e., provocation sufficient to cause a reasonable person to entertain the thought of killing another) simply because of V's name-calling, and, in any event, D had sufficient time within which to cool down (D walked from the pub to Homer's house, located the gun, and then walked back to the pub); and (2) as to the diminished capacity contention, no evidence of mental impairment should be permitted since the condition that allegedly caused the defendant to fail to possess the necessary *mens rea* was voluntarily self-induced. The prosecution should prevail on these issues, too. *See* ELO Ch. 3-II and 8-V(D)(1).

In summary, D should be convicted of first degree murder.

In the event, however, that D is not deemed to have the *mens rea* necessary for first-degree murder (i.e, because of his drunkenness he was unable to form the specific intent to kill or seriously injure V), D could be prosecuted for second-degree murder or, alternatively, involuntary manslaughter.

One is guilty of second-degree murder when he commits a homicide with a wanton *mens rea* (i.e., consciously disregards a risk that poses a high probability of death or serious injury to other human beings). One is guilty of involuntary manslaughter where he commits a homicide with a reckless *mens rea* (engages in conduct that poses a substantial risk of death or serious bodily harm). The prosecution could argue that D, being aware that excessive drinking exacerbates a paranoid schizophrenic condition, acted wantonly (or at least recklessly) by consuming the five beers and two bourbons. D could contend in rebuttal, however, that (1) he was not wanton or reckless, since he could not foresee that five beers over a several hours would constitute the "excessive drinking" necessary to aggravate his medical condition, and (2) assuming D had no history of felonious conduct while in a paranoid schizophrenic condition, there was no conscious disregard of a known risk or substantial probability of death or serious injury to others by becoming drunk. The prosecution would argue in rebuttal that violent behavior is a natural by-product of paranoid schizophrenia, and therefore D acted wantonly (or at least recklessly) in imbibing the beer (even if D is correct in his contention that his paranoid schizophrenic condition began prior to drinking the bourbon). If, however, D had no history of violent behavior as a consequence of his paranoid schizophrenia, his conduct probably would be characterized as merely reckless. Therefore, if D did not form the intent to commit murder because of his drunken state, he will probably be convicted only of involuntary manslaughter. *See* ELO Ch. 8-IV(D) and VI(A)(1)-(6).

D's crimes vis-á-vis Victoria

The prosecution would probably charge D with aggravated battery and assault of Victoria. Aggravated battery is ordinarily a battery (bodily injury or offensive touching of another) accomplished using a deadly weapon. The prosecution would contend that a battery against Victoria occurred by reason of (1) the transferred intent doctrine (where the defendant intended a particular harm to one party, and as a consequence of her conduct a similar type of harm occurred to another party, the defendant's intention toward the original person is deemed transferred to the latter victim), or (2) even if as a consequence of D's drinking he could not form the intent to commit a battery, D's drinking with the knowledge that intoxication could aggravate a dangerous mental condition was reckless. While D would assert basically the same arguments and defenses described above with respect to V's homicide (other than diminished capacity), the prosecution should prevail since (1) D probably was not sufficiently drunk to prevent him from forming the specific intention to kill V, or (2) alternatively, D's drinking with knowledge of his condition probably constituted reckless behavior. Thus, D could be prosecuted for aggravated battery on Victoria. *See* ELO Ch. 8-VII(A)(4).

In some jurisdictions, an assault occurs where the defendant has intentionally or recklessly placed the victim in imminent fear of bodily harm. Although D shot at V, since Victoria was right next to the victim, she probably felt apprehension for her physical well-being when the gun was pointed in her direction. Thus, D is also culpable of assault. *See* ELO Ch. 8-VII(B).

D's crimes vis-á-vis Valerie

The prosecution would also probably charge D with assault vis-á-vis Valerie assuming she was in the general area at which D pointed the gun. It is unclear from the facts whether Valerie was close to V when the shooting occurred. If Valerie was in close proximity to V, the discussion above would again apply.

Burglary of Valerie's house

A burglary is a trespassory breaking and entering into the dwelling of another, at night, with the intent to commit a felony (or, in most states, a theft offense) therein. Since it was already dark when D reached Homer's home, and D went to Valerie's house after leaving Homer's, the night-time element must be satisfied with respect to Valerie's house. Since D kicked down Valerie's door with the intention of shooting V therein, the intent element is also met. Finally, there was an "entering" because the bullet D shot (and probably D's foot) broke the plane of Valerie's doorway. Thus, D would probably be convicted of burglary with respect to Valerie's home. *See* ELO Ch. 9-VII.

Burglary of Homer's ("H") house

No burglary would have arisen by reason of D's initial entrance into H's house since the sliding door was standing open (i.e., no "breaking" occurred). In many jurisdictions, entering a closed area within which a person is capable of standing suffices to meet the "breaking" element of burglary. The prosecution could, therefore, contend that a burglary occurred when D opened the closet door and looked inside (assuming his face or body broke the plane of the closet doorway) for the purpose of locating H's Magnum (i.e., committing a larceny within the closet). In addition, in a few jurisdictions, the "breaking" element may be satisfied by conduct that constitutes a breaking at the time the structure is exited. If this is one of the latter states, D's conduct in closing the front door on his way out of H's home would constitute a "breaking" with respect to the initial entrance into H's home. *See* ELO Ch. 9-VII.

Larceny

Finally, D may have committed a larceny (the trespassory taking and carrying away of another's tangible personal property with the intent to permanently deprive the latter thereof) by taking H's gun and using it to shoot V. D could contend rebuttal that (1) the taking was not "trespassory" since H, as D's friend, probably would have loaned it to him, and (2) he had every intention of returning the gun. The prosecution would probably argue in rebuttal that (1) the "trespassory" element is satisfied since one may **not** presume a loan of personal property to them (in fact, if H were aware of the purpose for which D desired the firearm, he presumably would **not** have permitted D to borrow it), and (2) D should have realized that by using the gun in a murder, it would be confiscated as evidence for an indeterminate period of time (making it impossible to return it). Unless the prosecution can show that D did not intend to return the gun, the argument that it would be confiscated as evidence will not prevail and D would probably not be convicted of larceny. *See* ELO Ch. 9-II(B).

Answer to Question 10

Dr. Jones ("J") could be charged with the crime of murder.

Did J have a duty to perform the operation?

Where a defendant is charged with a crime based upon his inaction, he must have first had a duty to undertake the conduct in question. One is under a duty to act where he (1) is contractually obligated to perform the act in question, or (2) has commenced to act and subsequently leaves the victim in a worse position as a result of such intervention. J could contend that (1) nothing was said as to payment for the operation so consideration was lacking, and (2) since he never boarded the plane to perform the operation, it cannot be contended that he "commenced to act." However, the prosecution could contend successfully in rebuttal that (1) an implied-in-fact contract arose, whereby J would receive his normal and usual fee for such an operation, and (2) since J had assured the governmental officials that he would perform the operation, they probably ceased their search for another physician to perform it. Thus, J probably had a duty to perform the operation. See ELO Ch. 1-I(D)(4)(b) and (d).

Was J's failure to perform the operation the actual cause of the victim's death?

A defendant's failure to act must have been the "but for" cause of the victim's harm. J could contend that even if he had boarded the plane on April 11th, it is uncertain that the operation could have been performed successfully (especially in light of J's agitated condition resulting from his son's death). However, the prosecution could argue in rebuttal that since J had perfected the technique involved and the operation was a routine one for him, it could be established beyond a reasonable doubt that J would have been able to perform it successfully. Assuming J had a history of success with this type of operation, the prosecution should prevail on this issue. See ELO Ch. 2-II(A).

Was J's failure to act the proximate cause of the victim's death?

Where an unforeseeable cause or factor intervenes between the defendant's conduct and the victim's harm, the defendant's action (or nonaction) is **not** the proximate cause of the victim's misfortune. J could contend that given his initial reluctance to perform the operation and his obviously agitated condition, the State Department was grossly negligent in not retaining a backup physician in the event J was unable to go through with the operation. However, the prosecution could contend in rebuttal that, at most, the State Department was merely negligent in assuming that J (a responsible surgeon) would abide by the promise he had given to them. Since mere negligence by an intervening entity ordinarily is deemed to be foreseeable, the prosecution should prevail. See ELO Ch. 2-V(C)(6).

Did J commit first-degree murder?

Assuming the *actus reas* portion is satisfied, J must have (1) intended to kill or seriously injure the patient, *and* (2) acted with premeditation and deliberation to be culpable of first-degree murder. The prosecution would contend that given the rule that one is presumed to intend the natural consequences of one's conduct, J intended the patient to die (or at least knew that her death was substantially certain to occur) since (1) J was told that the patient would die without the operation, (2) his absence was unexpected, and therefore, it was likely that a qualified doctor might not be present, and (3) J had stated "I hope the bastard dies." Additionally, since J had the entire evening to contemplate his conduct, his failure to board the plane was premeditated and deliberate. J could contend in rebuttal that he (1) reasonably assumed that the State Department would have another competent doctor available to perform the operation if he were unable to do so, and (2) was too intoxicated (albeit voluntarily) to be able to form the specific intention necessary for first-degree murder. While the facts state that J was intoxicated, there is nothing to indicate that he failed to comprehend that the patient could die in his absence. Assume, however, that J might be successful in his argument that the intoxication prevented him from forming the specific intention required for first-degree murder. *See* ELO Ch. 8-II(C), IV(C)(1) and (3).

Did J commit second-degree murder or involuntary manslaughter?

Where a defendant had a wanton *mens rea* at the time of the homicide for which he is responsible, he is guilty of second-degree murder. One has a wanton state of mind where he consciously disregards a risk which she knew (or should have known) posed a high probability of death or serious injury to another human being. Voluntary intoxication is usually *not* a defense to a general intent crime where the lack of awareness results from the intoxication. Therefore, the prosecution will contend alternatively that J acted wantonly by becoming intoxicated the evening before he was to board a plane to perform a critical operation. J might argue in rebuttal that he did not act with a wanton *mens rea* because he reasonably presumed that (1) another doctor would be available to perform the operation, and (2) even if he did become intoxicated on the evening of the 10th, he would have an entire day to recover since the operation was not to be performed until the 12th. However, the prosecution would probably prevail on this issue. Thus, J probably would be guilty of second-degree murder. *See* ELO Ch. 1-II(H), Ch. 8-II(D) and IV(D).

As a third alternative, the prosecution could contend that J is culpable of involuntary manslaughter. This crime arises where the death for which the defendant is responsible occurred while the latter had a reckless *mens rea* (i.e., the defendant acted in a manner that created a substantial risk of death or serious injury to other human beings). The factual arguments described above with respect to whether J acted wantonly would again apply.

If J avoided culpability for second-degree murder, he probably would be prosecuted successfully for involuntary manslaughter. *See* ELO Ch. 8-VI.

Mistake of fact

It should be noted that even if the patient were the Russian general (rather than the wife of the Prime Minister of Canada), no defense to the crime charged would exist. Mistake of fact is only a defense where, were the facts as the defendant reasonably believed them to be, she would have possessed a defense to the crime charged. In this instance, since the Russian general would have been in the United States with the permission of the State Department, J would have had no justification to cause that person's death. *See* ELO Ch. 1-II(L)(3).

Culpability of J's friends

The crime of solicitation occurs where the defendant requests or encourages another to undertake a felony or misdemeanor involving a breach of the peace, with the intent to induce the latter to commit such crime. Where a solicitation has occurred, the soliciting party is vicariously culpable for the offense committed by the solicitee. The prosecution could contend that since the group "encouraged" J not to help the patient, they had solicited the patient's death. However, the group could contend in rebuttal that they were too intoxicated to form the specific intention to induce J to commit the crime in question. Like J, the group may have assumed that other competent physicians were available to perform the operation if J failed to meet the airplane which would arrive the very next day (since Walter Reed Hospital is in Washington D.C., there would presumably be an abundance of capable medical personnel). Finally, the group's lack of desire to persuade J to commit a crime is demonstrated by the fact that they urged J to inform the State Department of his decision to not perform the operation. It is, therefore, unlikely that the group could be prosecuted for J's crime. *See* ELO Ch. 7-IX(A).

Answer to Question 11

Crimes of T

T could be charged with burglary, larceny, and second-degree murder.

At common law, a burglary occurred where the defendant had, in a trespassory manner, broken and entered into the dwelling of another at night with the intent to commit a felony therein. (Assume that this jurisdiction extends the crime to any structure and any theft offense.) While T might contend that no "breaking" occurred because entrance into the building was gained without the necessity of damaging it in any manner, the prosecution probably could argue successfully in rebuttal that this element is usually deemed to be satisfied when any portion of the structure is moved (i.e., opening the door to X's premises). *See* ELO Ch. 9-VII.

There appears to be little question that T committed a larceny (the trespassory taking and carrying away of the personal property of another with the intent to permanently deprive the owner of such property) by placing X's jewelry in a bag and exiting the premises. Since the elements of larceny are subsumed within burglary, T would probably not be convicted for the larceny if the burglary charge were sustained. *See* ELO Ch. 9-II.

T could also be charged with second-degree murder under the felony-murder rule ("FMR"). Under this doctrine, when the victim's death occurred during and as the result of the defendant's participation in an inherently dangerous felony, the defendant is deemed to have the *mens rea* for murder (regardless of whether the defendant intended or desired the victim's death). The prosecution's assertion would be that T's burglary of X's store ultimately resulted in C's death. However, T probably could contend successfully in rebuttal that (1) no homicide (the killing of one human being by another) occurred since C caused his own death by firing the defective firearm, (2) many jurisdictions limit the FMR to situations where an innocent person is killed during the felony, and (3) there is an insufficient causal relationship between T's conduct and C's death (i.e., C's attempt to rob T and C's violent response to the police intervention superseded T's burglary of X's store). Thus, it is unlikely that T will be convicted of second-degree murder. *See* ELO Ch. 8-III(C).

Crimes of B

The prosecution conceivably could charge B with conspiracy to commit robbery, attempted robbery, and second-degree murder as a co-conspirator with A.

A conspiracy occurs where there is an agreement between two or more persons to commit a crime. Since B initially accompanied A in the car to the jewelry store after A explained the reason for his presence, there must have been at least a tacit agreement to rob T (even if B did not explicitly agree to assist A). The fact that B told A, "I've changed my mind," also indicates that there had been an agreement between them. B, therefore, would be culpable of conspiracy to commit robbery. *See* ELO Ch. 6-II(A).

B could argue that he withdrew from the conspiracy when he advised A that he no longer wished to go through with the robbery and left. However, if this jurisdiction requires that a conspirator actually make an effort to thwart the crime or contact the police, B would still be responsible for A's conduct to the extent that it was within the scope of the conspiracy or a natural outgrowth of it. In such event, B could probably be convicted for A's subsequent robbery of T (discussed below). However, B would probably not be liable for the attempted robbery of T by C (also discussed below). This is because B could not foresee criminal activity by a new, unanticipated co-conspirator. While it is not necessary that a co-conspirator know the actual identities of all of the members of the conspiracy, it is ordinarily required that he is aware of their likely existence. Also, due to similar reasons and factors discussed above relative to T, B would probably not be found liable for the murder of C under the FMR. *See* ELO Ch. 6-VII(B)(2).

Crimes of A

A could be charged with two counts of solicitation. This crime occurs where the defendant requests or encourages another to join in the commission of a crime, with the intent to induce the latter to perform the crime. A, therefore, committed a solicitation when she asked (1) C (even though she originally thought C was B), and later (2) B, to join her in the robbery of T. *See* ELO Ch. 7-IX(A).

A could also be charged with two counts of conspiracy: (1) when he agreed with B to rob T, and (2) when he apparently reached a tacit understanding with C to rob T. A could contend that he never agreed with C to perpetrate a robbery; rather, C having heard of T's intended burglary, was motivated by a desire to obtain the stolen jewelry for himself. It is unclear from the facts whether A should have realized that he had inadvertently spoken with C during her initial telephone call to B. Presumably, when B didn't know why A appeared at B's house, A should have recognized that he had spoken earlier with C (especially if there was no other male in B's home). Regardless, however, a tacit conspiratorial understanding would probably be found between A and C in light of their subsequent jointness of action—A's holding T's arms while C grabbed the bag, and then both running toward A's car. *See* ELO Ch. 6-II(A)(1).

In most states, a solicitation charge will merge into a conspiracy conviction.

Since a conspirator is culpable for acts committed by a co-conspirator that are within the scope of the conspiracy or a foreseeable outgrowth thereof, A would be culpable for the attempted robbery of T by C. This occurred when C "swiped" at T's bag (a robbery occurs where the defendant, in the victim's presence, by force or the threat of violence, commits a larceny). While A might contend that no robbery was attempted since the property that T had in his possession belonged to X, most jurisdictions hold that a robbery occurs even though the victim had previously stolen the property from another (the rationale being that robbery is a crime against mere possession, and does not depend on ownership).

Assuming a conspiracy between A and C was found to exist, A would also be culpable for the subsequent robbery of T (when A held T's arms and C grabbed the bag containing X's jewelry).

If no conspiracy was found (i.e., C was acting only for his individual benefit when he grabbed at T's bag), A would still probably be guilty of attempted robbery based upon his conduct in trying to wrest the bag from T (no robbery by A would have occurred in this instance, since it was C who actually carried away the bag containing X's jewelry). *See* ELO Ch. 6-IV(D).

C's death

The prosecution also could charge A with second-degree murder under the FMR. Points (1) and (2) of the discussion above explaining the inapplicability of the FMR with respect to T would apply in this instance as well.

Answer to Question 12

Is Axe ("A") guilty of solicitation to commit a burglary?

The crime of solicitation occurs where the defendant has requested or encouraged another to commit a felony or misdemeanor involving a breach of peace, with the intent to induce the latter to commit such crime. When A contacted Boss ("B") and Chum ("C") and asked them to participate in his plan to steal Carot's diamonds, the crime of solicitation probably occurred. However, since solicitation normally merges into the crime of conspiracy if there is agreement (discussed below), it is unlikely that A will be prosecuted for this crime. *See* ELO Ch. 7-IX(A).

Are A, B and C guilty of conspiracy to commit burglary?

A conspiracy occurs when two or more persons agree to commit a particular crime (i.e., the target crime). Today, many states also require that one of the co-conspirators commit an overt act in furtherance of the conspiracy. The three defendants agreed to commit a burglary, and driving to Carot's house would suffice for the overt act. Thus, A, B and C are culpable for conspiracy. *See* ELO Ch. 6-I(A).

Ordinarily, once a conspiracy occurs, the charge cannot be avoided. Thus, the fact that C may have withdrawn from the target crime (discussed below) would not absolve her of conspiracy.

Has C committed a theft of Wheel's ("W") car?

Ordinarily, a larceny occurs where the defendant has taken and carried away another's personal property with the intent of permanently depriving the owner of his property. C could contend that no theft occurred because she never intended to keep the car permanently, as evidenced by her return of the vehicle to W's house. The State would argue in rebuttal, however, that C had originally intended to keep the car. (She probably decided to return it only *after* she withdrew from the plan.) State should prevail on the charge of larceny. *See* ELO Ch. 9-II.

If the larceny charge were unsuccessful, C could be prosecuted for malicious mischief (generally, the intentional or reckless tampering with another's personal property) and State would probably prevail since C was arrested leaving W's car at W's house.

Are A and B vicariously guilty of C's crime?

Assuming C did commit a crime, State could attempt to hold A and B criminally responsible for it. Co-conspirators are ordinarily culpable for any crimes committed by any of the other co-conspirators, so long as the other co-conspirator's crimes were within the scope of the conspiracy or a foreseeable outgrowth of it. A and B could contend that there was never any discussion or agreement to steal a car, and that doing so was both outside the scope of the conspiracy and not a foreseeable outgrowth of it. A and B could argue that their understanding was that C would "borrow" the vehicle from a friend. State could contend that given C's prior history of car theft, A and B should have recognized that by "borrow," C meant "steal," but since C never said she was going to "steal" a car, A and B probably are not vicariously guilty for C's conduct in this instance. *See* ELO Ch. 6-IV(D).

Are A, B and C guilty of attempted burglary?

An attempt occurs when the defendant takes a substantial step toward the culmination of the target crime, with the intent to commit such crime. Since the defendants went to Carot's home and actually raised a window, an attempted burglary occurred. However, this crime would probably be merged into the completed burglary (discussed below). *See* ELO Ch. 5-VI(A)(1).

Are the defendants guilty of burglary?

Burglary is the trespassory breaking and entering into the dwelling of another, at night, with the intent to commit a felony (or in most states, a theft offense) therein. Since the element of a "breaking" is ordinarily interpreted as the movement of any part of the structure, opening the window would satisfy this aspect of the crime. (The facts indicate the crime took place at night and the defendants intended to commit a felony—the theft of Lady Carot's diamonds.) Thus, the defendants appear to be guilty of this crime since A and B entered Carot's home, and C was a co-conspirator. *See* ELO Ch. 9-VII.

C might, however, contend that she is not guilty of burglary since she withdrew from the conspiracy prior to the time that the target crime occurred (i.e., C never actually entered Carot's house). However, to be effective, a renunciation must ordinarily be (1) made without compulsion to do so (voluntarily), and (2) communicated to all members of the conspiracy. In addition, in some jurisdictions, the withdrawing party must make an effort to thwart the crime. Since C thought she heard Carot's car in the driveway, and presumably was afraid of being caught, she probably would not be considered to have acted voluntarily. Also, C made no effort to prevent the target crime. Therefore, C probably is culpable of the burglary committed by A and B. *See* ELO Ch. 6-VII(B)(2).

Is A guilty of assault and battery of Carot?

A battery occurs when the defendant causes either bodily injury or offensive touching. The crime of assault exists in two situations: (1) an attempted battery occurs; and (2) the victim is intentionally placed in fear of imminent injury. Since A confronted and struck Carot, an assault and battery occurred. While the first type of assault (attempted battery) would definitely merge into the battery, the second type would not because the additional element of apprehension of the battery by the victim also must be proved. *See* ELO Ch. 8-VII(A) and (B).

The fact that Carot pointed a gun at him, and threatened to shoot, would not constitute a defense to A's actions, since her conduct was privileged under both the arrest of felon and self-defense privileges (which ordinarily extends to invasions of one's home). *See* ELO Ch. 4-IV(E).

Are C and B vicariously guilty for A's assault and battery of Carot?

Both C and B would contend that the assault and battery upon Carot by A was not a foreseeable outcome of the conspiracy and, therefore, they are not culpable for those crimes. However, State probably could argue successfully in rebuttal that the assault and battery were foreseeable, since any time one enters another's home there is always the possibility that the occupant could return and physical violence might ensue. Thus, B and C probably will be culpable for A's actions toward Carot. *See* ELO Ch. 6-IV(D).

Answer to Question 13

A. DID DON ("D") COMMIT A BURGLARY?

In the removal of the stereo equipment

Burglary is the trespassory breaking and entering into another's dwelling, at night, with the intent to commit a felony therein. Today, many states extend this crime to any structure and the intent to commit any theft offense within the structure. Since the facts are silent, assume that (1) D acted at night, (2) taking the stereo equipment for the purpose of defrauding an insurance company constitutes a felony, and (3) this jurisdiction extends the definition of burglary to any structure. D could argue that no "trespassory breaking" occurred since he (1) was given the key by Oscar ("O"), and (2) simply opened the warehouse door with it. The "breaking" element would be satisfied by the fact that the warehouse door was opened (movement of any part of the structure will usually suffice). But D is probably correct in contending that the "trespassory" element is missing, since O gave him the key to the premises. Therefore, D probably did not commit a burglary with respect to the removal of the stereo equipment. *See* ELO Ch. 9-VII(A).

In the theft of the vehicle

The State will argue that a burglary occurred when D re-entered the warehouse for the purpose of stealing the vehicle behind it. While D might contend that the "therein" element is not satisfied since the car was not *in* the warehouse, entrance into a structure for the purpose of removing something within the fenced-in area behind the structure probably would satisfy this aspect of burglary, i.e., the vehicle would be deemed to be within the curtilage of the structure. Here, the trespassory element is probably met, since O never gave D permission to take the vehicle. Thus, D probably did commit a burglary with respect to the vehicle. *See* ELO Ch. 9-VII(A).

B. IS D GUILTY OF EITHER SECOND-DEGREE MURDER OR MANSLAUGHTER?

For State to show that D is guilty of second-degree murder or manslaughter, it would have to prove that (1) Allen ("A") is guilty of such a crime, and (2) D is vicariously culpable for A's crime(s).

Second-Degree Murder/Felony-Murder Rule ("FMR")

Under the FMR, where a homicide occurs during and as a consequence of the defendant's participation in an independent, inherently dangerous felony, the defendant is deemed to have the *mens rea* for second-degree murder (even though she did not intend or desire the victim's death). As noted above, a burglary charge against D and A for entering the warehouse with the purpose of removing the stereo equipment would probably be unsuccessful. Thus, this conduct could *not* serve as the underlying felony necessary to trigger the FMR. *See* ELO Ch. 8-III(A).

Second-Degree Murder/Wantonness

State alternatively could contend that A committed second-degree murder by causing the officer's death while possessing a wanton *mens rea* (consciously disregarding a risk that posed a high probability of death or serious bodily harm to others). While A might contend the highway patrol officer died when she lost control of her car, not as a consequence of A's conduct, a sufficient causal connection would probably be found between A's conduct and the officer's death (i.e., "but for" A's driving at an excessive speed and attempted escape, the officer would not have given chase and crashed). A also could argue that highway patrol officers presumably receive special training with respect to high speed driving, and therefore A's conduct did *not* create a high probability of death or serious bodily harm. However, A should have recognized that, despite a higher than normal level of driving expertise, a lethal accident was entirely possible at 100 mph. Thus, A is probably guilty of second-degree murder. *See* ELO Ch. 8-II(D) and IV(D).

Involuntary Manslaughter/Recklessness

Since State might be unsuccessful with respect to its second-degree murder assertion, it would alternatively contend that A committed involuntary manslaughter by causing the officer's death while possessing a reckless *mens rea* (acting in a manner that posed a substantial risk of death or serious injury to others). The same factual arguments described above with respect to second-degree murder based upon a wanton *mens rea* would apply equally in this instance. If A's conduct was deemed *not* wanton, it should be considered reckless. Thus, at a minimum, A should be found to have committed involuntary manslaughter. *See* ELO Ch. 8-VI(A).

Involuntary Manslaughter/Misdemeanor-Manslaughter Rule ("MMR")

The MMR probably would *not* be applicable since driving at an excessive rate of speed (if a misdemeanor) is probably only a *malum prohibitum* (rather than a *malum in se*) offense. *See* ELO Ch. 8-VI(B).

Is D culpable for the crimes of A?

A conspiracy exists where there is an agreement between two or more persons to commit a crime. The facts state that A agreed to help D in D's plan to take the stereo equipment for the purpose of defrauding the insurance company. Therefore, a conspiracy existed between A and D.

A conspirator is vicariously culpable for any crimes committed by other co-conspirators provided such offenses were within the scope of the conspiracy or were a reasonably foreseeable outgrowth thereof. State could argue that it was foreseeable that (1) the crime might be detected, (2) police would respond, and (3) someone would be killed in the course of an escape. D could contend in rebuttal that a homicide was not foreseeable in light of the fact that A and D had received a key to the premises by the owner and (apparently) no one was armed. State would probably prevail, on the issue of foreseeably notwithstanding the absence of a gun, and therefore D would be culpable of the degree of murder for which A could be convicted. Thus, D should be culpable for A's crimes if A is found to have committed second-degree murder or involuntary manslaughter. *See* ELO Ch. 6-IV(D).

C. IS O VICARIOUSLY CULPABLE FOR D'S CRIMES?

D is probably guilty of burglary (with respect to the vehicle), larceny (taking the vehicle), conspiracy to commit insurance fraud, and second-degree murder or involuntary manslaughter. O was certainly a member of the conspiracy to defraud his insurer. But O probably could contend successfully that the burglary and larceny of the vehicle were not contemplated by the conspiracy. (O presumably thought that D and A would bring their own vehicles.)

Further, with respect to the death of the patrol officer, State could argue that the officer's death was a foreseeable consequence of the conspiracy to commit insurance fraud, since there is always a possibility of detection and ensuing violence when a stranger enters a warehouse to remove goods from it. However, O would argue in rebuttal that here the possibility of detection and ensuing violence was practically nonexistent since D was not a stranger entering the warehouse, but rather knew O and obtained entry with a key. Thus, D would not have been worried about anyone detecting a "break-in" of the building. The facts indicate that A drove away with the goods without incident and was pursued by the highway patrol car only because he had been driving in excess of the speed limit. By speeding, first when the officer's attention was attracted and then in a high-speed chase in excess of 100 mph, A committed an independent, intervening act that was not a foreseeable consequence of a conspiracy to commit insurance fraud; O would argue that this was beyond what O should have expected D to do (i.e., drive the stereo equipment from O's premises). Thus, while O would be guilty of conspiracy to commit insurance fraud, he probably would not be found guilty of second-degree murder or involuntary manslaughter. *See* ELO Ch. 6-IV(D).

Answer to Question 14

The prosecution would probably charge Dave ("D") with murder (the unlawful killing of another person).

Can D assert the "fleeing felon" justification?

Where a dangerous felony has been committed in the presence of a private citizen, he may utilize whatever force is reasonably necessary to prevent the perpetrator from escaping. D could contend that since Bob ("B") presumably had just committed a dangerous felony with respect to the museum guard by striking the latter with such force that he was knocked unconscious and bleeding (an aggravated form of battery), D was privileged to use force (the lance) capable of causing B's death to prevent B from escaping. The prosecution could argue in rebuttal, however, that (1) the guard had not actually been attacked in D's presence, (2) B wasn't attempting to escape at the time D killed him, and (3) merely threatening to use deadly force against B might have restrained him until the police could be summoned. While the first argument might not be persuasive, the prosecution's second and third arguments probably would be successful, and therefore the "fleeing felon" justification should fail. *See* ELO Ch. 4-VII(B)(4)(d).

Can D successfully assert either the self-defense or protection of property justification?

It does **not** appear that D could successfully assert the self-defense or protection of property privileges. Self-defense does not appear to apply because there is no indication that B made any type of menacing movement toward D. Indeed, there is nothing in the facts that indicates B even knew D was there. Defense of property (D's paintings) would likewise not apply because one is not privileged to exercise deadly force (i.e., force capable of taking life) in defense of property. *See* ELO Ch. 4-IV(F) and VI(B).

Assuming none of D's defenses are successful, for what degree of murder is he likely to be convicted?

The prosecution could charge D with first-degree murder, arguing that he intentionally took B's life with premeditation and deliberation since D hesitated a moment before throwing the lance. However, since D was "stunned" by the fact that B was slashing D's valuable paintings, the mere passage of a moment or two for D to adjust to the gravity of B's actions probably would not be viewed as a sufficient interval to constitute premeditation and deliberation. The charge would thus be reduced to second-degree murder. *See* ELO Ch. 8-IV(C)(1) and (2).

D also would contend that his crime should be reduced from second-degree murder to voluntary manslaughter because he acted with adequate provocation.

While the prosecution might contend that seeing someone slash valuable paintings could never constitute adequate provocation (i.e., cause a reasonable person to consider taking life), given the fact that the paintings were irreplaceable, adequate provocation could be found. D probably would be convicted of voluntary manslaughter. *See* ELO Ch. 8-V(D).

What crimes could D be charged with as a consequence of the incident with Amos ("A")?

With respect to A, the prosecution could charge D with (1) robbery (where the defendant, by force or the threat of force, and in the presence of the victim, commits a larceny), (2) larceny (the trespassory taking and carrying away of another's personal property with the intent to permanently deprive the victim of that property), (3) assault (deliberately placing another in fear of imminent injury), and (4) battery (intentionally causing bodily injury or offensive touching). These crimes stem from Dave's conduct in sticking a pipe against A's back and pretending it was a gun to recover the memorandum.

One can ordinarily use reasonable, nondeadly force to recover wrongfully taken property, provided the person is in "hot pursuit" of the item(s) (the right of reclamation). D will contend that his action was a reasonable means of regaining possession of his memorandum, and this will be his defense to all of the above crimes. However, since D just happened to see A while driving to the museum, it would not appear that D was in "hot pursuit" (i.e., that he promptly discovered the wrongful taking and immediately set out in pursuit). In addition, the facts state that D only suspected A had taken the memorandum. Thus, this defense probably will fail. *See* ELO Ch. 4-VI(D)(1).

As to the battery and assault charges, D might contend that a pipe is really not a device that can be characterized as forceful or intimidating. However, the prosecution probably could argue successfully in rebuttal that the item used is irrelevant; all that matters is whether a reasonable person in the victim's position would have been intimidated under the circumstances. Since A reasonably believed a gun was pointed at his back, the "force or intimidation" element is satisfied. *See* ELO Ch. 8-VII(A) and (B).

As to the robbery and larceny charges, D also might argue that he did not have the intent to permanently deprive A of A's property. This is evidenced by the fact that D threw A's billfold (except for the memorandum which was D's property) under a street light where he expected A to find it. The prosecution would argue in rebuttal, however, that D's decision to return the billfold may have been formed subsequent to the taking and D should have realized that leaving a wallet under a street lamp probably would result in it not being found or returned to A. The prosecution probably would prevail. (If so, the larceny charge probably would be merged into the robbery conviction.) *See* ELO Ch. 9-II(F) and VIII.

Thus, D can be convicted of robbery, battery (unless this is a jurisdiction that requires actual physical injury) and assault.

Answer to Question 15

CRIMES OF CLYDE ("C")

C could be charged with the following crimes:

Solicitation

The crime of solicitation occurs where the defendant requests or encourages another to commit a crime, with the intent to induce the latter perform the crime. The prosecution would contend that C solicited (1) Bob ("B") to commit the crime of receiving stolen property, and (2) Tank ("T") to commit larceny or embezzlement. *See* ELO Ch. 7-IX(A).

Conspiracy

The crime of conspiracy occurs where there is an agreement between two or more persons to commit a crime. In many states, an overt act by one of the co-conspirators in furtherance of the crime is also necessary. No conspiracy appears to have arisen between C and B since B never agreed to assist C in obtaining Acme's whiskey (rather, B merely indicated a willingness to purchase the liquor after delivery). C could contend that T's statement, "What an unbelievable idea," did not constitute an agreement by T to commit larceny or embezzlement. However, since both C and T acted as if an agreement had been reached (C altered the records and had the truck loaded, while T acknowledged that she had "lost her nerve"), a conspiracy between C and T would probably be found. *See* ELO Ch. 6-II(A) and IV(B).

If a conspiracy between C and T were found, C's solicitation of T probably would be merged into the conspiracy conviction.

Larceny/Embezzlement

Larceny is the trespassory taking and carrying away of the personal property of another with the intent to permanently deprive the owner of such property. C could contend that there was no "trespassory taking" since (1), in his capacity as shipping manager, he had the right to direct whiskey from the warehouse into Acme trucks (i.e., the whiskey was already in his possession at the time of the alleged larceny), and (2) Sam ("S") was aware of C's plan and knowingly permitted it to occur. Furthermore, no "carrying away" occurred, since at the time the whiskey was driven away from Acme's premises, T was acting pursuant to police instructions. The prosecution could argue in rebuttal that a "trespassory taking" had occurred since (1) a shipping manager is not an employee with broad authority, and therefore a "trespassory taking" did occur when the whiskey was diverted from the warehouse to the truck pursuant to C's directions; and (2) Acme's knowledge and inaction do not prevent the defendant's subsequent taking from being "trespassory." A "carrying away" occurred when Acme's employees, pursuant to C's instructions, moved the whiskey from Acme's warehouse to the truck (it was not necessary for the liquor to actually be moved from Acme's premises). Assuming C was *not* a "trusted employee," he probably could be prosecuted successfully for larceny. *See* ELO Ch. 9-II(B).

Since C might, however, be considered a "trusted employee," the prosecution would alternatively charge C with embezzlement. (i.e., C had fraudulently converted the personal property of another that was rightfully in his possession.) While C would contend that no "misappropriation" occurred by causing whiskey to be placed onto a truck parked within Acme's premises, the prosecution probably could argue successfully in rebuttal that since C's use of the vehicle for his intended purposes was unauthorized, an embezzlement had occurred. *See* ELO Ch. 9-III(E)(2)(a).

Finally, in the unlikely event that the court concluded that C was a "trusted employee," but no misappropriation had occurred, C probably could be convicted of attempted embezzlement since he had taken a substantial step toward the culmination of the target crime by altering the shipping records and sending the truck to B's garage loaded with Acme's whiskey. *See* ELO Ch. 5-II(D).

Forgery

Forgery occurs where the defendant has fraudulently made a false document. A "document" for purposes of this crime is ordinarily viewed as a writing that purports to have legal significance (i.e., one that creates rights or obligations). The facts are unclear as to whether the shipping records that C altered purportedly affected rights or liabilities. If these writings required Acme to deliver whiskey to B, a forgery probably would have occurred since B would appear to have the right to have Acme whiskey delivered to him. However, if the records were only for Acme's internal use, they might not have a legal significance and, therefore, no forgery would have occurred. *See* ELO Ch. 9-IV(I)(3).

CRIMES OF TANK ("T")

Assuming T is found to have entered into a conspiracy with C, T would be culpable for all crimes of which C were convicted (except for the solicitation of B), since a co-conspirator is liable for all crimes committed by any other conspirator that are in furtherance of, or are within the scope of, the conspiracy. While T might argue in rebuttal that she was attempting to withdraw from the conspiracy when confronted by the police, the prosecution probably could contend successfully in rebuttal that withdrawal ordinarily results in avoidance of the crimes *subsequently* committed by other co-conspirators. Since C's offenses were complete prior to T's attempted withdrawal from the conspiracy, T probably *cannot* avoid them. *See* ELO Ch. 6-VII(B)(2).

If, however, no conspiracy were found between T and C, T probably would not be guilty of any crimes. This is because an aider and abettor must actually assist the principal perpetrator with the intent to help the principal accomplish the target crime. Since T would not have driven the truck unless instructed to do so by the authorities, the intent element is lacking.

CRIMES OF BOB ("B")

The prosecution could charge B with receiving stolen property (B knowingly took stolen property into his possession with the intent to continue depriving Acme of it). However, B could contend that this was legally impossible since the whiskey ceased to be "stolen" the moment the police intervened and instructed T to drive the truck to B's premises. While the prosecution could contend in rebuttal that (1) the whiskey was stolen when moved from the warehouse to the truck, and (2) their instructions to T only permitted the whiskey to reach its original destination, B should prevail on this issue. *See* ELO Ch. 9-VI.

However, B is probably culpable for attempting to receive stolen goods. Although the target crime is legally impossible, an attempt is complete where, had the facts been as the defendant thought them to be, the target crime would have been committed. Since B would have been culpable of receiving stolen property if the whiskey were stolen, B probably could be charged with attempting to commit this crime. *See* ELO Ch. 5-IV(E)(3).

Answer to Question 16

1. HOW SHOULD THE FEDERAL APPEALS COURT RULE?

Conspiracy

A conspiracy exists where two or more persons agree to commit a crime. Many states require that one of the parties commit an overt act in furtherance of such criminal objective. Both Dan ("D") and Paul ("P") would contend that neither could be guilty of conspiracy because P never actually agreed with D to rob Bank. While P accepted the pistol, the facts indicate that P feared for his physical safety and that he intended to try to thwart the crime. Neither P nor D ever had an "agreement" with Mike, since Mike was coerced into joining them. Therefore, the conspiracy conviction should be overturned. *See* ELO Ch. 6-II(A).

The federal statute

Both P and D could contend that they did not commit the crime described in the federal statute because (1) Fred was not "in the performance of his duties" at the time he was shot (arguing that the facts seem to indicate that Fred had *just arrived* at the bank), (2) while the statute appears to describe a general intent crime (that the defendant only have intended the *actus reas* portion of the statute), D and P would argue that it implies acting "knowingly," and (3) P and D were not aware Fred was a federal officer. First, it is necessary to interpret the phrase "in the performance of his duties." The facts state that F "was a federal bank examiner conducting an audit of Bank's accounts," using the present tense. It is arguable that F had already begun this audit and was walking into Bank that day to continue his work. Furthermore, even if P and D's contention is true (i.e., that F had just arrived at Bank to begin his auditing duties), it could be argued that F still would have been killed while performing his duties as a federal bank examiner. Only if F had been killed when he was not on the job as a federal bank examiner should P and D's position prevail. Next, whether Congress desired to punish for this offense only in the event that the perpetrators knew they were assaulting federal officials is a question of statutory intent (to be determined from the legislative history pertaining to this statute). However, the statutory language appears to reveal a decision to treat the entire class of federal officials in a particular manner, and the defendant's knowledge seems to be irrelevant. In summary, these statutory interpretation contentions by P and D probably would *not* be successful.

Assuming the federal statute was violated, P would contend that (given the absence of a conspiracy) he is not culpable for D's assault with a deadly weapon. An individual is culpable for the criminal acts of another where the former, with the intent to do so, aids or assists another in the commission of a crime. The facts seem to indicate that P probably lacked the intent to aid or assist D (as mentioned above, P apparently helped D because he feared for his safety).

Moreover, the crimes committed by the perpetrator must have been reasonably foreseeable by the aider and abettor. While it might have been foreseeable that D would use his pistol if someone obstructed their robbery attempt, it arguably could not be anticipated that D would shoot "a federal officer engaged in the performance of his duties" for no apparent reason. Because the specific intent element is lacking and because D shooting F was not reasonably foreseeable, P should *not* be guilty of the crime set forth in the federal statute. *See* ELO Ch. 7-III(B) and IV(A).

In summary, neither P nor D is guilty of conspiracy, and only D would be guilty under the federal statute.

2. HOW SHOULD THE STATE COURT RULE ON MIKE'S ("M") MOTION FOR A DIRECTED VERDICT?

The defense of duress exists where the defendant, as a consequence of threats to cause her imminent death or serious bodily harm, committed the crime with which she is charged; provided, however, the defendant (1) actually and reasonably believed the threatened acts would be carried out, and (2) is not charged with intentionally killing another human being. The facts indicate that (1) D pointed a gun at M and threatened M with death unless M assisted in the bank robbery, (2) M's pistol was unloaded, (3) D always had M "covered," and (4) M "reasonably believed" that D's threats were genuine. The prosecutor could argue that M, as an aider and abettor to D killing F, fits into the "intentional killing" exception to the defense of duress. For the same reasons that P should not be guilty of aiding and abetting D's assault with a deadly weapon, M also should be acquitted of this charge; M did not intend to be a part of (i.e., to aid or assist) any intentional killing. Thus, M probably is entitled to a directed verdict. *See* ELO Ch. 4-II(D).

Answer to Question 17

CRIMES OF ADAMS ("A")

Second-degree murder/involuntary manslaughter

Second-degree murder occurs where the defendant commits a homicide (the killing of one human being by another) with a wanton *mens rea* (i.e., consciously disregarding a risk that posed a high probability of death or serious bodily harm to others). However, if the defendant possessed a reckless *mens rea* when the homicide occurred (the defendant engaged in conduct that created a substantial risk of death or serious injury to others), she is culpable only of involuntary manslaughter. The facts are unclear as to the precise conduct undertaken by A (i.e., in what way was operation of the vehicle grossly negligent). To constitute wantonness, A would have had to have been acting in a manner that presented an obvious risk of serious harm to others (i.e., driving at 75 mph through crowded downtown streets). Since A had a prospective customer with her, it is more likely that her grossly negligent conduct would be equated with recklessness. Therefore, A probably could be convicted of involuntary manslaughter. *See* ELO Ch. 8-II(D), IV(D) and VI(A)(1)(a).

Note: No conviction under the misdemeanor-manslaughter rule ("MMR") would be appropriate since moving violations are ordinarily *malum prohibitum* misdemeanors (as opposed to *malum in se*) offenses. Only the latter type of crimes are generally the basis for a conviction under the MMR.

Larceny by trick/embezzlement

Larceny by trick occurs where the defendant obtains possession of the personal property of another, through fraud or deceit, and carries away such personal property with the intent to permanently deprive the victim thereof. If it could be shown that, at or before the time A received the $100 payment from Riley ("R"), A had already decided to sell the vehicle to Williams ("W"), A probably would be guilty of larceny by trick. If, however, it can be proved that A resolved to sell the car in question to W after receipt of R's $100 payment, then A probably could be convicted of embezzlement (fraudulently converting the personal property of another at the time when such property was rightfully in the former's possession). Thus, more facts are needed to determine whether larceny or embezzlement is the appropriate crime, but it appears that A would be guilty of one of them. *See* ELO Ch. 9-II(B)(6) and III.

CRIMES OF RILEY ("R")

The facts are unclear with respect to how R forcibly took possession of the car from Williams ("W"). Assuming she merely pushed W away from the vehicle, R probably would be culpable of assault (intentionally or recklessly placing another in fear of an imminent, injury), battery (intentionally or recklessly causing bodily injury or offensive touching) and robbery (committing larceny by force, or the threat of force, in the presence of the victim). While R could contend that he believed he had a superior right to the car, and therefore his actions were privileged, the prosecution could argue in rebuttal that a mistake of law is ordinarily not an excuse for the commission of a crime. Some jurisdictions, however, permit a mistake of law to negate an element of the prosecution's *prima facie* case. If this view were followed here, R probably could contend successfully that no robbery occurred since he lacked the intent to permanently deprive "another" of his personal property (because R believed the car belonged to him). In such event, R probably still could be successfully prosecuted for assault and battery (since R acted recklessly in not consulting an attorney prior to attempting to regain possession of the vehicle). If the robbery conviction were sustained, the assault and battery charges probably would merge into that offense. *See* ELO Ch. 1-II(L)(2), Ch. 8-VII(A) and (B), and Ch. 9-VIII.

CRIMES OF HAND ("H")

H could be charged with (1) larceny for obtaining an unsigned certified check from the bank (presumably without its authorization), (2) uttering a forged document (the knowing tender of a forged document to another) for giving a document that purported to be a certified check to Black ("B"), when H knew that the item was worthless, (3) forgery (the fraudulent creation of a false document) for signing the certified check with the signature of a purported bank officer, and (4) false pretenses (the fraudulent acquisition of title to another's property by means of a material misrepresentation of fact) for receiving a certificate of title to the vehicle from B in exchange for an item that H knew was worthless. Probably the only factual contention that H could make is that the larceny prosecution should be unsuccessful because the common law definition of this crime requires that "tangible" personal property be involved. At common law, items such as checks were sometimes deemed to have no intrinsic value (i.e., they only represent a chose in action for the right to acquire money). Today, however, most states extend this crime to documents such as checks. Therefore, whether H could be convicted of larceny would depend upon the applicable law of this jurisdiction. In addition, in many jurisdictions the crime of uttering a forged instrument is merged into a conviction for forgery. *See* ELO Ch. 9-II(D)(2).

CRIMES OF COOPER ("C")

The prosecution could charge C with embezzlement. By giving the finance company a lien upon ABC's car, C has arguably fraudulently converted property of the corporation. However, C could contend that (1) assuming the vehicle was not removed from ABC's premises, there was no conversion of the car (i.e., exercise of dominion or control by the financing entity); (2) there was no "fraudulent" intent to convert the car since he intended to repay the loan (and thereby remove the lien) within three days; and (3) since C held ABC stock, there was no conversion of "another's" property. The prosecution could argue that (1) a conversion occurred because the finance company acquired an interest in the vehicle, and (2) a corporation is a separate legal entity from its stockholders. However, there does not appear to be a successful rebuttal to C's claimed lack of intent unless C did not, in fact, repay the loan within the three-day period. Thus, C probably could *not* be convicted of embezzlement. *See* ELO Ch. 9-III(F)(3).

ABC CORPORATION

Whether ABC could be culpable for the crimes of A depends upon the applicable legislation, if any. Many states have enacted laws that permit a corporation to be fined for offenses committed by officers or directors. If such an ordinance exists and A's offenses fall within it, a monetary fine might be assessed against ABC for A's conduct.

Answer to Question 18

First, we will consider L's possible culpability for murder or manslaughter, since these offenses carry the greatest potential penalty.

Did a homicide occur?

Homicide is the killing of one human being by another. L could contend that the accidental explosion and fire, not L, caused Q's death. However, inaction can constitute the *actus reas* portion of a crime where the defendant had a legal duty to act and failed to do so. The State could argue in rebuttal that L, as the apartment house owner (and presumably the only party legally capable of inspecting and authorizing repairs to the central heating system) was contractually obligated to his tenants to maintain the building's heating system. State should prevail on this issue. *See* ELO Ch. 1-I(D)(4)(b).

L next might argue that his inaction was not the actual ("but for") cause of Q's death, since he was responsible for his own demise by electing to return to the burning dwelling. However, given the (1) legal duty of parents to care for their children, and (2) natural paternal instinct of a father toward his baby, this contention by L should fail. *See* ELO Ch. 2-II(A)(2).

Finally, L might contend that his inaction was not the proximate cause of Q's death (i.e., he died in a manner that was not reasonably foreseeable from his alleged failure to act) since he behaved in a bizarre manner by reentering a flaming structure. However, it probably is reasonably foreseeable that someone might return to a burning building to save a family member. *See* ELO Ch. 2-IV(H)(1)(a) and (b).

In summary, L probably will be deemed to have committed a homicide.

Assuming a homicide occurred, is L guilty of second-degree murder or involuntary manslaughter?

State might contend that L had the requisite *mens rea* for second degree murder, in that his failure to investigate X and Q's complaints about the building's heating system evidenced a conscious disregard for a risk that posed a high probability of death or serious bodily harm to others (i.e., wantonness). L, however, might argue successfully in rebuttal that merely having been advised on six occasions that the heating system was malfunctioning did not sufficiently apprise him of the likelihood of an explosion and fire (although, if L had an obligation under the state's landlord-tenant law to investigate the malfunction, there may be a different result). Without such knowledge, L may have lacked the wantonness necessary for murder. *See* ELO Ch. 8-II(D) and IV(D).

State alternatively could contend that L was culpable of involuntary manslaughter since his indifferent conduct (ignoring six requests to investigate) constituted at least a reckless *mens rea* (i.e., he behaved in a manner that posed a substantial risk of death or serious injury). State probably could argue successfully that L's conscious decision to remain ignorant about the heating problem constitutes recklessness; an explosion and subsequent fire are foreseeable consequences of a heating system malfunction. Again, L would respond that a heating system malfunction could occur from any number of causes and mere knowledge of a potentially defective condition would not adequately apprise L that a life-endangering risk was present. It is a close question, but L probably would be characterized as having a reckless *mens rea* and thus would be culpable of involuntary manslaughter. *See* ELO Ch. 8-VI(A)(1)(a).

Is X guilty of assault (possibly aggravated assault) and battery upon Y?

There is little doubt that X committed an assault (intentionally causing Y to fear imminent injury), battery (intentionally or recklessly causing bodily injury to, or offensive contact with, another), and possibly an aggravated assault (an assault with a deadly weapon) upon Y. These crimes occurred when X struck Y with the heavy metal ashtray. *See* ELO Ch. 8-VII(A) and (B)(4).

X could assert the self-defense privilege (i.e., where one reasonably believes she is in imminent danger from the unlawful exercise of force, she may exercise whatever force is reasonably necessary under the circumstances to prevent such contact). X will contend that, since she believed that Y was reaching for a weapon, hitting Y with the ashtray was reasonable under the circumstances. However, State could argue in rebuttal that X's belief was not reasonable (i.e., despite a previous argument, when someone puts their hands in their pockets there is no reason to assume that such person is reaching for a weapon). In addition, State would contend that hitting a person with a heavy metal ashtray constituted excessive (rather than reasonable) force. Presumably, X could have punched Y or grabbed her (although X could assert that she had to act spontaneously and the ashtray was the closest item). Since X's belief that Y was reaching for a firearm probably was not "reasonable" (unless Y had a reputation for carrying lethal weapons), the self-defense privilege should fail. *See* ELO Ch. 4-IV(D).

Did J embezzle or commit a larceny vis-á-vis X's watch?

Larceny by trick occurs where the defendant obtains possession of another's personal property by fraud, and carries such property away with the intent to permanently deprive the victim of it. Since J was heavily indebted to numerous bookies, State could contend that at the time J was received X's watch, he had no intention of returning the item. Therefore, J's receipt of the watch was fraudulent. However, the facts do not clearly indicate that J had formed the intent to sell the watch prior to the time it was delivered to him by X. Thus, a larceny charge should fail unless this jurisdiction has a special larceny by bailee statute that would apply to these facts. *See* ELO Ch. 9-II(B)(4), (6) and (F)(1).

Embezzlement occurs where the defendant fraudulently misappropriates the personal property of another, at a time when such property is rightfully in the defendant's possession. Since X had left her watch with J for repairs (and therefore the watch was "rightfully" in J's possession), J committed embezzlement when he sold the watch to Y. There is no possibility that J could assert the defense of necessity (if he failed to pay the bookies, they would kill him) since J put himself into the position that caused his predicament. *See* ELO Ch. 9-III(E).

Did J embezzle the second watch?

There also appears to be little doubt that J embezzled the second watch (the one he sold to the detective for $100), since there is no indication he intended to sell it at the time it was delivered to him. J could assert the defense of entrapment. Entrapment occurs where a law enforcement officer creates in the mind of the defendant the desire to commit a crime that the latter would not otherwise be predisposed to undertake. Some courts use an objective test (i.e., would a reasonable person have been induced to commit the crime for which he is charged). Under this test, J could contend that an ordinary person would accept $100 for a watch of lesser value, although the persuasiveness of this argument is questionable. Under the common law subjective test (i.e., whether the particular defendant was predisposed to commit the crime in question), entrapment probably could not be successfully asserted since J had previously demonstrated a disposition to commit embezzlement in the transaction with Y. *See* ELO Ch. 4-X(A)(2).

Answer to Question 19

1. CHARGES AGAINST ALEX ("A")

a. Burglary

At common law, burglary was the trespassory breaking and entering into the dwelling of another, at night, with the intent to commit a felony. Today, many jurisdictions have extended this crime to include (1) structures other than dwellings, and (2) situations where the defendant intended to commit a theft offense within the building. The breaking and entering requirements are, respectively, satisfied by A's (1) pushing the window upward, and (2) extending the pole into Ben's ("B") store (the pole would be deemed to be A's instrumentality). Since B and his family lived upstairs, the pawnshop might be considered a dwelling (i.e., a place of regular habitation), even if the common law definition were to apply.

At common law, the "night-time" requirement was met if a person's face could not be discerned by natural sunlight. Today, the night-time element has been eliminated except for higher degrees of burglary in approximately half the states. Assuming for this exam that the night-time element is an issue, the facts are unclear as to whether this element is satisfied. Whether the sun sets by 6:11 p.m. depends on the geographic location and time of year. Assume A's conduct occurred at night.

A could still contend that he did not have the intent to commit a felony or theft offense within B's premises. A's attempt to regain his watch might *not* constitute a larceny (discussed immediately below). *See* ELO Ch. 9-VII.

b. Larceny

A larceny occurs where the defendant, in a trespassory manner, has taken and carried away the personal property of another with the intent to permanently deprive the owner of that property. A could contend that (1) since the watch belonged to him, the property "of another" was not involved, and (2) there was no intent to "permanently deprive" B of the watch. (A merely wanted to re-obtain it temporarily for the purpose of showing it to his father and would have returned it as soon as his father left.) The prosecution could argue in rebuttal that (1) since A had pawned the watch to B, B's interest in the item was superior to that of A, and therefore the "of another" element was satisfied, and (2) since A had apparently not decided when he would return the watch to B, the "permanently deprive" element is satisfied. Since the issue is one of intent, a jury would probably infer that A intended to return the item to B as soon as his father had departed. Thus an interesting issue is raised: whether A is guilty of burglary because he entered the premises with the intent to take the watch, but is not guilty of larceny because he did not intend to permanently deprive B of it (i.e., unbeknownst to A, he did not satisfy all the elements of larceny). *See* ELO Ch. 9-II(E) and (F).

c. and d. Attempted burglary and larceny

An attempt occurs where the defendant has engaged in conduct for the specific purpose of committing a crime (the target offense), and such conduct represents a substantial step toward the culmination of that crime.

An attempted burglary charge would be inappropriate because A actually entered B's premises. Thus, A's conduct, if criminal, was complete. With respect to the attempted larceny charge, if the conduct A was seeking to accomplish was not criminal, it would be legally impossible for an attempt to have occurred (i.e., there would be no target crime). Thus, if A did not intend to permanently deprive B of the watch (as concluded above), the attempted larceny charge against A would also fail. *See* ELO Ch. 5-II(A).

2. CHARGE OF ASSAULT WITH A DEADLY WEAPON AGAINST BEN ("B")

An assault occurs where the defendant has intentionally or recklessly caused her victim to be in fear of imminent injury. Where this conduct is accomplished by means of a lethal instrumentality, assault with a deadly weapon occurs. Although B might contend that A never had the opportunity to be apprehensive of an injury (the shot was fired before A realized that B saw him), the prosecution could argue in rebuttal that (1) A must have heard the bullet ricocheting and, therefore, had a moment of apprehension wondering whether it would hit him, and (2) A would have feared a second shot once he heard the first one. In addition, in many jurisdictions, any attempted battery is an assault. *See* ELO Ch. 8-VII(B)(4).

B probably could assert the defense of home or self-defense. Under the modern view of the defense of home privilege, when a home occupier reasonably believes that an intruder is about to commit a dangerous felony within the premises, she may use deadly force (force capable of causing death or serious bodily harm) to expel the intruder. Since B's pawn shop was part of his home and A appeared to be holding a rifle, B's belief that he and his family were in grave danger probably would be considered reasonable. It is, therefore, unlikely that any prosecution against B would be successful. *See* ELO Ch. 4-V(B).

B also might assert the self-defense privilege (where one reasonably believes that he is in imminent danger of death or serious bodily injury from another, the former may respond with lethal force against the latter). However, it might be difficult to characterize B's fear of attack from A as being "imminent" since A was still outside the store and was unaware of B's existence. Thus, the self-defense privilege probably could *not* be successfully asserted. *See* ELO Ch. 4-IV(F).

3. CHARGE OF LARCENY AGAINST CLIFF ("C")

Lost or mislaid property is deemed to be in the constructive possession of the person with superior title to it (in this instance, B). Thus, Cliff's act of taking the watch into his possession would be "trespassory," if he had intended to keep it. The facts indicate he intended to return it (which might well have been possible since A's initials were engraved on it) at the time he picked it up in front of the store, so there was no intent to permanently deprive the owner of it at the time the "taking" occurred. It is therefore unlikely that C could be prosecuted successfully for larceny. (In a few jurisdictions, the crime of embezzlement might extend to situations such as this.) *See* ELO Ch. 9-II(F)(1).

4. CHARGES AGAINST DON ("D")

a. Receiving stolen property

The crime of receiving stolen property occurs where the defendant has received stolen property knowing that it has been stolen from another, with the intent to deprive the owner of it. Since (as discussed above) C probably did not commit a larceny, D probably could *not* be successfully prosecuted for receiving stolen property (the watch in question *not* having been the subject of a larceny). *See* ELO Ch. 9-VI(B)(1).

b. Attempting to receive stolen property

However, most jurisdictions will permit conviction for an ***attempt*** to receive stolen property where, had the facts been as the defendant thought them to be, the target crime would have actually occurred. Since D thought the watch was stolen (C told him that it was "hot"), D probably could be convicted of an attempt to receive stolen property. *See* ELO Ch. 5-II(A)(1).

Answer to Question 20

CRIMES OF SAM ("S")

Murders of Mac, Fred and Tom

Under the felony-murder rule ("FMR"), where a homicide occurs during and as a consequence of the defendant's perpetration of an independent, inherently dangerous felony, each of the felons is deemed to have the *mens rea* for second-degree murder. Since Mac, Fred and Tom were killed during the robbery (robbery is the trespassory taking and carrying away of another's property, from or in the presence of such person, via the use or threat of force, with the intent to permanently deprive the victim of such property), the State could contend that, under the FMR, S is culpable for the deaths of Mac, Fred and Tom. However, Fred's death was not a homicide (the killing of one human being by another). Rather, it was the result of an accident resulting from Fred's ineffectual utilization of the nitroglycerin. Mac's death was not a natural and probable consequence of the felony; it resulted from an independent, intervening event (Eb was unaware of what had transpired inside the casino) and thus there was no causal relationship between the robbery and Mac's death. Finally, Carlo probably was privileged to kill Tom under the "fleeing felon" justification. If this jurisdiction follows the rule that the FMR does not apply to situations where a felon is killed by the victim, S would not be charged with Tom's death. *See* ELO Ch. 8-III(A), (C)(2) and (4)(e).

Attempted Murder of Eb ("E")/Aggravated Battery

A murder occurs where one commits a homicide with the intent to kill or cause serious bodily harm to the victim. When S shot E, he probably was attempting to kill the latter (although S might not actually have desired to kill E, it may be assumed that one intends the natural consequences of his actions, and shooting at someone with a gun certainly has the potential of causing death or serious bodily harm). *See* ELO Ch. 8-II(C)(1).

If for any reason a court or jury held that S did not have sufficient intent to justify an attempted murder conviction for shooting E, S probably could be prosecuted successfully for aggravated battery (causing bodily injury with a lethal weapon). *See* ELO Ch. 8-VII(A)(4)(b).

However, S probably could assert the self-defense justification to these charges (i.e., he reasonably believed he was in imminent danger of serious bodily harm or death), since E had just killed Mac and turned the gun on S. Theoretically, under the "fleeing felon" doctrine (a private citizen can exercise force capable of causing serious bodily harm or death to prevent a felon from escaping where the latter has committed a felony in the former's presence), E could have been justified in shooting S, but since E had no knowledge of the felony (he only desired to kill gamblers), the "fleeing felon" doctrine does not apply to E and S should prevail. *See* ELO Ch. 4-VII(B)(4)(d).

Robbery/Larceny

Since S and his co-conspirators threatened Carlo ("C") and his employees with the threat of force (i.e., they were held at gunpoint), S is guilty of robbery (defined above). While the requisites of larceny (the trespassory taking and carrying away of another's property with the intent to permanently deprive the victim of such property) are also met, this crime would merge into the robbery. *See* ELO Ch. 9-II and VIII.

Burglary

The crime of burglary is the trespassory breaking and entering into another's structure, at night, with the intent to commit a felony or theft offense therein. Since S had apparently been permitted ingress into the casino before it closed, the "trespassory breaking" elements do not appear to be satisfied. However, in some states, these requisites are fulfilled where the defendant has trespassorily entered (moved the door of) any room or enclosed area within the structure. The safe (being of a size in which an individual could stand) could arguably be deemed to be such an enclosed room or area. If so, S could be guilty of burglary since the safe door was blown open for the purpose of taking the money within it (i.e., a larceny). *See* ELO Ch. 9-VII(B).

Arson/Malicious Mischief

Arson is the malicious burning of another's structure. State could contend that a "burning" occurred as a result of the explosion, and that the safe was actually a "part" of the casino since it could be moved only by heavy equipment. While in many states an explosion will constitute the "burning" necessary for arson, the facts indicate that the safe was not attached to the building and there is no indication in the facts that the blast affected any other part of the casino. Consequently, it is unlikely that the "structure" element is satisfied, and a charge of arson probably could not be successfully prosecuted. However, the crime of malicious mischief (maliciously causing injury to another's property) apparently has occurred since the safe is no longer usable.

Conspiracy

Since S, Mac, Fred and Tom (apparently) had agreed to commit a robbery (we can infer an agreement to act in concert from their actions of entering the casino and hiding together, and of holding the employees at gunpoint while F blew up the safe), S could be guilty of conspiracy (an agreement between two or more persons to commit a crime) to commit robbery. *See* ELO Ch. 6-II(A)(2).

CRIMES OF EB ("E")

Murder of Mac

E probably could be successfully charged with the murder of Mac. There is little doubt that a homicide occurred, E showed the necessary malice aforethought (intent to kill or cause serious bodily harm) when he yelled, "Death to gamblers," and when he fired at Mac. Waiting outside the casino with a gun indicates premeditation and deliberation. *See* ELO Ch. 8-II(C) and (D).

As discussed above, the "fleeing felon" justification is probably unavailable to E. *See* ELO Ch. 4-VII(B)(4)(d).

E might contend that he was insane at the time of the shooting since his life was wrecked. Although E apparently understood the nature of his act (by shouting, "Death to gamblers," and then shooting a person whom he thought to be a member of this group) and understood that it was morally wrong (the *M'Naghten* test), E might contend that he was acting under an irresistible impulse (i.e., he was unable to control his actions at that moment). The irresistible impulse that affects a defendant's mind may be the culmination of sustained brooding. State, of course, will argue in rebuttal that E seemed to be in full control of his faculties. While E was obviously upset with his experiences at the casino, there probably is not sufficient proof that the urge to kill gamblers had become irresistible. *See* ELO Ch. 3-I(D).

A few states recognize the diminished capacity doctrine. Under this theory, where a mental deficiency (not rising to the level of insanity) prevents the defendant from possessing the specific intention *mens rea* necessary for murder, his crime is reduced to voluntary manslaughter. If this were such a state, E might be culpable of only the latter offense if he could show that his brooding hostility vis-á-vis the casino ripened into a mental defect that precluded him from forming the requisite specific intention *mens rea* for murder. *See* ELO Ch. 3-II(D)(1)(a).

Attempted Murder of Sam ("S")

Where a defendant commits some act in furtherance (as opposed to mere preparation) of a criminal offense, an attempt has occurred. Since E was about to pull the trigger of his gun and shoot S, an attempted murder appears to have occurred. While E's actions toward S probably would constitute an assault as well, that crime probably would merge into the attempted murder. *See* ELO Ch. 5-III(A).

CRIMES OF CARLO ("C")

Operating a casino

The facts stipulate that C "operated" the casino, and so he would be guilty of a misdemeanor under the state's gambling statute.

Murder

State probably could not successfully charge C with murder in the killing of Tom. While there is no privilege to exercise force capable of causing death or serious injury in defense of property (the money), C probably could successfully avail himself of the "fleeing felon" justification (since Tom had just perpetrated a robbery upon C). The fact that C was responding to the taking of illicit property (the gambling proceeds had been obtained in violation of a criminal statute) would not, in most states, prevent C from asserting this defense. *See* ELO Ch. 4-VII(B)(4)(d).

Involuntary manslaughter

It is conceivable that State could charge C with the involuntary manslaughter of Tom, Mac and Fred under the misdemeanor-manslaughter rule. Under this doctrine, where a homicide occurs in the course and as a consequence of a *malum in se* misdemeanor, the perpetrator of the misdemeanor is guilty of manslaughter for any death that results from that misdemeanor. However, there does not appear to be a sufficient causal relationship between the misdemeanor in which C was engaged (gambling) and the deaths of the three co-felons. These deaths occurred as a consequence of the robbery that they had perpetrated, not because of C's gambling activities. Also, gambling probably is only a *malum prohibitum* misdemeanor. Thus, this assertion by State should fail. *See* ELO Ch. 8-VI(B)(2).

Multiple-Choice Questions

1. The State of Ames has a statute which defines Criminal Assault as occurring when one person "causes bodily injury to another." The case law of Ames defines Criminal Assault as a "general intent crime."

    George and Kramer are drivers searching for a parking spot at a mall in the State of Ames. Both drivers approach an empty spot at about the same time. They begin to argue over who is entitled to the spot. During the argument, Kramer, intending to scare George away, walks over to George's car and touches George's throat with a screwdriver. Unfortunately, when George twists his head to look at Kramer, he cuts his throat seriously against the screwdriver point.

    Based on these facts, if Kramer is prosecuted for Criminal Assault, it is most likely that:

    (A) Kramer is culpable because he intended to place the screwdriver against George's throat.
    (B) Kramer is culpable because he created an inherently dangerous situation.
    (C) Kramer is not culpable because he could not reasonably foresee George's actions.
    (D) Kramer is not culpable because he lacked the intent to physically injure George.

2. Responding to a recent trend in gang violence, the California legislature enacted a statute which makes it a capital offense for any motorist to "knowingly" kill another motorist with an explosive device. (Assume that California law follows the Model Penal Code's definition of "knowingly.")

    One day, Freddy, a member of a gang called the Hooters, pulls alongside a car driven by Richie, a member of the Rockers gang. Richie makes a derogatory finger gesture towards Freddy. Enraged, Freddy lights a stick of dynamite, throws the stick into Richie's car, and then races away. Richie is killed when the dynamite explodes. Jack, who was sleeping in the back seat of Richie's car, is also killed. Freddy had no way of knowing that Jack was in Richie's car.

    Based on these facts, can Freddy be successfully prosecuted under the California statute for Jack's death?

    (A) Yes, because he knowingly threw the dynamite into Richie's car.
    (B) Yes, because Jack was clearly within the zone of danger created by Freddy's conduct.
    (C) No, because Freddy did not know Jack was in the car.
    (D) No, because Richie's conduct constituted "provocation."

3. Joe, desperately needing money for his drug habit, steals a television from a friend's house. (Assume that, under applicable law, no burglary has occurred.) Three days later, Joe holds a garage sale and offers to sell the TV to Molly for $50. When Molly asks Joe how he could sell the item for "such a bargain," Joe replies that he needs the money "quickly" to relocate to another city. Molly pays Joe $50 and takes the television without ever getting proof of title for the item.

    Based on these facts, it is most likely that Joe could be successfully prosecuted for:

    (A) False pretenses because Joe implicitly represented to Molly that he owned the television.
    (B) Larceny by trick because Joe received $50 for the television, but gave no instrument of title to Molly.
    (C) No crime because Joe made no express representations of ownership to Molly.
    (D) No crime because purchasers assume the risk of defective title at events such as garage sales.

4. After Jethro was fired from his job, he decided to "get even" with his ex-employer. So, one night, Jethro broke into Farmer John's barn and set fire to John's favorite tractor. The barn was located approximately 100 feet from the main house.

    One of Farmer John's neighbors, Leroy, saw smoke coming from the barn. Leroy ran over and put out the fire before any part of the barn was destroyed. There was, however, extensive charring to the barn. Also, several of the items in the barn were burned. (Assume that the common law view of arson is adhered to in this jurisdiction.)

    Based on these facts, if Jethro is prosecuted for arson, it is most likely that:

    (A) Jethro is not guilty because the barn was only charred.
    (B) Jethro is guilty because the fire caused damage to a structure adjacent to the main house.
    (C) Jethro is not guilty because he did not specifically intend to damage any structure (only Farmer John's tractor).
    (D) Jethro is not guilty because the barn isn't part of Farmer John's house.

5. Mr. Barnes, a senior partner at the We Sue For You law firm, gave a fax machine to Andrew, a file room clerk, to deliver to a repair shop. Andrew, who felt slighted because he was not given a Christmas bonus by Mr. Barnes, took the fax machine to a local pawn shop and obtained $200 for it. He then told Mr. Barnes that a thug had taken the fax machine from him at

gunpoint. Two days later, Mr. Barnes happened to see the fax machine in the pawn shop window and called the police. Andrew was subsequently arrested. (Assume that common law principles are applicable in this jurisdiction.)

Based on these facts, if Andrew is prosecuted for larceny, it is most likely that:

(A) Andrew is guilty because he pawned Barnes' fax machine.
(B) Andrew is guilty because he lied to Barnes when he said the fax machine was taken from him.
(C) Andrew is not guilty because Barnes voluntarily gave him the fax machine.
(D) Andrew is not guilty if he intended to redeem the fax machine from the pawn shop when he was arrested.

6. Anita Badcheck decides that she simply has to have a new Mercedes convertible. She goes to the local Mercedes dealer and writes a check for the price of the car from her personal account. She knows that she only has $50 in her account. Before the salesperson can verify that the check is good, he has a heart attack. After the manager calls for an ambulance, he tells Anita to "take the car" and he gives her the car's title documents. Three days after Anita drives off in the new Mercedes, her check is returned to the dealership, marked "insufficient funds."

    If Anita is prosecuted for false pretenses, it is most likely that:

    (A) Anita is guilty because she took possession of the vehicle.
    (B) Anita is guilty because she took title to the vehicle.
    (C) Anita is not guilty because she only received possession of the vehicle.
    (D) Anita is not guilty because the vehicle and attendant documents of title were turned over to her voluntarily by the dealer.

7. Erica offered to sell her computer to Jamie for $1,000. Erica told Jamie the computer was worth at least $2,000. However, just the day before, Erica had been told by an expert appraiser that the computer was worth" $500, at most." Jamie, believing that the computer was worth $2,000, gave Erica a money order for $1,000. Erica, however, lost the money order before she could cash it.

    Based on these facts, if Erica is prosecuted for false pretenses, it is most likely that:

    (A) Erica is guilty because she fraudulently obtained Jamie's money order.
    (B) Erica is guilty because Jamie took possession of the computer.

(C) Erica is not guilty because she never cashed the money order.

(D) Erica is not guilty because her comment about the computer's value was merely her opinion, not a factual statement.

8. Allison was shopping at Bruno Magli, when she spotted an extraordinary pair of loafers. Allison checked the price tag and saw the shoes were marked at $350. She had only $200 in her pocketbook. Undaunted by her shortage of funds, Allison calmly took a $200 price tag from another pair of shoes and switched it with the price tag on the loafers she wanted to buy. The teenage cashier failed to notice the change in price tags. Allison happily took her new pair of shoes home. Two days later, she was arrested when the store manager's inventory check revealed the tag switch.

If Allison is prosecuted for larceny by trick, it is most likely that:

(A) Allison is guilty because she acquired the shoes by deceit.

(B) Allison is guilty because she fraudulently switched price tags.

(C) Allison is not guilty because she acquired legal title to the shoes.

(D) Allison is not guilty because she altered no digits on either of the price tags.

9. Mary asked Brian Beagal if she could borrow his new Toyota. She told Brian that she needed the car to go to a party at a professor's house. When she made the statement, she had no other purpose in mind. Brian gave her the keys and told Mary to have a good time. At the professor's party, Mary had a violent argument with her fiance and decided that she had to get as far away from him as possible. Mary drove back to her house, put her most valuable possessions in Brian's car, and started on a trip to the West. Mary was arrested one week later when a custom's official checked the car's license plate at the US-Mexican border.

Based on these facts, it is most likely that Mary could be successfully prosecuted for:

(A) Larceny.

(B) False pretenses.

(C) Larceny by trick.

(D) Embezzlement.

10. Sid was the manager of the local Domino's Pizza. One night, while he was working at Domino's, he opened the safe in the back office with the key the owner had given to him. Sid was given the key in order to pay for any unexpected expenditures that might arise while the owner was away. Sid took $250 from the safe. He did not use this money to pay for any business

expenses. Rather, he used the money to buy an expensive watch for his girlfriend. Sid was arrested a few days later when the manager discovered the money was missing.

Based on these facts, it is most likely that Sid could be successfully prosecuted for:

(A) Larceny.
(B) False pretenses.
(C) Larceny by trick.
(D) Embezzlement.

11. Kevin, an eighteen year old with an addiction to silly practical jokes, took a plastic gun from his closet and went outside in search of his friends. Kevin saw his cousin Mary and her friend Pam walking towards his house. He decided to have a little fun with them and hid behind a bush, waiting for them to walk past. As they walked by, Kevin jumped out and yelled, "Give me your money or I'll shoot." Mary, who knew Kevin's addiction and suspected that Kevin's gun was just an old toy, pretended to be frightened and gave Kevin $5 from her purse. Kevin took the money and ran back into his house. Pam was genuinely frightened, but Kevin ran off before she could give him any money.

Based on these facts, it is most likely that Kevin can be successfully prosecuted for:

(A) Robbery.
(B) Larceny.
(C) Embezzlement.
(D) No crime at all.

12. Tommy Nimblefingers is a professional pickpocket. One evening, he was lounging at a popular tourist resort in California, "checking out" the passing crowd. As he watched, a rich-looking couple walked by, arm-in-arm. They were obviously focused on each other, and not paying much attention to anything else around them. Spying a good "target," Tommy got up and began walking behind them. When he was close enough, he deftly removed the wallet from the man's back pocket. A nearby shopkeeper saw Tommy take the wallet and he tackled Tommy before he could get away.

Based on these facts, which crime has Tommy committed:

(A) Robbery.
(B) Larceny by trick.

(C) Embezzlement.

(D) None of the above.

13. Kristen works as a live-in maid for Ward and June Cleaver. Feeling that she is underpaid, Kristen decides to steal an antique Chinese vase from the Cleaver mansion. She takes the vase, puts it under her coat, and leaves the house. About an hour later, June Cleaver notices the missing vase and calls the police. Policeman Joe Friday spots Kristen walking in the seedy part of town with a big bulge under her coat. Friday stops Kristen, who admits that she stole the vase. She turns the vase over to Friday.

Kristen tells Friday that she was going to sell the vase to Beaver, a well known "fence" for antique artifacts. Hoping to earn a few commendation points on his record by catching the notorious Beaver, Friday hands the vase back to Kristen and asks her to go ahead with the sale to Beaver. Beaver, intending to add the vase to his own private collection of rare Chinese antiques, buys the vase from Kristen for a small fraction of its real value.

Based on these facts, if Beaver is prosecuted for receiving stolen property, it is most likely that:

(A) Beaver is guilty because the low purchase price establishes that he either knew or suspected that the vase was stolen.

(B) Beaver is guilty because the vase was stolen.

(C) Beaver is not guilty because Friday had recovered the stolen vase.

(D) Beaver is not guilty because he did not intend to resell the vase.

14. Morgan runs the largest "fencing" operation in the City of Broken Arrow. One day, his "employees" call and tell him that a large shipment of stolen televisions has arrived from an adjoining state. Morgan directs his "employees" to placed the goods in a warehouse owned by Pete, an innocent third party who is completely unaware of Morgan's "fencing" operation. Two weeks before he can remove any of the stolen televisions from the warehouse, Morgan is arrested by the police, who received an anonymous "tip" about Morgan's operation.

Based on these facts, it is most likely that the most serious crime for which Morgan can be successfully prosecuted is:

(A) Receipt of stolen property.

(B) Attempted receipt of stolen property.

(C) Conspiring to receive stolen property.

(D) None of the above crimes.

15. Tom and Alex were both rejected for admission by Avery Law School though they had excellent college grades. Tom suspected that the sole reason for their rejection was the blind predjudice of the Admissions Director against students from Fairmount College. One night, after many beers, Tom asked Alex, "Wouldn't it be great if someone simply got rid of the Admissions Director?" Alex did not answer, but Tom continued, "If I could just get him alone, I could do it."

The next day, Tom asked Alex to accompany him to the Admissions Office "so I can talk to that SOB once more." When they got there, the Director was talking with his secretary. Tom asked Alex to get the secretary to leave the office. Alex responded "Fine." He succeeded in luring the secretary out of the office on the pretext of showing her a mistake on one of the school's bulletin boards. Tom then closed the door to the Director's office, took out a gun, and fatally shot the Admissions Director. Alex knew that Tom owned a gun, but he didn't believe that Tom actually was carrying it with him.

Based on these facts, if Alex is prosecuted as an accomplice to murder, it is most likely that:

(A) Alex is guilty because he distracted the Admissions Director's secretary.

(B) Alex is guilty because he helped Tom carry out the murder plan.

(C) Alex is not guilty because he did not participate in the actual murder of the Admissions Director.

(D) Alex is not guilty because he lacked the necessary *mens rea*.

16. Timmy wanted to join the Jets gang. Brian "Mad Dog" Harriman, the leader of the gang, wouldn't let Timmy join because he thought Timmy was a wimp. To prove his point, Brian publicly dared Timmy to "do something important, like showing those religious fanatics who's in charge." Timmy responded, "What do you mean? What do you want me to do?" Brian laughed and then said, "I knew it, you're not really one of us." The following night Timmy set fire to the local church. When Timmy told Brian what he had done, Brian responded, "That's cool. Welcome to the gang."

Based on these facts, if Brian is prosecuted for solicitation, it is most likely that:

(A) He is guilty because he "dared" Timmy to commit a crime.

(B) He is guilty because he complimented Timmy for burning down the church.

(C) He is not guilty because a dare is insufficient to impose criminal liability if it results in commission of a crime.

(D) He is not guilty because he didn't specifically intend that Timmy burn down the church.

17. Dillinger and Capone were prison cellmates at Alcatraz. Six months ago, Capone was released from prison after serving his three year term for tax fraud. Dillinger, who is still serving a life term for murder, wants Capone to kill the police officer who captured him. He sends Capone a letter offering him $50,000 for the hit. Unknown to Dillinger, Capone has been sent to Papillion prison after a new conviction for Armed Robbery. The letter is forwarded to Capone at his new prison. After Capone receives the letter, he throws the letter in the garbage and mutters, "I'd never help that rat."

Based on these facts, if Dillinger is prosecuted for solicitation of murder in a jurisdiction following the Model Penal Code, it is most likely that:

(A) Dillinger is guilty because the letter was read by Capone.
(B) Dillinger is guilty because he sent a letter requesting the policeman's murder.
(C) Dillinger is not guilty because it was impossible for Capone to kill the policeman.
(D) Dillinger is not guilty because Capone had not yet taken a "substantial step" toward killing the policeman.

18. Tina and Inez are roomates who hate their snobbish neighbor, Patricia. One day, Tina tells Inez that Patricia is going out of town for the weekend and that this would be a "perfect" time to steal Patricia's prize brooch. She also tells Inez that Patricia keeps a spare house key under the big flowerpot in the backyard. She says, "all you have to do is take the key and find the brooch. I'll take care of getting rid of it."

The next evening, while Tina waits at home, Inez takes the key under the flower pot and enters Patricia's apartment. Patricia cuts her trip short and surprises Inez in her bedroom, putting the brooch into her handbag. Patricia chases Inez and throws her against the kitchen counter. Inez grabs a kitchen knife and turns to face Patricia. Patricia overpowers Inez, siezes the knife and plunges it into Inez's chest, killing her instantly.

Based on these facts, if Tina is prosecuted as an accomplice to Inez's murder, it is most likely that:

(A) Tina is guilty because Inez's death is a "natural and probable consequence" of the burglary.
(B) Tina is guilty because she expects to profit from Inez's actions.
(C) Tina is not guilty because she could not foresee Inez's death.
(D) Tina is not guilty because Inez was the victim of the homicide.

19. Jake met a tough-looking guy named Marty at a bar in the State of Ames. (Ames follows the Model Penal Code). They hit it off well and began to talk.

After determining that they had a lot in common, Jake proposed to Marty that they rob the nearby 7-Eleven together. Marty said, "Okay, let's do it, man. " Jake did not know it, but Marty was actually an undercover police officer.

Jake and Marty entered the store together. Jake pointed his gun at the cashier and demanded "all of the cash in the register." Marty then pointed his gun at Jake, and advised Jake to "drop the gun and put your hands in the air." Jake dropped the gun and was arrested by Marty.

Based on these facts, if Jake is prosecuted for conspiracy to commit armed robbery, it is most likely that:

(A) Jake is guilty because he agreed to rob the 7-Eleven with Marty.
(B) Jake is guilty because he had undertaken a "substantial step" toward commission of the crime.
(C) Jake is not guilty because he was entrapped.
(D) Jake is not guilty because Marty's agreement was feigned.

20. Amanda and Corrine are friends at Portside High School. One day, Amanda says to Corrine, "Let's rob the Gap and get some cool clothes." Corrine, assuming that Amanda is joking, responds, "Sounds like fun, let's do it." Amanda, who has a reputation as a gang tough, pulls two guns from her purse and hands one to Corrine. Corrine wants to run away, but she's afraid that Amanda will hurt her if she doesn't go through with the plan. Corrine goes with Amanda to the Gap & Snap Mall. Before going into the Gap, Corrine says she has to go to the bathroom, hoping somehow to get away. While Corrine is in the bathroom, a security guard sees a bulge in Amanda's purse and suspects it's a gun. He arrests Amanda, who tells him that Corrine is her accomplice. Corrine is arrested as she leaves the ladies room.

Based on these facts, if Corrine is prosecuted for conspiracy to commit robbery, it is most likely that:

(A) Corrine is guilty because she took the gun and went with Amanda to the mall.
(B) Corrine is guilty because she did not renounce the crime after separating from Amanda.
(C) Corrine is not guilty because she never entered the Gap.
(D) Corrine is not guilty because she never agreed with Amanda to rob the Gap.

21. Bill and Ted are partners in a major drug distribution operation. They agree to sell 10 kilos of cocaine to Mickey, a drug dealer in the town of Bedrock. One night, Bill and Ted drive over to an abandoned warehouse to make the

sale to Mickey. Bill notices several police cars cruising the neighborhood and he becomes alarmed. He tells Ted, "I don't want any part of this one. It's too dangerous. You should pull out, too." Bill responds, "You no good wimp. I can do this without your help." Bill leaves and Ted goes through with the sale to Mickey. Hoping to make a deal for a lighter sentence, he tells the police that Bill helped him to plan the sale.

Based on these facts, if Bill is prosecuted for conspiracy to sell illegal drugs, it is most likely that:

(A) Bill is guilty because he agreed with Mickey to sell drugs.

(B) Bill is guilty because Ted completed the drug deal.

(C) Bill is not guilty because he withdrew from the conspiracy and attempted to dissuade Ted.

(D) Bill is not guilty because he didn't participate in the actual sale of the drugs.

22. Sam and Jim own a store, Minks-On-Us, which sells fur coats and jackets. After several anti-fur demonstrations in front of the store, the store's sales plummet. Facing bankruptcy, Sam and Jim decide that they will arrange a theft of the store's inventory so that they can collect from their insurance company. They contact Bart, a local handyman, and offer him a portion of the insurance proceeds if he will "steal" the coats and jackets. Bart agrees and Sam and Jim give him a key to the store and the codes to the various store alarms.

The next night, Bart enters the store to take the fur coats. While he is removing a coat from the display window, he accidentally trips and shatters the window. Afraid he's been seen, Bart flees in his van. An off-duty policeman, who is eating dinner at a nearby restaurant, hears the glass shatter. When he runs outside to see what happened, he sees Bart race off in his van. The policeman gets in his car, and a high speed chase ensues. During the chase, the policeman misses a turn and slams into a marble statue. He dies in the ambulance carrying him to the local hospital.

Based on these facts, if Sam and Jim are prosecuted for homicide, it is most likely that:

(A) The defendants are guilty because they had arranged for the burglary to occur.

(B) The defendants are guilty because the officer's death was reasonably foreseeable.

(C) The defendants are not guilty because the officer's death was *not* likely to occur.

(D) The defendants are not guilty because the "target" crime of their conspiracy was not a homicide.

23. Barker and Samantha are violence-prone computer hacks. They decide to rob a local Egghead Software store. Each uses a handgun. They agree in advance to split up after the robbery and to meet at Samantha's home one hour later to divide their booty. The robbery comes off without a hitch, but on her way home, Samantha is stopped by Frank, a local policeman. She begins to run, but is brought down by Kipper, Frank's police dog. Samantha reaches for a knife concealed in her left stocking and slashes Kipper across the throat. Kipper dies immediately. (Assume that in this jurisdiction, killing a police dog during commission of a felony is itself a felony.)

Based upon the foregoing, if **Barker** is prosecuted for the killing of Kipper, it is most likely that:

(A) Barker is guilty because it was reasonably foreseeable that Samantha would use force to avoid capture.

(B) Barker is guilty because conspirators are culpable for the acts of their co-conspirators.

(C) Barker is not guilty because Samantha's killing of Kipper was not reasonably foreseeable.

(D) Barker is not guilty because the conspiracy was concluded when the robbery of the Egghead Software store was concluded.

24. Beatrice left a Halloween party dressed in her John Dillinger costume. On the way to her car, she spotted an elderly couple walking down the street. Beatrice decided to play a Halloween prank on the couple. She pulled a 4-inch-blade rubber pocket knife from her coat and ran towards the couple, pointing the blade at them. Beatrice was acting out her idea of Halloween fun and did not intend to rob or harm the couple. However, the couple, seeing Beatrice in her gangster outfit brandishing the knife, thought they were going to be stabbed and robbed. They started to run. They ran into the street directly into the path of an oncoming car. They were hit by the car, and both died instantly. (Assume that common law principles are applicable in this jurisdiction.)

Based on these facts, if Beatrice is prosecuted for multiple homicide, it is most likely that:

(A) She is guilty of murder (under the felony-murder rule).

(B) She is guilty of involuntary manslaughter.

(C) She is guilty of voluntary manslaughter.

(D) She is not guilty of homicide.

25. Frank was devastated when his girlfriend, Louise, broke up with him. He tried for months to win her back, but she rebuffed him every time. Finally, Frank decided that if he couldn't have Louise, no one else would either. He bought a gun and drove to her apartment, intent on killing her. When he got there, the janitor told Frank that Louise had moved to the North Side. Frank asked for the address, but the janitor said he didn't know. Frank drove to the North Side with the gun in his pocket, hoping to spot Louise. As he cruised through the neighborhood, Frank was stopped by a police officer for going through a red light. A check revealed a warrant for Frank's arrest for robbery. Frank was arrested and the gun was confiscated. (Assume this jurisdiction follows the Model Penal Code).

Based on these facts, if Frank is prosecuted for attempted murder, it is most likely that:

(A) He's guilty because he armed himself with a deadly weapon.

(B) He's guilty because he made every effort to locate Louise with the intent of killing her.

(C) He's not guilty because he never actually shot at Louise.

(D) He's not guilty because he never found Louise.

26. Frank found his girl friend Louise in the arms of his best friend, Antonio. Enraged, he bought a gun and drove to her apartment, intending to kill her. Unknown to Frank, the gun he had purchased was defective and would not fire.

When he got to the apartment, Louise was not at home. He waited in the shadows outside until she finally arrived. As soon as he saw her, he pointed the gun at her forehead. Suddenly, he began to whimper softly and put the gun away. He said, "I don't know what made me think I could do this. I love you very much."

Based on these facts, if Frank is prosecuted for attempted murder, it is most likely that:

(A) Frank is guilty because he pointed the gun at Louise.

(B) Frank is guilty if he did not report the incident to the police.

(C) Frank is not guilty because he voluntarily abandoned his plan to kill Louise.

(D) Frank is not guilty because the defective gun made it impossible for him to commit the murder.

27. On her way home one night, Margot saw Thomas sleeping in a cardboard box outside the entrance to her luxury apartment building. Margot hated the presence of homeless people in her wealthy neighborhood. Determined to send a message to the homeless, she took out a pair of scissors from her purse and stabbed Thomas several times in the neck and back. Margot's intent was not to kill Thomas but to frighten the homeless away from her posh neighborhood. However, the wounds she inflicted were deep enough to kill any ordinary man. The autopsy revealed the extent of the stab wounds but, also, that Thomas was already dead when Margot stabbed him. He had died an hour earlier from dehydration and hypothermia.

Based on these facts, if Margot is prosecuted for murder, it is most likely that:

(A) She is guilty because she stabbed Thomas with the intent to seriously injure him.
(B) She is guilty because Margot's stab wounds would have killed the average person.
(C) She is not guilty because she did not intend to kill Thomas.
(D) She is not guilty because Thomas was already dead.

28. Coyotes have invaded the suburban neighborhood. Their howling has kept Mark from getting a good night's sleep for weeks. Most of all, Mark is afraid the coyotes will harm or kill his two infant children, who often play in the backyard. Mark would like to kill the coyotes, but hesitates because he read in a nature magazine that coyotes are on the endangered species list and must not be killed. In fact, coyotes have been removed from the endangered species list in this one area because there are so many of them. After another week of sleepless nights, Mark takes his shotgun down and tells his wife, "the law be damned." He procedes to kill every coyote in sight or hearing.

Based on these facts, if Mark's neighbor files a complaint against Mark for killing the coyotes, it is most likely that the magistrate will:

(A) Arraign Mark because his intent was to violate the law.
(B) Arraign Mark because he contributed to the decimation of coyotes.
(C) Refuse to arraign Mark because he was defending his children.
(D) Refuse to arraign Mark because his conduct was not illegal.

29. Harry has been convicted of drug-dealing on several occasions. One day, he is standing on a street corner waiting for the bus to take him to his new job. Matthew, a plain-clothes police officer, recognizes Harry as a convicted drug-dealer. He approaches Harry and asks, "Know where I can get some crack?" Harry replies, "If the price is right, sure." Harry has no crack in his

possession at the time but knows where he can get some. Matthew immediately arrests Harry for attempting to sell an illegal substance.

Based on these facts, if Harry asserts the defense of entrapment, it is most likely that:

(A) Harry is guilty because he was predisposed to sell drugs.
(B) Harry is guilty because the defense of entrapment is not available to former convicts for the same or a similar crime.
(C) Harry is not guilty because Matthew proposed the transaction to him.
(D) Harry is not guilty because he did not intend to sell drugs until Matthew approached him.

30. Mandy and Samantha are invited to a lavish party at the home of a rich Hollywood producer. Mandy drinks seven glasses of champagne and is quite drunk when she goes to the powder room. As she leaves the powder room, Mandy spots a diamond and sapphire necklace on the dresser in the adjoining bedroom. After admiring it for a few minutes, she puts the necklace in her purse, intending only to show it to Samantha. Returning to the party, she is greeted by a famous movie actor. Under his spell, she forgets that she has the necklace. When Samantha tells her it's time to go, she leaves the house with the necklace still in her purse. Unfortunately, another guest saw Mandy put the necklace in her purse and tells the Pinkerton guard who is on hand to guard the family jewels. Mandy is arrested while she is waiting for Samantha to bring her car to the door.

If Mandy is prosecuted for larceny, it is most likely that:

(A) She is guilty because she put the necklace in her purse.
(B) She is guilty because she left the house with the necklace.
(C) She is not guilty because she lacked the requisite *mens rea*.
(D) She is not guilty because the requisite *actus reus* elements are lacking.

31. Gerry has never drunk anything alcoholic because she is convinced it is unhealthful. At her eighteenth birthday party she is pressed by her friends to drink two glasses of red wine. As it happens, Gerry is abnormally sensitive to alcohol. Upon finishing the second glass, she goes into a wild, uncontrolled frenzy and begins to swing her glass round and round. She strikes one of the guests and slashes his cheek and forehead. He bleeds profusely and is driven to the local hospital. He presses the charge of battery against Gerry. (Assume that Gerry knew that it was morally wrong to strike people.).

If Gerry is prosecuted for battery, it is most likely that:

(A) Gerry is guilty because she voluntarily drank the wine.

(B) Gerry is guilty because battery is a general intent crime.

(C) Gerry is not guilty because she didn't expect to become intoxicated.

(D) Gerry is not guilty if the legal age of majority in this jurisdiction is 21.

32. Eric, Dan, and Paul are all incoming freshmen in a dormitory at Podunk College. One night, the whole dorm decides to have a beer bash. Dan announces that he will not participate because he thinks social drinking is disgusting. Eric and Paul respond: "If you're going to be a killjoy all year, we don't want you as a roommate." Dan replies, "OK, you guys," and proceeds to chug down five large beers. He begins to shout and curse, seizes a chair and begins to wave it wildly around his head, striking three students who happen to be in his path.

Based on these facts, if Dan is prosecuted for battery, it is most likely that:

(A) Dan is guilty because he voluntarily drank the beer which led to his violent outburst.

(B) Dan is guilty because he deliberately struck three students.

(C) Dan is not guilty because battery is a specific intent crime.

(D) Dan is not guilty if he no longer realized that hitting people was wrong.

33. Looking for an easy mark, Carl decided to burglarize the home of Mary Murphy, an 80-year-old recluse who lived alone. Carl suspected that Mary was away visiting her sister in another state. The lock was not as easy to pry open as Mark thought it would be. Determined to get in, Mark broke the lock and used a crowbar in his effort to pry the door. Despite all his strength and efforts, he could not get the door to open and he finally left in disgust.

Unknown to Mark, Mary was actually home and heard all the noise. She hid in a closet until the noise stopped. She then tried to leave the house by the only available exit--the front door. However, Carl had succeeded in jamming the door against the door jamb. Mary was unable to get out of the house, though she tried for two hours to get the door open. She finally called the police, who broke the door down and rescued her. The jurisdiction defines kidnapping as "the intentional and unlawful confinement of another for a substantial period of time...."

Assuming that the "substantial period of time" element is satisfied, if Carl is prosecuted for kidnapping, it is most likely that:

(A) Carl is not guilty because Mary was able to call the police and obtain help.

(B) Carl is not guilty because he didn't know Mary was home.

(C) Carl is guilty because Mary was confined to her home by Carl's actions in jamming the door.

(D) Carl is guilty because Mary was unable to leave her home for two hours.

34. One summer evening, Alison decided to go swimming in the roof-top pool of her apartment building. She stepped out onto the roof to find only Jamie, her neighbor's seven year old. Alison watched in horror while Jamie fell into the deep end of the pool and began to thrash around. Alison had been a lifeguard in high school and could easily have saved Jamie without any risk to herself. Fearing that she might be accused of pushing Jamie in the first place, she decided not to intervene and went back downstairs. She did, however, call the police when she got back to her apartment. The police came immediately, but Jamie had already drowned.

If Alison is prosecuted for homicide, it is most likely that:

(A) Alison is not guilty because she was under no legal duty to save Jamie.

(B) Alison is not guilty because she made a reasonable effort to save Jamie by calling the police.

(C) Alison is guilty because she could have saved Jamie without serious risk of harm to herself.

(D) Alison is guilty because there is a special duty to help minors in danger.

35. Kevin's Furniture Store was facing bankruptcy. The store occupied the first floor of a two-story building. One evening, Kevin set fire to the building. He planned to collect on the store's insurance policy. Unbeknownst to Kevin, Ben, a 42-year-old homeless derelict, was asleep on the second floor, which was vacant. Ben was burned to death. Before the fire could be put out, the entire building was destroyed. Tormented by this tragedy, Kevin confessed his crime to the police.

Based on these facts, if Kevin is prosecuted for murder, it is most likely that:

(A) Kevin is not guilty because he did not intend to kill Ben.

(B) Kevin is not guilty because it was not reasonably foreseeable that someone would be killed by the fire.

(C) Kevin is not guilty because he was only attempting to commit insurance fraud (a felony which is not inherently dangerous).

(D) Kevin is guilty because Ben was killed in the fire Kevin started.

36. Seth asked Daniel if he could borrow a VCR to watch a video with his girlfriend. Daniel loaned Seth his VCR, but before he could get it back, the two had a big argument. Daniel demanded his VCR back, but Seth responded, "I'll get to it when I get to it." The next evening, Daniel opened

an unlocked window at Seth's home and went inside, intent only on recovering his VCR. Inside Seth's house, Daniel saw and instantly decided to take Seth's new Macintosh Powerbook. Daniel loaded the VCR and Powerbook into his van, and drove home. A neighbor, who had seen Daniel climb through the window, called the police and gave them Daniel's license number. He was arrested shortly thereafter.

Based on these facts, if Daniel is prosecuted for burglary, it is most likely that:

(A) Daniel is not guilty because he entered Seth's home only for the purpose of retrieving his VCR.
(B) Daniel is not guilty because no "breaking" occurred.
(C) Daniel is guilty because he had no legal right to enter Seth's house.
(D) Daniel is guilty because he took the Powerbook with the intent to permanently deprive Seth of its possession.

37. David has been telling malicious lies about his sister Janice to their parents. Janice is convinced that David is out to get them to disinherit her. Home from college on Christmas vacation, Janice decides to "excise David, once and for all." She makes a batch of poison-laced cookies, puts them on a plate, and leaves the plate on David's desk. Janice then drives downtown to finish her holiday shopping. The holiday music at the mall fills her with remorse and guilt. She calls home to tell David what she's done, but the line is busy. Janice rushes home, intending to throw the poisonous cookies away, but she finds that David has already eaten the cookies and is lying unconscious. She rushes David to the nearest hospital, but David dies in the emergency room.

Based on these facts, if Janice is prosecuted for murder, it is most likely that:

(A) Janice is not guilty because the *mens rea* element necessary for murder was lacking when David ate the cookies.
(B) Janice is guilty of voluntary manslaughter, not murder, because Janice was provoked by David's malicious lies.
(C) Janice is guilty of murder because she intended to cause David's death.
(D) Janice is guilty only of attempted murder because she tried to warn David about the cookies.

38. Jonathan and Peter are classmates at Podunk Law School in the State of Pretoria. One evening they begin to discuss the proposed Pretoria legislation forbidding any school to promote or utilize affirmative action as a basis for admission. Before long, Jonathan and Peter are on their feet, arguing and shouting at one another. Peter calls Jonathan a "a warped, opinionated,

prejudiced, calloused, stupid idiot who doesn't belong in law school."
Enraged by these remarks, Jonathan pushes Peter, who loses his balance and
falls backwards, hitting his head against the edge of an oak table. Peter dies
instantly. (Assume that common law principles are applicable in Pretoria.)

Based on these facts, if Jonathan is prosecuted for homicide, it is most likely
that:

(A) Jonathan is guilty of first-degree murder.
(B) Jonathan is guilty of voluntary manslaughter.
(C) Jonathan is guilty of involuntary manslaughter.
(D) Jonathan is **not** criminally culpable for Peter's death.

39. Erica and Pat are law school roommates. They live in a large duplex which is
located in a nice, quiet section of Houston. They argue constantly about
Pat's tendency to let dirty dishes pile up in their sink and her refusal to share
in the housekeeping. One day, Erica decides to "teach Pat a lesson." She
leaves Pat's new mountain bike unlocked and unattended on the sidewalk in
front of their apartment house. Erica keeps an eye on it from the apartment
hallway, but, when she returns to the apartment for a moment to get a
cigarette, the mountain bike is stolen. Pat is definitely **not** amused by Erica's
excuse and explanation. She decides to flex her law-school-student muscles
and files a charge of larceny against Erica.

If Erica is prosecuted for larceny, it is most likely that:

(A) Erica is guilty because it was reasonably likely that the theft would occur.
(B) Erica is guilty because her actions were undertaken for the improper
purpose of teaching Pat a lesson.
(C) Erica is not guilty because she didn't participate in taking Pat's
mountain bike.
(D) Erica is not guilty because her intent was only to teach Pat a lesson.

40. Sheila asked her neighbor, Max, if she could borrow his car to go grocery
shopping. Max said "yes" and gave Sheila the keys. Instead of going to the
grocery store, Sheila took the car and drove to another state to spend the
weekend with her boyfriend, a securities analyst who was required to be at
his desk at 7:00 AM on Monday. Sheila never intended to go shopping, but
used the grocery shopping story to induce Max to let her use the car. On her
way to her rendezvous, Sheila was in an accident which seriously damaged
Max's car. When Sheila didn't return that night, Max called the police and
told them his car had been stolen.

Based on these facts, it is most likely that Sheila could be successfully
prosecuted for:

(A) Larceny.

(B) Larceny by trick.

(C) Robbery.

(D) Malicious mischief.

41. Molly and Samantha were neighbors. Molly became convinced that Samantha was having an affair with her husband. This was not the fact. One day, Molly, an employee of Wow Chemical, hid a bottle of acid under her smock as she left work. When Molly arrived home, she saw Samantha sunbathing on her porch. Molly uncorked the bottle and splashed acid on Samantha's face, intending to disfigure her. Reacting quickly, Samantha ran to the pool in her backyard and dove in to dilute the acid. In her panic she dove into the shallow part of the pool and fractured her cheekbone. Her fracture healed, but despite excellent plastic surgery, her smile was permanently, although only slightly, distorted.

The crime of mayhem is defined in this jurisdiction as "the intentional infliction of a disfiguring bodily injury."

Based on these facts, if Molly is prosecuted for mayhem, it is most likely that:

(A) Molly is guilty because she intended to cause a disfiguring bodily injury to Samantha.

(B) Molly is not guilty because Samantha's response was a supervening cause of her injury.

(C) Molly is not guilty because her conduct was not the proximate cause of Samantha's injuries.

(D) Molly is not guilty because the acid caused Samantha no disfigurement.

42. David sacrificed seven children during a bizarre religious ritual. At his murder trial, all four defense psychiatrists agreed that (1) David honestly believed Satan had ordered him to kill the children, and (2) David lacked the cognitive ability to recognize that his conduct was morally or legally wrong. The court-appointed psychiatrist also testified that, in his opinion, David was insane. The prosecution tried to discredit these witnesses, but each held firm to his conclusions. The state presented no psychiatrists of its own to rebut the psychiatric testimony. Nevertheless, the jury rejected all of the expert testimony, and found David guilty of murder.

Based on these facts, an appeals court would most likely:

(A) Reverse the verdict because all of the expert testimony was in David's favor.

(B) Order a new trial because all of the expert testimony was in David's favor.

(C) Sustain the verdict because the jury was free to disregard the experts' testimony.

(D) Sustain the verdict only if the trial judge found that the prosecution had "clearly impeached" David's expert witnesses.

43. Assume for the purposes of this question that the jurisdiction involved defines rape as a crime which is committed only if the defendant "knows or reasonably believes" that the woman has not consented, or "recklessly disregards" that possibility.

Donald walked Debbie back to her dorm after a wild fraternity party. He had consumed nine beers at the party and was legally intoxicated. When they got to her room, Donald and Debbie exchanged a few kisses. Donald soon became more aggressive and started to undo the buttons on Debbie's blouse. Debbie immediately said, "No! I don't want to do that." Donald decided that Debbie was teasing him. Though she began to cry and continue to say "no," Donald forced Debbie onto the bed and had forcible intercourse with her.

Based on these facts, if Donald is prosecuted for rape, it is most likely that:

(A) Donald is guilty because he wrongly believed Debbie consented.

(B) Donald is guilty because he should have realized that nine beers would cause him to become drunk.

(C) Donald is not guilty because he thought Debbie had consented.

(D) Donald is not guilty because he was legally drunk.

44. Assume that the jurisdiction in this case does not permit a claim of imperfect self-defense.

Steve and Jenny have been married for five years. Steve has a "temper problem," and has beaten Jenny many times during their marriage. One Saturday night, Steve begins to yell at Jenny when she suggests that he get counseling for his temper. Jenny has never seen Steve so enraged. Steve hits Jenny several times and then says, "Your time is almost up." Steve then turns away and goes to sleep. Two hours later, Jenny, fearing that Steve intends to kill her when he awakes, quietly removes a gun from the kitchen cabinet and shoots Mark in the temple, killing him instantly.

Based on these facts, if Jenny is prosecuted for murder, it is most likely that she would be convicted of:

(A) Murder.

(B) Voluntary manslaughter.

(C) Involuntary manslaughter.

(D) No crime at all.

45. Jeremy works as a prosecutor in the Juvenile Division of the Euphoria State Attorney's Office. In response to a series of anonymous death threats, Jeremy has started carrying a gun. One night, when Jeremy leaves work, he spots a teenager running towards him carrying a gun which he points towards's Jeremy's chest. The youth, who appears to Jeremy to be about fifteen, is 18 feet away from Jeremy when he first sees him. When the boy shouts "Look out, honky," Jeremy shoots him, killing him instantly. When the police come, they find the boy is only twelve and that the "gun" is only a toy rubber gun. Later, they discover that the boy was taking part in an initiation by a local gang.

If Jeremy is prosecuted for homicide, it is most likely that he will be convicted of:

(A) Murder.
(B) Voluntary manslaughter.
(C) Involuntary manslaughter.
(D) No crime at all.

46. Phi-Ro fraternity had a long tradition of making its new pledges run through a wall of fire at the conclusion of "Hell Week." Because other fraternities had been sued by pledges for "Hell Week" injuries, Phi-Ro required that its pledges sign a consent and waiver form, specifically relieving the fraternity and its individual members of responsibility for injuries resulting from hazing.

Biff, Phi-Ro's current president, supervised this year's wall of fire activities. After the fire wall was built, Biff instructed Morton to run through it. Though scared, Morton was determined to become a member of Phi Rho. He ran toward the fire, but tripped and fell as he reached the "wall." Before he could be pulled away, he had received multiple second-degree burns. An ambulance was called but he died in the hospital that night. The cause of death was a contaminated blood transfusion administered by the hospital staff.

Based on these facts, if Biff is prosecuted for involuntary manslaughter, it is most likely that:

(A) Biff is guilty because he acted negligently.
(B) Biff is guilty because he manifested a reckless disregard for Morton's safety.
(C) Biff is not guilty because Morton signed a waiver.
(D) Biff is not guilty because Morton's death was caused by the hospital's negligence.

47. Barney was exposed to Jordan's driving ambition and ruthlessness when
they were classmates at Harpert Law School. Years later, when Jordan, after
a meteoric but unprincipled career, announced his candidacy for Governor
of Utopia, Barney felt it was his patriotic duty to stop him before he
destroyed the state. Barney read in the local paper that Jordan was going to
be making a speech in the public square of Harpert Village the next day.
Barney also knew that there was an abandoned office building located
opposite the square, where he could position himself in order to fire at
Jordan.

About 30 minutes before Jordan's speech, Barney entered the building facing
the square, carrying a high-powered rifle. A vigilant police officer saw
Barney at the window holding what appeared to be a rifle, "casing" the
square. The officer immediately broke into the building and arrested Barney.
(You may assume that the Model Penal Code is operative in Utopia.)

Based on these facts, if Barney if prosecuted for attempted murder, it is most
likely that:

(A) Barney is guilty because he undertook a substantial step towards the
assassination with the intent to kill.
(B) Barney is not guilty because he was waiting for Jordan to begin his
speech.
(C) Barney is not guilty because Jordan had not yet arrived.
(D) Barney is not guilty if his rifle's range could not reach the spot at which
Jordan would be standing.

48. David was laid off from his job at Federal Motors because more Americans
were buying Japanese cars. He was so angry that he decided to go to a bridge
and throw stones at Japanese cars as they drove through the underpass. He
didn't want to hurt anyone; he only wanted to dent a few rooftops. He
picked up a few small pebbles and threw them, but they just seemed to
bounce off without leaving any damage. Frustrated, David picked up a
slightly larger stone and threw it at an oncoming Toyota. This rock made a
"direct" hit upon the front window of the Toyota driven by Ralph, which
caused him to lose control of the car. The car smashed into a concrete wall,
killing Ralph.

Based on these facts, it is most likely that David could be successfully
prosecuted for:

(A) Murder in the First Degree.
(B) Murder in the Second Degree.
(C) Voluntary Manslaughter.
(D) Involuntary Manslaughter.

49. Martin and his wife Doris owned a manufacturing plant. The business was doing poorly and they were desperate for cash. They decided to burn down the plant to obtain the insurance proceeds. After they had purchased the gasoline, Doris changed her mind and decided she couldn't go through with it. Doris thought about notifying the police, but was afraid that Martin would leave her if she did.

Doris told Martin that she no longer wanted to take part in the arson and vigorously encouraged Martin to abandon the plan. Martin disregarded Doris' advice and burned the building down. Martin was apprehended as he left the scene. (You may assume that, under applicable law, Martin committed arson.)

Based on these facts, if Doris is prosecuted for arson, it is most likely that:

(A) Doris is not guilty because she did not set the plant on fire.
(B) Doris is not guilty because she withdrew and tried to dissuade Martin from setting the plant on fire.
(C) Doris is guilty because she did not notify the police when she withdrew from the conspiracy.
(D) Doris is guilty.

50. Larry and Francine saw a neighborhood "thug" selling drugs to several young children at a local schoolyard. Larry, who knew that Francine always carried a gun in her purse, said to her, "Someone should kill the scum." Francine nodded. Larry then suggested that they wait behind a trash bin so that Francine could shoot the dealer as he walked past. While they were waiting behind the trash bin, Larry had second thoughts about participating in a murder. Without saying anything to Francine, he quietly slipped away. Unaware that she was alone, Francine shot and killed the drug dealer.

If Larry is prosecuted as an accomplice to murder, it is most likely that:

(A) Larry is guilty because he did not stop Francine from committing the murder.
(B) Larry is guilty because he left the area without specifically advising Francine not to kill the drug dealer.
(C) Larry is not guilty because it was Francine who shot the drug dealer.
(D) Larry is not guilty because he had already left the vicinity before the shooting occurred.

51. Josh told Aaron, his friend and classmate, that he didn't have enough money to pay for a coronary bypass. A couple of days later, Aaron, worried about his friend, left a note on Josh's locker. It read: "I know you need money. Meet me at the corner of Fifth and Hazel on Thursday at 2, and we'll 'take' the

Bank of America branch. I'll have the weapons. Your friend, Aaron." When Josh saw the note, he decided that Aaron was joking and threw the note away. A security guard found the note and Aaron was arrested. There is no evidence that Aaron actually waited for Josh at Fifth and Hazel on Thursday.

Based on these facts, if Aaron is prosecuted for solicitation to commit bank robbery, it is most likely that:

(A) Aaron is guilty because he was serious about robbing the bank when he wrote the note.

(B) Aaron is guilty because a reasonable person reading the note would have believed that he was serious about robbing the bank.

(C) Aaron is not guilty because Josh did not take the note seriously.

(D) Aaron is not guilty because no substantial step toward commission of the crime was undertaken.

52. Ethan borrowed $10,000 from Carl, a professional loan shark. When Ethan missed his first payment, Carl decided to teach Ethan a lesson. He went to Ethan's house and threw Ethan against the wall. Carl smashed several vases and then told Ethan, "If you don't pay up, this is what's going to happen to you." At this point, Ethan called Carl "a no good SOB." Carl stared menacingly at Ethan for several minutes, but finally turned and left, slamming the door behind him.

Ethan was so frightened that he had a massive heart attack and died. Ethan's death was the last thing Carl wanted because it meant that now he would never get his money back. Carl had only wanted to scare Ethan into making his future loan payments on time.

Based on these facts, if Carl is prosecuted for Ethan's death, it is most likely he will be guilty of:

(A) First Degree Murder.

(B) Second Degree Murder.

(C) Voluntary Manslaughter.

(D) Involuntary Manslaughter.

53. Late one night, Jim was walking home alone from the library. Ilya, the "Chicago slasher," began to trail him. Ilya's plan was to kill Jim as soon as they reached a secluded area. Ilya knew of a dark alley that would be "the perfect" spot. When Jim was only a block away from the alley, Ilya took a knife from his knapsack and began to run towards Jim. A police officer saw Ilya holding the knife as he moved closer to Jim. Ilya spotted the police officer out of the corner of his eye. He quickly put the knife into his pocket and began walking in the opposite direction.

Based on these facts, if Ilya is prosecuted for attempted murder, it is most likely that:

(A) Ilya is not guilty because he didn't take a substantial step towards commission of the murder.
(B) Ilya is not guilty because he terminated his plan to murder Jim prior to his arrest.
(C) Ilya is guilty because he intended to kill Jim.
(D) Ilya is guilty because he drew the knife from his knapsack with the intent to kill.

54. Angie, a 22 year old cover model, married a wealthy 80 year old widower. Seven years later, Angie's husband was still in good health and it appeared he would easily live several more years. Impatient to collect her inheritance, Angie decided to speed up the old man's death.

She asked her favorite bartender if he knew anyone who could "do a hit." The bartender gave her a phone number and told her to ask for Danny. She called the number and made arrangements to meet with Danny to discuss the deal. When they met, Angie offered to pay Danny $20,000 upon the successful "elimination" of her husband. Danny then informed Angie that he was an undercover police officer, and arrested her.

Based on these facts, if Angie is prosecuted for conspiracy to commit murder, it is most likely that:

(A) Angie is guilty because she offered to pay Danny to have her husband killed.
(B) Angie is guilty because she specifically intended to have her husband killed.
(C) Angie is not guilty because no actual agreement occurred.
(D) Angie is not guilty because a substantial step had not yet been taken to carry out the murder.

55. John, Brian and David were teammates on the Valley High soccer team. Mindy, a cheerleader, was on the bus carrying the team home from a game at Hillsdale High. When the bus stopped to get gas, the three players decided to have a little "fun" with Mindy. They agreed that they would remove their shirts and surround Mindy as she came out of the women's restroom. They would then all point to their genitals and scream, "Please, please, touch me here." As soon as they saw Mindy, they carried out their plan.

Mindy became so upset by their behavior that she had stomach cramps for several days. Mindy decided to take no action, but the local prosecutor, an ambitious and fearless young man, charged the three players with "conspiracy to commit sexual harassment." Sexual harassment is not a crime in that jurisdiction.

Based on these facts, if John, Brian and David are prosecuted for conspiracy to commit sexual harassment, it is most likely that:

(A) The three players are not guilty because they did not agree to perform a criminal act.

(B) The three players are not guilty because Mindy never actually filed a criminal complaint against them.

(C) The three players are guilty because the act they agreed to perform is an immoral act.

(D) The three players are guilty because Mindy became physically ill as a result of their rude behavior.

56. Dexter, a physician, has sexual intercourse in his office with a new patient, Caroline. Caroline is a married woman. If she is charged with the crime of adultery, her **best** defense would be which of the following?

(A) She promptly reported the incident to her husband, who condoned her conduct.

(B) Dexter induced her to believe that sexual intercourse would improve her condition.

(C) Dexter told her that she was pregnant, that childbirth would be dangerous to her life, and that he could abort the pregnancy by sexual intercourse.

(D) Dexter told her he was inserting a medical instrument.

57. Read the summaries of the decisions in the four cases (A-D) below. Then discuss which is most applicable as precedent to the facts that follow:

(A) Defendant hit a fellow worker on the head with an iron crowbar, crushing his skull. Although Defendant testified she did not intend to kill, her conviction of murder was affirmed.

(B) Defendant and Doaks held up a bank and tried to escape in their car. Shots from pursuing police disabled the car, and Defendant was captured. Doaks fled on foot, commandeered a passing car, and, at gunpoint, forced the driver to drive off. A chase ensued extending over twenty miles. In an exchange of shots, a police officer was killed and Doaks escaped. Defendant's conviction of murder was affirmed.

(C) Smythe owed Defendant $500. Impatient with Smythe's failure to pay, Defendant went to Smythe's home. He demanded payment, brandished a revolver, and threatened to shoot Smythe if she did not pay up. All this occurred in the presence of Smythe's aged aunt, who, as a result of the excitement, died of heart failure on the spot. Defendant's conviction of manslaughter was affirmed.

(D) Defendant saw his wife and Ares go into the woods under circumstances that made him suspect adultery. As they came out of the woods, Defendant was told by Brent that he had seen them commit adultery the day before. Defendant got a rifle and killed Ares. Defendant's conviction of murder was reversed on the grounds that the evidence showed him guilty only of manslaughter.

Facts: A Police Officer undertook to arrest Fan for throwing a pop bottle that hit a baseball umpire. Fan was innocent and indignantly objected to being arrested. Because Police Officer had no warrant, the arrest was illegal. Fan resisted Police Officer forcibly, succeeded in seizing Police Officer's revolver and shot him dead.

Questions 58-60 are based on the following fact situation:

Frederick, who had a local reputation for unreasonable violence, threatened Bruce with a severe beating unless Bruce wrote, signed, and mailed a letter to the President of the United States threatening the President's life. Bruce complied. A statute makes it a felony "knowingly to mail to any person a letter that threatens the life of the President of the United States."

58. Is Bruce guilty of violating that statute?

(A) Yes, because Bruce knowingly mailed the letter.
(B) No, because he acted under duress.
(C) Yes, if Bruce believes that Frederick will carry out his threat against the president.
(D) Yes, because Bruce was not threatened with loss of his life.

59. If Frederick and Bruce are prosecuted for violating the statute and Bruce is acquitted, may Frederick be convicted?

(A) Yes, under the doctrine of transferred intent.
(B) Yes, because a person can commit a crime through an innocent agent.
(C) No, because Frederick did not write or mail the letter.
(D) No, because Frederick cannot be vicariously liable for Bruce's act.

60. If Frederick and Bruce are charged with the crime of conspiracy to violate the statute, they will most likely be found

(A) Not guilty, because the conspiracy was merged into the completed crime.
(B) Not guilty, because Bruce was not a willing participant.

(C) Guilty, because Bruce participated in the commission of the crime.

(D) Guilty, because Bruce complied with Frederick's threat.

61. Bill borrowed a television set from Len to watch a football game on Sunday afternoon. Bill promised that he would return the set to Len by 7:00 Sunday night because Len wanted to watch a program beginning at 10:00. When Bill did not return the set by 9:00, Len went to Bill's house. Bill was not at home, so Len entered Bill's house through an open window, took his television set, and walked out with it.

Did Len commit burglary?

(A) Yes, because Len entered Bill's house at night.

(B) Yes, because Bill was in lawful possession of the television set.

(C) No, because Bill had promised to return the set by 7:00 p.m.

(D) No, because Len was retrieving his own television set.

62. Bank had a substantial increase in the number of robberies at its main office. During one of these robberies, a teller was wounded when the robber became impatient with the speed with which she handed over the money. Bank hired Sharp, a former FBI agent, and placed him at a position where he could observe the entire bank floor through an opening in the ceiling. Several days after Sharp was hired, Rob entered the bank, pointed a gun at a cashier, and demanded money. When Sharp saw Rob point a gun at a cashier, he fired at and killed Rob.

What criminal offense, if any, did Sharp commit?

(A) None, because Sharp reasonably believed his act was necessary to prevent a dangerous felony.

(B) Voluntary manslaughter, because Sharp used deadly force to protect private property.

(C) Voluntary manslaughter, because Sharp did not first warn Rob.

(D) Murder, because Sharp deliberately aimed to kill Rob.

63. Mike was employed as a salesperson in Leo's store. Leo owned a beautiful clock that Mike had often admired. The clock needed repairs and Leo asked Mike to take it with him on his way home and leave it at the repair shop. Mike saw an opportunity to keep the clock for himself. He took the clock, did not deliver it to the shop, and did not return to work for Leo.

Did Mike commit larceny?

(A) Yes, because Mike decided not to take it to the repair shop after he received the clock.

(B) Yes, because Mike was a mere employee of Leo.

(C) No, because Leo personally handed the clock to Mike.

(D) No, because Mike did not induce or trick Leo into giving him the clock.

Questions 64-65 are based on the following fact situation (Assume the jurisdiction follows the Model Penal Code):

Deft intended to kill Vic. Deft deliberately shot at Vic, but missed and hit Cal. Cal was wounded only slightly. Cal was able to get up and saw Deft running away. Cal yelled at Deft, "Stop or I'll shoot." When Deft continued to run, Cal took out his gun and shot Deft, killing him instantly.

64. Is Deft guilty of the attempted murder of Cal?

(A) Yes, because Deft attempted to kill Vic.

(B) Yes, because Deft acted with premeditation and malice towards Vic.

(C) No, because Cal was wounded only slightly.

(D) No, because Deft intended to kill Vic, not Cal.

65. What crime, if any, did Cal commit?

(A) Voluntary Manslaughter.

(B) Murder.

(C) Involuntary Manslaughter.

(D) No crime.

Questions 66-67 are based on the following fact situation.

Borrower owed Lender $5,000. Payment was overdue and Lender retained Ace Inc., to collect the debt. Washington, the President of Ace Inc., assigned Little, an employee of Ace, to collect the account. At the time Washington assigned Little to collect the debt, Washington and Ace were also indebted to Lender for $5,000. Washington intended to apply the funds paid by Borrower in discharge of the debt from him and Ace to Lender. Little collected the $5,000. The amount collected was immediately remitted to Lender by Washington as payment of the debt for which Ace Inc. and Washington were jointly liable. Lender was not told that Little had collected Borrower's debt.

66. Based on these facts, it is most likely that Washington can be successfully prosecuted for:

(A) Embezzlement, because Lender's money was entrusted to Ace Inc.

(B) False pretenses, because at the time Little collected the funds, Washington intended to use them for his own benefit.

(C) Larceny, because at the time the funds were collected, Washington intended to use them for his own benefit.

(D) No crime, because Lender received all of the funds that were due from Borrower.

67. If a crime was committed by Washington, can Ace Inc. be convicted for the same offense?

(A) Yes, because Washington was President of Ace Inc.

(B) Yes, but only provided Washington is also convicted for the same offense.

(C) No, because a corporation cannot be imprisoned.

(D) No, if the crime involved requires a specific intent.

68. Agent was an undercover police officer. Agent received information from a reliable source that Deft, recently released from prison after serving a sentence for selling narcotics, was again selling narcotics, but that he was being very cautious and would sell only to persons who knew a designated code word. Agent's source told Agent the current code word.

Agent approached Deft, offered to make a buy of narcotics "at the going rate," and said the code word. Deft agreed to the sale and to the time and place of delivery. When Deft accepted the cash for the narcotics, he was arrested.

If Deft claims he was entrapped, will he prevail?

(A) Yes, because Deft would not have made the sale if Agent had not said the code word.

(B) Yes, because Agent approached Deft and offered to make a buy.

(C) No, because Deft was already predisposed to sell narcotics.

(D) No, because Deft accepted the Agent's cash.

69. Roger, walking down a city street, found a wallet on the sidewalk. He picked up the wallet and examined its contents. He found a driver's license reciting the owner's name and address. In the belief that the law was "finders keepers," he removed the cash from the wallet, put it in his pocket and tossed the wallet into the trash can.

Did Roger commit a theft crime? If the answer is yes, describe the crime.

(A) Yes, because Roger kept the money knowing the owner's identity.

(B) Yes, because Roger had lawful possession when he formed the intent to keep the money.

(C) No, because Roger did not commit a trespassory taking.

(D) No, because he was right on the law and was entitled to keep the money.

70. Mike, Leo, and Frank planned to rob a local liquor store. The agreement was that Mike would supply the guns and ammunition, and Leo and Frank would actually commit the robbery. Mike told Leo and Frank that all he wanted was to be paid for the guns and ammunition, that he would have nothing to do with the actual robbery, and that he would not be present at the time or share in the proceeds. Mike supplied Leo and Frank with guns and ammunition, which they then used to rob the liquor store.

Can Mike be held criminally liable for the robbery of the liquor store as:

I. A co-conspirator?
II. An accessory before the fact?

(A) No, neither I nor II.

(B) Yes, I but not II.

(C) Yes, II but not I.

(D) Yes, both I and II.

71. Intending to get Art arrested, Bob and Sam threatened him at gunpoint and told him, "If you don't immediately hold up the bank on the corner, we will kill you." They handed Art a loaded gun. Bob and Sam then positioned themselves so they could observe Art's actions. Art entered the bank and pointed the gun at a teller. Before the teller could respond, Art saw that a bank guard was pointing a gun at him and was about to shoot him. Art dropped his gun and held up his hands in surrender.

Did Art commit the crime of attempted robbery?

(A) Yes, because Art carried a loaded gun.

(B) Yes, because he took a substantial step towards the completion of the robbery.

(C) No, because he surrendered before the robbery was completed.

(D) No, because Art did not intend to take the bank's funds.

Questions 72-73 are based on the following fact situation:

When Dave saw his girlfriend Sally walking down the street holding hands with Abel, he was infuriated. Dave drove to Sally's house, hid in the bushes outside, and waited. A short time later, Dave saw Abel and Sally sitting at the kitchen table drinking coffee. Still angry, Dave went to his car and got a pistol. When he returned, Abel and Sally were still sitting at the kitchen table. Intending only to scare Abel by shooting in his direction, Dave fired through the window.

72. The bullet from Dave's pistol missed Abel but struck the coffee cup Abel was holding, shattering the mug in his hands. Which of the following crimes did Dave commit?

(A) Battery.

(B) Assault with a deadly weapon.

(C) Attempted murder.

(D) Battery and Assault with a deadly weapon.

73. If the bullet from Dave's pistol struck and killed Abel, the most serious crime with which Dave could be charged is:

(A) First-degree murder.

(B) Second-degree murder.

(C) Voluntary manslaughter.

(D) Involuntary manslaughter.

Questions 74-75 are based on the following fact situation (Assume the Model Penal Code is applicable in this jurisdiction):

Wimp wanted to get even with her boss, Vic, for the poor job evaluation he had just given her. She called Tough, who owed her a favor. Tough was out, so she left a message on his answering machine asking him to "rough Vic up." Wimp cautioned Tough that he wasn't to beat Vic so severely as to send him to the hospital. Wimp did not know that Tough was out of town. That afternoon, Tough's friend, Ready, went into Tough's apartment to feed Tough's cats. While in the apartment, Ready listened to his telephone messages. Because Ready also owed Wimp a favor, she decided to take care of Vic herself. She erased the message and then went out immediately to look for Vic. She found Vic in his office and beat him viciously. The next day, Vic died from the beating. Two days later, Tough telephoned Wimp from a distant city. Wimp, unaware that Ready had already dealt with Vic, told Tough what she wanted done to Vic. Tough agreed to beat Vic up after he returned to the city.

74. Did Wimp commit the crime of soliciting Ready to do an unlawful act?

(A) Yes, because Wimp asked that Vic be beaten.

(B) Yes, because Ready acted on Wimp's request.

(C) No, because Ready was not the person Wimp intended the message for.

(D) No, unless Ready reasonably believed the message was intended for anyone who heard it.

75. Was there a conspiracy to assault Vic?

(A) Yes, between Wimp and Tough.

(B) Yes, between Wimp and Ready.

(C) Yes, among Wimp, Tough and Ready.

(D) No.

Questions 76-77 are based on the following fact situation:

Art talked Bob into giving him $200 to buy a gun and ammo for the burglary of a bakery and the theft of its receipts, in return for a one-quarter share of the proceeds. On his way to complete the purchase after receiving the $200 from Bob, Art changed his mind. He never bought the gun or committed the burglary. Instead, he gave the $200 to the local YMCA.

76. Did Art commit the common law crime of conspiracy to commit burglary?

(A) Yes, when Art asked Bob for the money.

(B) Yes, when Bob furnished the money to buy the gun and ammo.

(C) No, because Bob did not agree to take part in the burglary.

(D) No, because Art never bought the gun.

77. If Art did not return the $200 to Bob, did he commit a crime?

(A) No, because the parties were in *pari delicto*.

(B) Yes, larceny.

(C) Yes, embezzlement.

(D) Yes, obtaining property by false pretenses.

78. It is against the law in West Dakona to sell the drug Xtol if the seller sells it "knowingly," or "under the belief" that the drug is Xtol. Defendant druggist takes Ytol drug off his shelf, believing it to be Xtol, and sells it to Customer. If the defendant is prosecuted for the sale of Xtol, which of the following is true?

(A) Defendant is not guilty of selling Xtol because her mistake negates any knowledge.

(B) Defendant is guilty of selling Xtol because her mistake was unreasonable.

(C) Defendant is not guilty of selling Xtol because an element of the crime is lacking.

(D) Defendant is guilty of the sale of Xtol if West Dakona holds that legal impossibility is no defense to the crime of attempt.

79. It is against the law in East Dakona to "knowingly" sell Xtol drug without reporting the sale to state authorities. Defendant believes the law is unconstitutional and refuses to report his sales of Xtol. His attorney advises him that she also believes the law to be unconstitutional. The law is later declared to be constitutional. Which of the following is true?

(A) The opinion of the attorney is irrelevant because a misunderstanding of the law is never a defense to a crime.

(B) Defendant's belief that the law was unconstitutional is a defense because it negated the *mens rea* for the crime.

(C) Defendant has a defense if the attorney's opinion was reasonably based on her interpretation of lower court decisions in that jurisdiction.

(D) Defendant acted under a reasonable mistake of fact rather than a mistake of law.

80. Dr. Alexandra X told Defendant Jimmy James (a pharmacist) that she had inadvertently prescribed a banned (but not ordinarily dangerous) drug for Mrs. Jones. Pharmacists are under a statutory duty to report violations of the drug laws and failure to report is a misdemeanor. Defendant did not report Dr. X's violation. He did try to contact Mrs. Jones at the address she had given him, but the address was obviously wrong. Mrs. Jones took the drug and died. Defendant is charged with involuntary manslaughter. Defendant's **best** defense would be:

(A) He did not do anything culpable.

(B) He could not reasonably foresee the death.

(C) Dr. X alone is responsible.

(D) He tried to contact Mrs. Jones.

81. The applicable jurisdiction requires a defendant to prove an affirmative defense to a criminal charge by a preponderance of the evidence. Which of the following defenses would the State be required to **disprove** beyond a reasonable doubt?

(A) That the Defendant was insane at the time he committed the crime.

(B) That the Defendant was acting under duress at the time he committed the crime.

(C) That the Defendant honestly believed his victim was about to kill the Defendant's wife.

(D) That the Defendant's conduct was reflexive (i.e., he was not fully conscious of his actions at the time of the crime).

82. Arthur and Dan were walking on a mountain road, arguing about affirmative action, when Arthur called Dan a "stupid idiot." Dan, enraged by this remark, pushed Arthur as hard as he could. Unfortunately, Arthur's head snapped backwards and struck a rock. As a consequence, Arthur died a few days later. Which of the following is true?

(A) Dan is guilty of involuntary manslaughter.

(B) Dan is not guilty of involuntary manslaughter because he did not intend Arthur's death.

(C) Dan is not criminally responsible for Arthur's death.

(D) Dan is guilty of voluntary manslaughter because Dan's insult was adequate to provoke a reasonable person.

83. After meeting Mary at a bar, John persuaded her to go back to his apartment with him. Although Mary initially rejected John's advances, they eventually had sexual intercourse. John would be most likely to escape liability for rape if:

(A) Mary was so intoxicated that she did not know what was happening.

(B) John convinced her that he was a doctor and was performing a vaginal inspection.

(C) John told Mary that if she did not cooperate, he would "beat you till you bleed and scar."

(D) John deceitfully told Mary that he would commit suicide on the spot if she didn't comply.

84. Dick was planning to rob Bailey's Bank. He asked John if he would drive the getaway car in exchange for 1/3 of the loot. John agreed on condition that they use toy guns to avoid the risk of injury to anyone. When they got to the bank, Dick got out of the car and began to walk towards the Bank. Realizing that the moment of truth was approaching, John got cold feet, left the car and hailed a taxi back home. Unaware that John had left the scene, Dick entered the bank and pulled out his toy gun. A bank guard saw him and ordered him to put up his hands. Dick turned toward the guard without lowering his gun and the guard fired. His shot missed Dick, but struck and killed an innocent bystander.

If John is charged with felony-murder, he will be

(A) Acquitted, because he did not participate in the robbery.

(B) Acquitted, because he withdrew from the conspiracy before any criminal acts were completed.

(C) Acquitted, because John's desire to use toy guns indicates he wanted to avoid violence.

(D) Convicted, because John was a conspirator.

85. Frank borrowed money from Bill and failed to pay it back. Two years passed. Bill was not very concerned about getting the money back, but he did enjoy teasing Frank about the debt. Bill, who thought Frank was a wimp, often taunted Frank by telling him that a bank robbery would be the best way to get the money quickly. Unknown to Bill, Frank had once been convicted of armed robbery. If Frank took up Bill's suggestion and held up an on-duty bank teller at knifepoint, it is *most likely* that Bill would be convicted of:

(A) Solicitation.

(B) Conspiracy.

(C) Robbery.

(D) No crime at all.

86. Bill works as a teller in USA Bank. One day, Jim comes into the bank and hands Bill an envelope containing $10,000 in payment of a loan he owes the bank. After Jim leaves, Bill takes the envelope and puts it in his pocket. At the end of the day, Bill deposits the money in his personal account at USA Bank.What crime did Bill commit?

(A) Embezzlement.

(B) Larceny.

(C) False Pretenses.

(D) Larceny by trick.

Questions 87-89 are based on the following fact situation:

Mick confided to Maud while they were having lunch one day that he had recently made a lot of extra money robbing supermarkets. Mick told Maud that if she would drive the getaway car, while he "knocked over" Jim's grocery, he would take care of her rent for a year. Maud said that she could use some extra money, but that her license had recently been revoked for "drunk driving." Sue, their waitress, heard Mick brag about his record and his plan to rob Jim's grocery. Sue said, "I hate that SOB, Jim. If I weren't working now, I'd drive that car for you in a minute." Bill, who was sitting in the booth behind Mick and Maud, overheard the entire conversation. Bill went over to Mick and offered to drive the getaway car for a third of the proceeds. Mick accepted and they went off together to rob the grocery. After the robbery, Mick went back to the restaurant and gave Maud $1,000 just to show her how lucrative a life of crime could be. Maud accepted the money.

87. If Maud is charged with conspiracy to commit robbery, she will probably be found

   (A) Guilty, because she never advised the police of Mick's plans.
   (B) Guilty, because she knowingly received part of the proceeds from Mick's robbery.
   (C) Not guilty, because she didn't participate in the robbery.
   (D) Not guilty, because she didn't agree to commit a robbery with Mick.

88. If Sue is charged with aiding and abetting in the commission of a robbery, she will probably be found

   (A) Guilty, because Sue knew of Mick's plans to rob Jim and failed to warn Jim.
   (B) Guilty, because Sue failed to tell the police of Mick's robbery plans.
   (C) Guilty, because she told Mick she would participate if she could.
   (D) Not guilty.

89. If Mick and Bill are tried separately on charges of robbery and conspiracy to commit robbery and Bill is tried first and is acquitted of both charges, Mick could be convicted of

   (A) Conspiracy only.
   (B) Robbery only.
   (C) Both crimes.
   (D) Neither crime.

Questions 90-94 are based on the following fact situation:

John believed that Michael, who lived down the street, had taken several tools from his truck. One night, John found his power saw missing. Outraged, John grabbed a hammer and ran to Michael's home. He entered it through the front door, which was wide open. John saw Michael in the backyard, ran outside and hit Michael repeatedly with the hammer, killing him. Anne, Michael's wife, fainted when she saw Michael fall to the ground. As she fell, she struck her head against a porch step, knocking herself unconscious. Thinking that both Michael and Anne were dead, John quickly pulled them into the house and placed them on a sofa in the living room. He then set fire to the sofa. He hoped the fire would destroy the sofa and conceal how Michael and Anne had died. He then left. Firefighters extinguished the fire quickly; the only damage was a charred wall, but Ellwood, who was the first firefighter to arrive on the scene, died of smoke inhalation as he tried to pull the dead bodies of Anne and Michael outside. The autopsies showed that the cause of Anne's death was smoke inhalation.

90. Is John guilty of burglary?

(A) Yes, because he intended serious injury to Michael when he entered Michael's house.

(B) Yes, because his action occurred at night.

(C) No, because there was no breaking.

(D) No, because John did not intend to commit a larceny.

91. John's killing of Michael is most likely to be characterized as

(A) Voluntary manslaughter.

(B) Involuntary manslaughter.

(C) Murder.

(D) Justifiable homicide.

92. Is John guilty of arson?

(A) Yes, because John maliciously burned Michael's house.

(B) Yes, because John was involved in the commission of a burglary.

(C) No, because the house was only charred.

(D) No, because John did not intend to burn the house.

93. John's killing of Anne is probably

(A) Voluntary manslaughter.

(B) Involuntary manslaughter.

(C) Murder.

(D) No murder at all, since Anne's death was fortuitous.

94. Is John guilty of Ellwood's murder?

(A) Yes, if John's suspicion that Michael had taken his power saw was incorrect.

(B) Yes, because he set the fire in Michael's sofa.

(C) No, because John did not intend to kill Ellwood.

(D) No, because the missing power saw constituted reasonable provocation for John's actions.

Questions 95-98 are based on the following bigamy statute of North Dakona:

I. Every person who has previously married a person of the opposite sex and who marries any other person, except in the cases specified in the next section, is guilty of bigamy.

II. The previous section does not extend to any person

    a. who has no living spouse;

    b. whose prior spouse has been absent for five years without knowledge by such person that such prior spouse is still living;

    c. whose prior marriage was dissolved by divorce or annulment; or

    d. who reasonably believes that the prior marriage was dissolved by divorce or annulment in another state.

III. Every person who marries another person with knowledge of circumstances that would render such other person guilty of bigamy under the laws of this state is also guilty of bigamy.

IV. Bigamy is punishable by a fine of not more than $2,000, imprisonment in the county jail not to exceed 6 months, or both.

95. Fred, lawfully married to Agnes, left his home late one night to purchase an evening paper and did not return. Agnes never heard from Fred again. Agnes concluded that Fred was dead, and four years later married Clyde. Before their marriage, Agnes told Clyde she had previously been married but that her husband was dead. Fred reappeared one year after Agnes's marriage to Clyde. Under these circumstances, if Agnes and Clyde are charged with bigamy, the statute should be applied so that

(A) Neither Agnes nor Clyde is guilty.
(B) Both Agnes and Clyde are guilty.
(C) Only Agnes is guilty.
(D) Only Clyde is guilty.

96. Betty, lawfully married to John, flew to Mexico and obtained a "quickie" divorce; John was aware of this. Thereafter, John proposed to Lois, relying on the opinion of his lawyer, who told him that the Mexican divorce would be recognized in North Dakona. John's lawyer was incorrect on the law. Before the wedding, Lois consulted her own lawyer, who told her--correctly--that the Mexican divorce was invalid in North Dakona. Lois decided to keep her lawyer's opinion to herself and proceeded to marry John without telling him what her attorney had advised her. Under these circumstances, if John and Lois are charged with attempted bigamy, the statute should be applied so that

(A) Neither John nor Lois is guilty.

(B) Both John and Lois are guilty.

(C) Only John is guilty.

(D) Only Lois is guilty.

97. Roger was lawfully married to Ann in North Dakona. With Roger's knowledge, Ann commenced divorce proceedings in that state. After several months, Roger received a document from the court phrased in obscure legalese, which he erroneously interpreted as the final divorce decree. In fact, the document was an interim decree stating that the divorce would become final after the passage of three months. Six weeks after receipt of the document, Roger married Nancy. If Roger is now prosecuted for bigamy, the statute should be applied so that Roger is

(A) Not guilty of bigamy if his misinterpretation of the document is properly characterized as a mistake of law.

(B) Not guilty of bigamy if his misinterpretation of the document is properly characterized as a mistake of fact.

(C) Not guilty of bigamy if his misinterpretation of the document is properly characterized as either a mistake of fact or a mistake of law.

(D) Guilty of bigamy regardless of whether his misinterpretation of the document is properly characterized as either a mistake of fact or a mistake of law.

98. Victor was lawfully married to Susan, who left him and moved to another city. Victor proposed to Peggy and falsely told her that Susan was dead. Irwin, another suitor for Peggy's hand, told her that Susan was still alive and produced a recent letter from Susan to support his contention. However, Peggy was intoxicated at the time and did not understand or remember what Irwin told her. Thereafter, Peggy married Victor. On these facts, if Peggy is charged with bigamy, she is

(A) Not guilty only if her intoxication was voluntary.

(B) Not guilty only if her intoxication was involuntary.

(C) Not guilty regardless of whether her intoxication was voluntary or involuntary.

(D) Guilty regardless of whether her intoxication was voluntary or involuntary.

Multiple-Choice Answers

1. **A** A general intent crime requires proof only that the accused intended to commit the act which served as the *actus reus*, not that he intended the injury which might result. (*See* ELO Ch. 1-II(B).) Since Kramer intended to place the screwdriver against George's throat, and George was hurt when he twisted his head, Kramer is culpable of criminal assault. Choice **A** is correct. Choice **D** is incorrect because proof that the accused intended injury is unnecessary for a general intent crime. Choice **C** is incorrect because George's reaction was a reasonable response to Kramer's actions and Kramer should reasonably have expected that his placing an object against a person's neck might lead the victim to turn his head to view the source of the pressure. Finally, Choice **B** is incorrect because the critical issue is not the inherent danger of the perpetrator's actions, but his intent to commit the act which causes the danger. Kramer would be innocent if he had not intended to place the screwdriver on George's throat.

2. **C** Under the Model Penal Code, a defendant acts "knowingly" if "he is aware that it is **practically certain** that his conduct will cause that result." M.P.C. § 2.02(b)(ii). Since Freddy was unaware that anyone except Richie was in the car, he could not reasonably be considered "practically certain" that his conduct would cause Jack's death. (*See* ELO Ch. 1-II(G).) The correct answer is Choice **C**. Choice **D** is incorrect because, as applied to capital crimes, the "provocation" must be such as would lead a reasonable man to lose his self-control. It seems extremely unlikely that a reasonable man would throw dynamite in response to a derogatory finger gesture. Choice **A** is incorrect because the definition of "knowingly" relates not only to the act committed but to the consequences of the act. The accused must be considered "practically certain" that his actions will produce the result produced. Choice **B** is incorrect because, although Jack was clearly within the zone of danger created by Freddy's conduct, Freddy did not have actual knowledge that Jack was in the car.

3. **A** The correct answer is Choice **A**. The crime of false pretenses occurs when the defendant obtains title to the property of another by knowingly misrepresenting a material fact. (*See* ELO Ch. 9-IV.) Here, Joe obtained "title" to Molly's $50 by misrepresenting his ownership of the television. Selling a television at a garage sale implies ownership of the item by the seller. Choice **B** is incorrect because in larceny by trick only possession of the property is obtained. If ownership of property is obtained, the crime is false pretenses. Since Molly did not intend to get back her $50, she was giving up ownership rather than mere possession of the money. The fact that the television did not come with title

is irrelevant to the issue. Choice **C** is incorrect because Joe implicitly represented to Molly that he owned the TV by conducting the garage sale. Finally, Choice **D** is incorrect because purchasers at a garage sale do *not* (despite the relative informality) assume the risk of defective title.

4. **B** Common law arson occurs where the defendant, at night, maliciously burns the dwelling house of another. Charring ordinarily satisfies the "burning" element and arson occurred because the barn would be considered part of the dwelling house. Although the barn was a separate structure located 100 feet from Farmer John's house, it is regarded as part of the dwelling because of its proximity to the main building. In this sense, it comes within the definition of *curtilage,* which was originally applied to all the buildings adjacent to a main dwelling and surrounded by the same fence as the dwelling. This definition of dwelling also applies in the crime of burglary. Choice **B** is the correct answer. Choice **C** is incorrect because no specific intent is necessary for the crime of arson to occur. The defendant must only have acted maliciously (i.e., *intentionally* or *recklessly*). Choice **A** is not correct because the charring of a building is sufficient to constitute arson. Finally, Choice **D** is incorrect because arson extends to structures located within an area adjacent to the house which can reasonably be fenced in.

5. **A** The crime of larceny occurs if the accused, in a trespassory manner, takes and carries away personal property of another, with the intent to permanently deprive the owner of the item. The "taking-and-carrying away" element is satisfied here because Andrew, as a minor employee, has only custody of the fax machine (possession remained with Mr. Barnes). (*See* ELO Ch. 9-II(B).) In most states, the "permanently deprived" element is satisfied if the accused pawns the item, even if he intends ultimately to redeem and return it to the rightful owner. Thus, Andrew is culpable of the crime charged. Choice **A** is the correct answer. Choice **B** is incorrect because Andrew's lie to Barnes about the thug's theft of the fax machine is irrelevant to the crime of larceny. Choice **C** is incorrect because, since Andrew was a low-level employee with temporary custody and under specific instructions about the repair of the machine, the machine is still deemed to be in Mr. Barnes's possession. Finally, Choice **D** is incorrect because, even if Andrew intended to redeem the fax machine, the majority view is that his actions have still "permanently deprived" Mr. Barnes of the item.

6. **B** The crime of false pretenses occurs when the accused has fraudulently obtained title to another's property. Since Anita knew that she had insufficient funds to cover the check to the Mercedes dealer, she obtained title to the vehicle by fraudulent means. Thus, she is guilty. The correct answer is Choice **B**. (*See* ELO Ch. 9-IV(I).) Choice **A** is incorrect because, to commit false pretenses, the defendant must obtain title to (rather than mere possession of) the item involved. Choice **C** is incorrect on the facts as stated, which tell us that Anita received the car's documents of title as well as the car. Finally, Choice **D** is incorrect because Anita knew that the dealership would not have given her the car and the title documents if it had known her check was bad.

7. **A** The crime of false pretenses requires that the accused, with the intent to defraud, knowingly make a misrepresentation of a material fact that causes the person to whom it is made to give the accused title to his property. The statement is material if it would induce a reasonable person to part with title to the property. Erica's statement is material because a reasonable person would not pay $1000 for a computer worth $500. Since Erica knew her statement was false, and she obviously made it to get more money for the computer, she committed the crime of false pretenses when she permitted Jamie to give her the $1000 money order for the computer. The fact that Erica was not able to cash the money order is irrelevant. Erica had title to the money once she received the money order. Choice **A** is the correct answer. Choice **B** is incorrect; Jamie took possession only because he was induced to do so by Erica's fraudulent statements. Choice **C** is incorrect because the fact that Erica never cashed her money order is irrelevant. Her crime was complete when she took possession and title to the money order. Finally, Choice **D** is incorrect because Erica's statement that the computer's value was $2,000 was not an opinion but an outright lie; she knew the actual value was lower.

8. **C** Larceny by trick occurs when, with the intent to steal, the accused has fraudulently obtained ***possession*** of (but not ***title*** to) another's personal property. When the defendant has obtained ***title*** to the property, she cannot be convicted of larceny by trick. She can only be convicted of false pretenses. (*See* ELO Ch. 9-IV(B).) Therefore, the key issue here is whether Allison obtained title to the shoes. The rule is that a transfer of title occurs when the victim parts with property as the result of a **sale**. (*See* ELO Ch. 9-IV(E).) Since Allison bought the loafers from the store, she acquired title and, therefore, she cannot be successfully prosecuted for larceny by trick. She is, however, guilty of false pretenses.

The correct answer is Choice **C**. Choice **D** is incorrect because whether or not Allison altered the numbers on the price tags, Allison could be convicted of larceny by trick if she obtained possession of the shoes by switching the tags, and of the crime of false pretenses if she obtained title to the shoes. Finally, Choices **A** and **B** are incorrect because, as discussed above, Allison cannot be guilty of the crime of larceny by trick because she acquired title to the shoes (rather than mere possession of them).

9. **D**   The crime of embezzlement occurs when the accused has fraudulently converted the property of another at a time when the property was lawfully in her possession. (*See* ELO Ch. 9-III(A).) If the accused obtained the property lawfully, she cannot be guilty of embezzlement. Since Brian had voluntarily loaned the car to Mary at a time when her intent was only to use it to drive to a party, Mary committed the crime of embezzlement when she appropriated the car for her escape to the West. The correct answer is Choice **D**. Embezzlement and larceny are distinct crimes which cannot overlap. Choice **A** is incorrect because the crime of larceny requires a trespassory taking; it is a crime against possession and cannot occur when possession is obtained lawfully. Choice **B** is incorrect because the crime of false pretenses requires that title to property pass as the result of a false misrepresentation of a material fact. Mary made no misrepresentation and she never acquired title to Brian's Toyota. Finally, Choice **C** is incorrect because an individual cannot be convicted of larceny by trick if she was in rightful possession of the property at the time she appropriated it for her own use. Larceny by trick is simply one way in which the crime of larceny can be committed. (*See* ELO Ch. 9-II(B)(6).)

10. **D**   The crime of embezzlement occurs when the defendant fraudulently converts another's personal property at a time when the property was lawfully in his possession. The key issue here is whether Sid was in a position to acquire lawful possession of the money as the store manager, when he took it from the safe. A minor employee may have only temporary custody of an item, rather than possession. But managerial employees are deemed to be in lawful possession of property with which they have been entrusted by their employers. (*See* ELO Ch. 9-III(E).) Sid was the store manager; he had been given a key to the safe; and he had the authority to take money from the safe. The owner entrusted Sid with the money in the safe and, therefore, Sid was in lawful possession of the money when he took it. Thus, the crime of embezzlement occurred. Choice **D** is the correct answer. Choices **A** and **C** are incorrect because larceny—and larceny by trick is only one

manifestation of the broad crime of larceny—requires that the defendant wrongfully take property from another's possession. If the defendant is in rightful possession of the property at the time he appropriates it, he cannot be guilty of larceny. Finally, Choice **B** is incorrect because Sid did **not** acquire title to the cash he took from the safe. He obtained possession of the money through the voluntary act of his employer. The crime of false pretenses requires that title pass to a person who acquires property by a false representation of a material fact.

11. **D**   Each one of the crimes listed requires the unlawful taking of property by the accused. None of these crimes was committed against Pam because Kevin did not get any money from her. While Mary did give $5 to Kevin, she was not frightened into giving Kevin the money but did so voluntarily to go along with Kevin's prank. Mary's impulsiveness in playing along with Kevin's game does not create an unlawful taking. In addition, it is reasonably clear that Kevin did not intend to deprive Mary of her money. Kevin was only playing a game. He cannot be convicted of any of these crimes unless it is proved that he had the intent to steal. If Kevin had acted with the intent to steal, and either Mary or Pam had been frightened into giving Kevin her money, he would have committed the crime of robbery. A robbery occurs when the accused, by force or the threat of force, takes and carries away from her person or presence, the personal property of his victim, with the intent to steal. (*See* ELO Ch. 9-VIII(A).) The correct answer is Choice **D**. Choice **A** is incorrect because the facts do not establish the crime of robbery. Choice **B** is incorrect because the crime of larceny requires a trespassory taking and no trespassory taking occurred. Finally, Choice **C** is incorrect because no embezzlement occurred. Kevin did not have lawful possession of Mary's money before he took it from her.

12. **D**   The correct answer is **D**. Tommy is not guilty of any of the three listed crimes. Larceny by trick is a form of larceny, but it requires two ingredients which are not necessary for simple larceny: 1) the property taken by the accused must be **converted** by him, i.e., it must be destroyed, sold, or otherwise deprived of its utility to the victim; and 2) title to the stolen property must not have passed to the accused. (*See* ELO Ch. 9-II(B)(6)(a)-(b).) Larceny by trick also requires that the property be taken by fraud or deceit. None of these requirements is present here, and Choice **B** is therefor incorrect. Choice **A** is incorrect because the wallet was not obtained by Tommy by force or the threat of force, an essential element of the crime of robbery. Finally, Choice **C** is incorrect because Tommy did not convert property which was law-

fully in his possession. The crime of embezzlement can occur only with respect to property which is lawfully in the possession of the accused when it is fraudulently converted. Lest we conclude that no crime is committed by pickpockets, let us state that Tommy has committed the crime of common law larceny, which requires only a trespassory taking and carrying away of the property of another with intent to steal. (*See* ELO Ch. 9-II(A).)

13. C   The best answer is Choice **C**. The crime of receiving stolen property occurs when the accused receives *stolen goods* which he knows to be stolen, with the intention of permanently depriving the owner of the goods. The low price which Beaver paid for the vase justifies the conclusion that Beaver knew he was purchasing stolen property. Further, Beaver's intent to keep the vase establishes that he intended to deprive the true owner of the vase. However, we are lacking one essential element of the crime of receiving stolen property. The key issue is whether the vase was *stolen property* at the time of the sale to Beaver. The rule is that once the police recover the property in question, it ceases to be "stolen." (*See* ELO Ch. 9-VI(B)(2).) Since the vase was recovered by the police when Friday took it from Kristen, Beaver cannot be convicted for receiving stolen property. He may be successfully prosecuted for *attempted* receipt of stolen property, but even here he may be able to assert the defense of legal impossibility, on the theory that what he tried to do could not have been construed as a crime because the goods were not stolen when offered to him. Choice **D** is incorrect because the crime of receiving stolen property occurs whether or not the accused intends to resell the article; he may, as here, simpy wish to retain it. Choice **A** would be correct if the vase had not been recovered by the police. Once the property is no longer considered stolen goods, the accused is not guilty even if he believed he was purchasing stolen property. Finally, Choice **B** is also incorrect because the vase had ceased to be "stolen." In addition, even if the vase was considered stolen, Choice **B** would be incorrect because it fails to include one of the essential elements of the crime of receiving stolen property, i.e., that the accused know (or have reason to believe) that the goods were stolen.

14. A   The crime of receiving stolen property occurs when the accused has voluntarily taken into his possession goods which he knows to be stolen, with the intention of permanently depriving the owner of the goods. The key issue here is whether Morgan can be convicted of receiving stolen property even if he never personally handled the television sets himself. The accused need not handle the goods. He is

guilty if he exercises control over the goods. On these facts, Morgan exercised control over the goods when he directed his "employees" to deposit the goods in Pete's warehouse. The correct answer is **A**. Choice **B** is incorrect because **attempts** are ordinarily merged into the completed crime, and carry a lesser penalty than the completed crime. Choice **C** is incorrect. The crime of conspiracy requires agreement by two or more parties to carry out an unlawful act or to carry out a lawful act by unlawful means. (*See* ELO Ch. 6-I(A).) The requirements are not met here because the facts fail to indicate that Morgan agreed with anyone else to receive the TV sets. Also, conspiracy to commit a particular crime ordinarily carries a lesser penalty than the completed crime, and the question calls for the most serious crime committed by Morgan. Finally, Choice **D** is incorrect because, as explained above, Morgan is guilty of receiving stolen property because he took custody of the sets by depositing them in Pete's warehouse even though he did not handle the goods and did not own the warehouse.

15. **D**   A person becomes an accomplice when he aids, abets, encourages or assists another in the commission of a crime. (*See* ELO Ch. 7-II(A).) It is generally said that the accomplice's state of mind must be essentially the same as that of the perpetrator of the crime, i.e., he must have the same *mens rea* as the perpetrator. (*See* ELO Ch. 7-III(B)(3).) Here, Alex knew that Tom was angry with the Director and that he intended to "have words with him". But he did not know that Tom was carrying his gun, and, as we are told, he didn't believe that Tom intended to murder the Director. Thus, even though Alex did help Tom to commit the crime by luring the secretary out of the office, he lacked the *mens rea* necessary to the crime. The correct answer is **D**. Choice **A** is incorrect because it's not enough that a person commit an act which helps the perpetrator; he must **intend** that that act result in the crime itself. Choice **B** is incorrect for the same reason. Choice **C** is incorrect on the facts because in the strictest factual sense, Alex did "participate" in the crime. He is not guilty as an accomplice, however, because an accomplice must also intend that the criminal act itself occur.

16. **D**   Solicitation occurs when the accused requests, counsels, incites or encourages another to commit a crime. The accused must intend that the solicitee commit the crime. It is not necessary to the crime that the solicitee agree; or that the crime itself be committed. (*See* ELO Ch. 7-IX(A,D).) In this case, even though Timmy responded to Mad Dog's dare by burning down the church, there is no evidence that Mad Dog intended Timmy to commit this crime. Since the specific intent element is missing, Choice **D** is the correct answer. Choice **A** is wrong

because although, under some circumstances, a dare might be construed as an act of solicitation (example: a group of mobsters decides that a rival gang member must be "eliminated" and the leader of the group "dares" anyone to volunteer to commit the crime), the dare in this set of facts is not sufficiently pointed and direct to constitute solicitation; clearly, Mad Dog did not ask or direct Timmy to burn down a church. The correct answer is **D**. Choice **A** is wrong for the same reasons which make Choice **D** correct. Choice **B** is incorrect; the crime of solicitation, by its very nature, can occur only before the commission of a crime, not after it. Choice **C** is wrong because a dare can sometimes be enough to constitute solicitation.

17. **B**   The crime of solicitation occurs when the accused requests another to commit a crime, with the specific intent that the crime be committed. Under the Model Penal Code, the accused is guilty of solicitation even if he "fails to communicate with the person he solicits." M.P.C. § 5.02(2). This means that when Dillinger sent the letter asking Capone to kill the policeman, all the elements for solicitation were satisfied. Choice **B** is the correct answer. Choice **A** is incorrect because Dillinger would still be guilty even if Capone never saw or read his letter. The crime was complete when the letter was mailed. Choice **C** is incorrect because there is no general defense of impossibility to a solicitation charge. (*See* ELO Ch. 7-IX(I)(3).) It doesn't matter that the solicitee cannot actually commit the crime; all that's necessary is that the solicitor believe that the crime can be committed. Finally, Choice **D** is incorrect because there is no requirement that the solicitee take any action for the crime of solicitation. As soon as the defendant makes the request, the crime is complete. (*See* ELO Ch. 7-IX(B).)

18. **D**   Accomplice liability occurs when one aids, abets, encourages or assists another in the commission of a crime. The accused must intend 1) to commit the act which constitutes the assistance or encouragement; and 2) to help bring about the other perpetrator's criminal act. In this case, Tina encouraged Inez to steal the brooch and aided Inez by informing her that Patricia would be out of town and that she could find a key to Patricia's apartment in the backyard. Based on these facts, it is reasonable to assume that Tina intended to help Inez commit the burglary. The issue then is whether Tina, as an accomplice to the burglary, can be held responsible for Inez's death.

At first glance, it may appear that Tina's intent to aid in the burglary is sufficient to hold her responsible for the murder under the felony-murder rule. The felony-murder rule holds a defendant liable for a murder committed during certain dangerous felonies, even if the defendant did not intend the homicide. Since this murder occurred during the commission of a dangerous felony, it is not necessary that Tina have had an intent to kill. Tina can be convicted of murder, under the felony-murder rule, because she intended to help Inez commit the burglary. (*See* ELO Ch. 7-III(A).) *However*, when the person murdered is not the intended victim but the felon herself, most jurisdictions do not apply the felony-murder rule. *Commonwealth v. Redline*, 137 A.2d 472 (Pa. 1958). (*See* ELO Ch. 7-III(C)(4)(e)(i).) (*See* the criticism in the Emanuel outline of this exception to the felony-murder rule.) Thus Tina will not be liable for Inez's murder. The correct answer is Choice **D**. Choice **C** is incorrect because it is generally foreseeable that a homicide will result during the commission of a burglary. Choice **A** is incorrect because, although violence was a "natural and probable consequence" of the burglary, the felony-murder rule does not apply to the killing of a felon by her intended victim. Choice **B** is incorrect because the expectation of profits is not one of the requirements for homicide; a person may be guilty of murder, including felony-murder, whether or not she expects to profit.

19. **A** The crime of conspiracy requires the agreement of two or more persons to commit an unlawful act or a lawful act by unlawful means. The key word is "agreement". The traditional rule was that a conspiracy could not be found unless there was an actual agreement of two or more persons to commit a crime. Under this traditional view, a conspiracy could not exist when one party, such as an undercover police officer, feigned agreement. The more modern view, however, holds that a defendant can be convicted of conspiracy even if the other party lacks the intent to commit the object crime. This means that a defendant can be convicted of conspiracy if he agrees with a police officer to commit a crime, even though the police officer is feigning agreement. The Model Penal Code has adopted this modern view. The Code reaches its conclusion by reasoning that any person who agrees with another, whatever the circumstances, to commit a crime is guilty of conspiracy. Under this approach, conspiracy is not defined as an agreement between two or more parties, but rather, as the commitment of one defendant to the other(s). M.P.C. § 5.03(1)(a). (*See* ELO Ch. 5-II(D).) Since Jake agreed to rob the 7-Eleven, he is guilty of conspiracy. The correct answer is Choice **A**. Choice **C** is incorrect because the defense of entrapment is available to an accused only if the police officer *induces* commitment of the crime. Here, Jake proposed the robbery, not Marty. (*See* ELO Ch. 3-X(A).) Choice **D** is incorrect because, as explained above, under the modern view, it does not matter that Marty never really agreed or intended to rob the store. Finally,

Choice **B** is incorrect because it's not necessary for the crime of conspiracy that a "substantial step" be taken towards commission of the target crime. [The "substantial step" requirement can be a factor in assessing "attempt "crimes. (*See* ELO Ch. 4-(III)(D))].

20. **D** Under common law principles, a conspiracy occurs when there is an agreement between two or more persons to commit an unlawful act, or an lawful act by unlawful means. Half the jurisdictions also require an overt act by one of the conspirators in furtherance of the conspiracy. (*See* ELO Ch. 5-IV(B).) The Model Penal Code requires an overt act only in the case of non-serious crimes. In the case of felonies of the first or second degree, the Code does not require an overt act because it wishes to encourage "preventive intervention". In this case, the robbery was aborted before any act could be committed. In at least half the states, the overt-act rule would prevent Corrine from being convicted of conspiracy. Further, the general rule is that a defendant cannot be charged with conspiracy unless she has agreed to join in the commission of the crime. (Even under the Model Penal Code, which has adopted the "unilateral" approach to conspiracy, Corrine could not be the one charged because she never agreed with Amanda to rob the Gap. She went with Amanda to the mall only because she feared that Amanda would harm her. Since she did not voluntarily agree to commit the crime, she cannot be convicted of conspiracy. The correct answer is Choice **D**. Choice **C** is incorrect because the act of entering the store is not a necessary element of this crime. Even if this jurisdiction is one which requires an overt act, the overt act probably occurred when Amanda pulled the two guns from her purse and handed one to Corrine. Choice **A** is incorrect because Corrine took the gun and went to the mall only because she felt threatened, not because she intended to rob the store. Finally, Choice **B** is incorrect. Since Corrine did not intend to commit a crime, she did not have to repudiate it in order to avoid culpability.

21. **A** Bill and Ted formed a criminal conspiracy when they agreed to sell cocaine to Mickey. The key issue is whether Ted can escape culpability for the crime of conspiracy because he left the scene before the deal was consummated. The common law rule is that an act of withdrawal is not a defense to a conspiracy charge because the conspiracy is complete once the agreement has been made. (*See* ELO Ch. 6-VII(B)(2)(b).) The Model Penal Code does permit a withdrawal defense, but only if: 1) the accused's renunciation was voluntary; and 2) the accused thwarts the success of the conspiracy. MPC § 5.03(6). (*See* ELO Ch. 6-VII(B)(2)(b)(i).) Ted's withdrawal satisfies neither

view: it was not voluntary because it was motivated only by a desire to avoid arrrest, and it did not thwart the success of the conspiracy. The correct answer is Choice **A.** Choice **B** is incorrect because completion of the drug sale is not required. If Bill dropped the bag with the cocaine and was unable to complete the sale, Ted and Bill would still be guilty of conspiracy. Choice **C** is incorrect because Bill's withdrawal cannot be motivated by the desire to avoid arrest, especially since the success of the conspiracy was not thwarted. (Under the common law rule a voluntary withdrawal would not save Ted from culpability in any event.) Finally, Choice **D** is incorrect because a co-conspirator need not participate in the target crime to be culpable of conspiracy.

22. **C**   Sam, Jim and Bart are all conspirators to commit the crimes of robbery and insurance fraud, both felonies. Even in those states which require an overt act to complete the conspiracy, all three would be guilty here because Bart's actions were overt. (Editor's notes: 1) The Model Penal Code does not require an overt act in the case of serious crimes. 2) The acts of Sam and Jim in giving Bart the keys and the codes would also probably satisfy the overt act requirement.) (*See* ELO Ch. 6-IV(B).) A conspirator is culpable for the substantive crime committed by a co-conspirator in furtherance of the conspiracy, and for those consequences which are a reasonably foreseeable outgrowth of the substantive crime. (For an extended discussion of prevailing judicial and Model Penal Code attitudes on the issue of a conspirator's liability for the commission by his co-conspirator of the target crime, *see* ELO Ch. 6-IV(D).) Here, the officer's death was probably not a reasonably foreseeable outgrowth of the conspiracy, unless all burglary is deemed to carry with it the threat of violent police intervention. The best answer is probably **C.** Choice **D** is incorrect because the fact that a conspiracy does not anticipate the exact felony which culminates as its result does not *per se* preclude culpability. Choices **A** and **B** are wrong because although the conspirators had planned the crimes of burglary and fraud, the resulting homicide was probably not a reasonably forseeable consequence of their conspiracy.

23. **A**   A conspirator is liable for the criminal acts of a co-conspirator which occur in the furtherance of the conspiracy, or which are a reasonably foreseeable outgrowth of it. (*See* ELO Ch. 6-IV(D).) Since Barker and Samantha agreed to rob the store at gunpoint, it is reasonable to conclude that Barker foresaw that some violence would ensue, including the use by Samantha of a deadly weapon. The correct answer is Choice **A.** Choice **B** is incorrect because it is too broad. Conspirators are *not* always liable for the acts of their co-conspirators. The modern view is

that a conspirator will not be liable simply because he is a member of the conspiracy. This view imposes liability only if the crime committed is: 1) within the scope of the conspiracy, or (2) a reasonably foreseeable outgrowth of it. Model Penal Code § 2.06(3), Comment 6(a). Choice **C** is incorrect because, under the circumstances, the killing of Kipper was reasonably foreseeable. Finally, Choice **D** is incorrect because the conspiratorial objectives would not be concluded until the money taken from the store had been divided between Barker and Samantha. Also, this choice cannot be right because it would enable co-conspirators to limit their liability by defining their target crime in such a way as to eliminate the possibility of liability for other crimes growing foreseeably out of the target crime.

24. **B**   In analyzing a homicide to determine whether it is felony murder, we must first consider the crime during which the homicide is committed. On these facts, the crime committed by Beatrice is simple assault, which results when the defendant intentionally frightens his victim into fearing immediate bodily harm. Simple assault is a misdemeanor. (*See* ELO Ch. 8-VII(B)(2).) (Some jurisdictions recognize the felony of aggravated assault, which results when the accused commits the assault with the intent to kill; that is not the case here). Choice **A** is not the right answer because felony murder can occur only in connection with the commission of a felony. On the other hand, involuntary manslaughter occurs when 1) the defendant's gross negligence results in the accidental death of another (the Model Penal Code requires that the defendant act recklessly); or 2) death occurs accidentally during the commission of a misdemeanor or other unlawful act. The couple's death occurred during the commission of the misdemeanor of simple assault when Beatrice ran towards the couple brandishing the rubber knife. This assault led to the couple's death when they ran into the street to flee. The doctrine of misdemeanor-manslaughter is similar to the doctrine of felony-murder: if a person commits a homicide during commission of a misdemeanor, she is guilty of involuntary manslaughter. (*See* ELO Ch. 8-VI(B).) Choice **B** is the correct answer. Choice **C** is incorrect because the killing was not intentional. Voluntary manslaughter is generally applicable only when there are circumstances which reduce murder to this lesser crime, i.e, the killing is provoked, the accused acts "in the heat of passion"; the time elapsing between the provocation and the killing is not so great as to justify the conclusion that a reasonable person would have "cooled off"; and the accused has not in fact cooled off. (*See* ELO Ch. 8-V(C).) Finally, Choice **D** is incorrect because, as discussed above, Beatrice's conduct constitutes a homicide with the label of "involuntary manslaughter."

25. **B**   The Model Penal Code imposes attempt liability if 1) the accused
intends to commit the crime which is attempted, and 2) the accused
has taken a substantial step towards completion of the crime. M.P.C.
§ 5.01(1). The intent element is satisfied under these facts, which tell
us that Frank was "intent on killing her." Although Frank never found
Louise, he did cruise around the neighborhood hoping to spot her.
Under the Code, this conduct is sufficient to constitute the required
"substantial step" towards completion of the crime. The Code example is "lying in wait, searching for or following the contemplated victim, of the crime." (*See* ELO Ch. 5-III(D)(3)(a)(i).) Thus Frank is
guilty of attempted murder. (Note, however, that the act of searching
for the victim is not enough to constitute a substantial step under the
more traditional "proximity test" used by some courts. *People v. Rizzo*,
158 N.E. 888 (N.Y. 1927). Choice **A** is incorrect because the purchase
of a gun, without more, would not be considered a step substantial
enough to impose attempt liability. Choice **C** is incorrect because the
crime of attempted murder can occur without the firing of a shot.
Under the Code especially, the crime of attempted murder occurs
many steps ahead of the actual gunshot. Choice **D** is incorrect because,
as noted above, the crime of attempt occurs as soon as the accused,
intending to commit the crime, begins to search for his intended victim. The correct answer is Choice **B**.

26. **C**   The correct answer is Choice **C**. Frank is not guilty of attempted murder because he voluntarily withdrew from the attempt. Frank may
originally have intended to kill Louise. And, by lurking in the shad-
sows waiting for her and pointing the gun at her forehead, he certainly
took substantial steps towards killing her. [The Model Penal Code
imposes attempt liability if 1) the accused intends to commit the crime
which is attempted, and 2) the accused has taken a substantial step
towards completion of the crime. M.P.C. § 5.01(1).] However, the
Model Penal Code and many courts allow the defense of abandon-
ment so long as it is voluntary. M.P.C. § 5.01(4). Since Frank's decision to put the gun down was voluntary, he is not guilty of attempted
murder. (*See* ELO Ch. 5-V(B,C).) Choice **A** is incorrect because Frank
voluntarily abandoned the killing by putting down the gun. . If Frank
had put down the gun not because he could not bring himself to kill
Louise, but because he feared immediate apprehension, then Choice **A**
would be correct. The facts do not support this conclusion because
Louise was alone and Frank's remarks indicate that he may never have
been capable of killing Louise. Choice **D** is incorrect. The defect in the
gun is only a factor which made the crime impossible. The courts do
not regard factual impossibility as a defense to an attempt charge (*See*

ELO Ch. 5-IV(B)(2)(a).) There would seem to be no rationale for the
contrary view, which would allow a criminal to escape only because
some factor external to his intent and his own acts thwarted his crime.
Finally, Choice **B** is incorrect because there is no requirement that a
person report to the police an attempt which he voluntarily abandoned.

27. **D**   The crime of murder cannot occur unless a life has been taken. The
crime requires proof that the action, or inaction, of the accused caused
another's death. Since the autopsy revealed that Thomas was already
dead when Margot stabbed him, she did not cause his death and,
therefore, she cannot be guilty of murder. (*See* ELO Ch. 8-II(A)(2).)
The correct answer is Choice **D**. Under these facts, the prosecution
could have prosecuted Margot successfully for attempted murder
because she stabbed Thomas with the intent to inflict serious bodily
injury. A killing caused with intent to inflict serious bodily injury satisfies the *mens rea* for murder. (*See* ELO Ch. 8-II(D).) Choice **C** is
wrong because a person can be guilty of murder even if she did not
intend to kill. The *mens rea* requirement for murder is satisfied if the
accused had the intent to cause serious bodily harm. Choices **A** and **B**
are incorrect because, as explained above, Thomas had already died.
Thus, no homicide occurred despite Margot's actions or intent.

28. **D**   If the accused commits an act which is not legally a crime, he is not
guilty of anything even if he thinks his act is illegal. This situation can
occur, for example, if the accused misconstrues the meaning of a statute or honestly believes that his conduct violates a statute when it
doesn't. Thus, "true legal impossibility" is always a successful defense.
(*See* ELO Ch. 5-IV(C).) Because the killing of coyotes was legal in his
neighborhood when Mark shot at them, he is not guilty. The correct
answer is Choice **D**. Choice **C** is incorrect because Mark was not
defending his children against attack when he killed the coyotes. The
claim of defense of others is always available when one is defending his
child, but the child must be in imminent danger of bodily harm. That
was not the case here. (*See* ELO Ch. 4-V(C).) Choice **A** is incorrect
because Mark's intent to commit an act which he thought illegal is
irrelevant; in truth, his act was not illegal. Choice **B** is incorrect; the
killing of coyotes is not inherently illegal, whatever the consequences
to coyotes as a species. It must be made illegal by some statute or regu-
lation.

29. A Courts use one of two tests to determine whether entrapment of the accused by a police officer has occurred. A majority of courts, including the Supreme Court, use the "predisposition" test. Under this test entrapment exists where: 1) the government proposes the crime and induces the defendant to commit it; and 2) the defendant is "innocent", i.e., not predisposed to commit the crime. (*See* ELO Ch. 4-X(A)(2)(a).) In this case, Harry immediately offered to sell drugs "for the right price" in response to the officer's request. This offer, combined with Harry's prior record, establishes a predisposition to sell drugs. Therefore, Harry's entrapment defense will fail. In the minority of courts which use the "police conduct" test instead of the "predisposition" test, the defense will also fail on these facts. Under this test, the government's inducement and participation must be such as to lead "innocent" or unpredisposed individuals to commit the crime, whether or not the defendant himself is actually predisposed. (*See* ELO Ch. 4-X(A)(2)(b).) Harry's entrapment defense would fail under this test because, clearly, Harry was not an "innocent" or unpredisposed person. An innocent person would have remained silent, walked away, or said "no". The correct answer is Choice **A**. Choice **B** is incorrect because there is no legal rule which says that the defense of entrapment is unavailable to former convicts for the same or a similar crime. Evidence of the same or similar prior crimes can be used as evidence of predisposition but it would not be dispositive. Choice **C** is incorrect because it is not enough to show that government inducement initiated the crime; under the majority view, the defendant must also show that he was not predisposed to commit the crime. Finally, Choice **D** is incorrect because Harry can still be convicted even if he did not have the immediate intent to sell drugs. If he was ready and willing to accept the first offer to buy drugs, it doesn't matter that he didn't intend to sell drugs until the officer approached him.

30. C One of the essential ingredients of the crime of larceny is the intent to deprive the owner of his property. (*See* ELO Ch. 9-II(A),(F).) The term *mens rea* is a euphemism for the culpable state of mind which includes specific intent. (*See* ELO Ch. 1-II(A).) Although Mandy took and carried away the necklace, she did not intend to steal the necklace. She intended to show it to Samantha and simply forgot that she still had it in her purse when she left the party. The correct answer is therefore Choice **C**. Choice **D** is incorrect. So long as an act is *voluntary*, it satisfies the definition of the term *actus reus*. Mandy wanted to take the necklace so her act was voluntary; but she lacked the intent to steal it and is not guilty of larceny. Choice **A** is incorrect because she lacked the intent to steal when she put the necklace in her purse. Finally, Choice **B** is incorrect because the facts do not show that she had a different intent when she left the house.

31. **C**   The crime of battery occurs when the accused intentionally or recklessly causes either bodily injury or an offensive touching upon the victim. (*See* ELO Ch. 8-VII(A).) The crime requires that the accused *intend* the injury or the offensive touching (i.e., possess the *mens rea* necessary for the crime). Although the facts show that Gerry struck another person, the key issue is whether Gerry's intoxication prevents her from having the necessary *mens rea* to be convicted of battery. (*See* ELO Ch. 3-IV(B)(5).) Criminal defendants often rely on intoxication as a defense, on the theory that intoxication destroys the *means rea* necessary to the crime. The issue is an involved one, but it is clear that if the defendant can show that the intoxication was "involuntary", she has a good chance of acquittal. One form of involuntary intoxication, called pathological intoxication, occurs when the defendant takes a small amount of intoxicant, but suffers a reaction which is much more severe than for a normal person, because of an abnormal sensitivity to alcohol. Pathological intoxication allows the defendant to argue that she could not control her actions and therefore acted neither intentionally nor recklessly. (*See* ELO Ch. 3-IV(C)(1)(d).) As a consequence of Gerry's unusual and unsuspected reaction to wine, she lost control of her physical actions. Her intoxication was "involuntary" and will serve as a defense to battery. The correct answer is Choice **C**. Choice **D** is incorrect because the legal age of majority is irrelevant to Gerry's guilt or innocence. Children over the age of fourteen are generally treated as adults with respect to criminal capacity. (*See* ELO Ch. 3-V(A)(3).) Choice **A** is incorrect because although Gerry's actions in drinking two glasses of wine were voluntary, the resulting intoxication was involuntary (i.e., she had no reason to know that this condition would occur). Finally, Choice **B** is incorrect because, although battery is a general intent crime, Gerry lacked the necessary *mens rea*.

32. **A**   The crime of battery requires that the accused ***intend*** bodily injury or an offensive touching upon the victim. The key issue here is whether Dan's intoxication prevents him from having the necessary intent (i,e., state of mind or *mens rea*). Voluntary drunkenness will not usually constitute a successful defense to a crime which can be committed through recklessness. (*See* ELO Ch. 3-IV(B)(5).) Since the crime of battery requires merely a reckless disregard of the risk of inflicting bodily harm on another, voluntary intoxication is not available as a defense. As a reasonable person, Dan should have realized that drink-

ing five large beers in a row would result in intoxication. Intoxication does not negate the *mens rea* of crimes that are satisfied by proof of recklessness. The correct answer is Choice **A**. Choice **D** is wrong because it depends on the defense of temporary insanity. This defense is not available when the inability to distinguish right from wrong is caused by the intoxication. (*See* ELO Ch. 3-IV(B)(8).) Choice **B** is incorrect because Dan did not "deliberately" strike the three students. His conduct in gulping down five beers and waving the chair around was reckless, not "deliberate." Choice **C** is incorrect because battery is *not* a specific intent crime. It is a general intent crime in which recklessness satisfies the required *mens rea*. (*See* the discussion of intoxication and recklessness in crimes of general intent under the Model Penal Code, ELO Ch. 3-IV(B)(5)(b).)

33. **B** The kidnapping statute at issue requires that the accused commit the confinement of another "intentionally." Under common law principles, intent (*mens rea*) is satisfied when the accused (1) intended the result which occurred, or (2) should have realized that the result would be substantially certain to follow from his actions. Here, Carl intended to commit a burglary. He did not intend to commit the crime of kidnapping as defined in the statute. On the contrary, he believed that Mary was visiting her sister in another state. When one commits one crime with the requisite intent but inadvertently and unintentionally also commits the acts defining another crime, he is not guilty of the second crime because there is a failure of "temporal concurrence", i.e., the concurrence between the mental state (*mens rea*) and the act (*actus reus*). (*See* ELO Ch. 1-III(B).) The correct answer is **B**. Choice **A** is incorrect because it is not the best reason to find Carl not guilty. Mary was unlawfully confined for a substantial period of time. Nothing required her to call the police before attempting to free herself. The better answer is **B**, which relies on Carl's lack of intent. Finally, Choices **C** and **D** are incorrect because Carl never intended to cause Mary's confinement.

34. **A** The American legal system does not generally impose criminal liability for a failure or omission to act. Under some circumstances, however, there may be a duty to act to avoid or prevent an undesirable result. An accused will be found guilty if (1) he had a a legal duty to act; (2) was aware of the facts or circumstances which obliged her to act; and (3) was capable of performing the act required. A legal duty to act can be based upon (1) the personal relationship of the parties, (2) statutory law, (3) contract, (4) a voluntary assumption of care, (5) creation of the risk or danger by the accused, or (6) status as a landlord. (*See* ELO

Ch. 1-I(D)(1-5).) Because the relationship between Alison and Jamie does not fall within any of these categories, Alison had no legal duty to rescue Jamie and she is not guilty of murder (or any other crime). The correct answer is Choice **A**. (However, it is probably safe to say that Alison will not win the "Good Citizenship" award for this or any-month; nor would she be well advised to use the pool again.) Choice **B** is incorrect because this is not the basis for exonerating Alison; even if Alison had made no effort to call the police, she would still **not** be guilty of murder. Choice **C** is incorrect because, as explained above, although Alison could have saved Jamie without any risk of harm to herself, she was under no legal duty to do so. Choice **D** is incorrect because there is no special duty in the general public to come to the aid of a minor. The duty would arise, for example, because of the special relationship between a minor and his parents, or by virtue of a statute.

35. D If a defendant kills another, even accidentally, during the commission of a felony, he becomes guilty of murder under what is now called the felony-murder rule. (*See* ELO Ch. 8-III(A).) Although Kevin's ulti-mate intent was to commit the felony of insurance fraud, a felony which is not inherently dangerous, he elected to do so by committing arson, a felony which is very dangerous. In most jurisdictions, arson has now been extended to include commercial buildings. (Under common law, it was limited to a residence and its adjoining struc-tures.) To hold the defendant guilty of the killing resulting from com-mission of the felony, there must be a causal relationship between the two. The defendant will be liable only when the death is the "natural and probable consequence of his act." The key issue is whether Kevin's act of arson satisfies the proximate cause element despite his igno-rance of the fact that Ben was in the building. The rule with respect to arson is that the requisite causal relationship exists with anyone who is in the building at the time the fire is set and who dies in the fire. (*See* ELO Ch. 8-III(C)(3).) Therefore, Kevin is guilty of murder. The cor-rect answer is Choice **D**. Choice **C** is incorrect because Kevin commit-ted arson, an inherently dangerous felony (as well as attempting insurance fraud). Choice **A** is incorrect because the felony-murder rule does not require that the defendant have a specific intent to kill. Finally, Choice **B** is incorrect because it was reasonably foreseeable that a human being might die as a consequence of his actions, e.g., a fireman fighting the fire rather than an unknown derelict.

36. A Common law burglary requires several specific ingredients: 1) a break-ing; 2) and an entry; 3) into the dwelling of another; 4) at night; and 5) with the intent to commit a felony. The intent to commit a felony must be present at the moment of breaking and entering. It cannot be formed after the accused enters the dwelling. (*See* ELO Ch. 9-VII(F).) When Daniel entered the house, his sole purpose was to retrieve his VCR. Obviously, the act of retrieving your own property is not a felony. Because the intent to take the computer was not formed until after he was in the house, Daniel cannot be convicted of the crime of burglary. The correct answer is Choice **A**. Choice **B** is incorrect because the facts tell us that Daniel opened the unlocked window, and the slightest opening created by the accused constitutes a "breaking" for purposes of this crime. (*See* ELO Ch. 9-VII(B).) Choice **C** is incorrect because it does not state all the ingredients of the crime of burglary: 1) the illegal entry must be a "breaking" and 2) the defendant must intend to commit a felony once inside the house. Finally, Choice **D** is incorrect because the fact that Daniel took the Powerbook after he entered the house would make him guilty of larceny [the trespassory taking and carrying away of the personal property of another with intent to steal (*See* ELO Ch. 9-II(A))], but not burglary.

37. **C**   The crime of murder requires three essential ingredients: an affirmative act by the accused (*actus reus*); resulting in a death; committed with malice aforethought (*mens rea*). In addition, there must be a causal relationship between the act and the death, i.e., the act must be both the "cause in fact" and the "proximate" cause of the death. (*See* ELO Ch. 8-II(B)(4).) Janice laced the cookies with poison and placed them on David's desk, with the intent to kill, and David died as a result of eating the cookies. Thus, all the elements for a murder conviction are satisfied. It doesn't help Janice that she relented and attempted to undo her actions. The correct answer is Choice **C**. Choice **A** is wrong because Janice had the necessary *mens rea* when she committed the acts which caused her brother's death. Choice **D** is incorrect because the time to measure Janice's state of mind was at the moment she committed the acts that led to David's death—at that time she had the necessary *mens rea*, i.e., the intent to kill. A subsequent change of heart does not absolve Janice of responsibility for the murder. Choice **B** is incorrect. The provocation that is required to justify the reduction of a homicide from murder to voluntary manslaughter is not satisfied by Janice's impulse to preserve her interest in her parents' estate, whether or not David was telling malicious lies. (For an extended discussion of the elements of involuntary manslaughter, *see* ELO Ch. 8-V).

38. **C**   The crime of involuntary manslaughter results when the accused, through grossly negligent conduct, causes the accidental death of another person. It also results when the accused has committed a mis-

demeanor or other unlawful act which causes the accidental death. The latter is called the ***misdemeanor-manslaughter rule***. The reasoning behind the rule is similar to the reasoning behind the ***felony-murder rule***. (*See* ELO Ch. 8-VI(B).) (The Model Penal Code rejects the misdemeanor-manslaughter rule in its entirety, and it has been criticised by others because it often converts conduct which cannot be characterized as more than mere negligence, into a homicide.) In this case, however, the correct answer is Choice **C** because Jonathan committed a criminal battery. Simple battery, a misdemeanor, occurs when the accused intentionally causes either: 1) bodily injury; or 2) offensive touching. The crime can be committed intentionally, or, in some states, recklessly or with criminal negligence. Jonathan committed a battery when he pushed Peter and he is guilty of involuntary misdemeanor-manslaughter. (*See* ELO Ch. 8-VII(A).) Choice **A** is incorrect because Jonathan did not intend to kill Peter, and the crime of murder requires malice aforethought.. Choice **B** is incorrect because voluntary manslaughter also requires an intentional killing. The crime occurs when an act that would otherwise constitute murder is reduced to manslaughter because of provocation, "heat of passion", or the relationship in time between the provocation and the killing. (*See* ELO Ch. 8-V(C).) Finally Choice **D** is incorrect because, as discussed above, Jonathan is criminally responsible for Peter's death under the misdemeanor-manslaughter rule.

39. **D** A larceny occurs when the defendant, in a trespassory manner, takes and carries away the personal property of another, with the intent to steal. The "intent" element is crucial to the crime, which cannot be committed negligently or recklessly. Furthermore, the intent must be to deprive the owner of possession permanently, not temporarily (*See* ELO Ch. 9-II(F)(1).) The facts make it clear that Erica intended only to "teach Pat a lesson," not to deprive her permanently of the bike. Erica's lack of larcenous intent is shown also by her vigil in the hallway. Thus, Erica is not guilty of larceny, and the correct answer is Choice **D**. Choice **C** is incorrect because the fact that Erica did not take part in the actual removal of the bike is immaterial to the issue of her intent. Choice **A** is incorrect because the issue is Erica's intent, not the consequence of her actions. (*See* ELO Ch. 9-II(F)(1)(c).) Finally, Choice **B** is incorrect because the crime of larceny requires the intent to steal, not the intent to inconvenience someone or "teach her a lesson." Erica intended to return the bike, and the intent to return is inconsistent with the intent to steal.

40. D   The common law misdemeanor of malicious mischief occurs when the accused has intentionally (some cases accept criminal negligence in place of specific intent) destroyed or damaged the personal property of another. Sheila's conduct in lying about her intended use of the car, removing the car for a weekend lark and then damaging the car, are probably enough to constitute malicious mischief. The correct answer is **D**. Choices **A** and **B** are incorrect because both simple larceny and larceny by trick require proof that the accused intended to deprive the owner of his property permanently. Sheila intended to return Max's car at the end of the weekend. Although the element of "permanency" can be satisfied if the defendant takes the property for such a long time that the owner is deprived of a significant portion of its economic value, that is not the case here.(*See* ELO Ch. 9-II(F)(1).) Finally, Choice **C** is incorrect because an essential element of robbery—the use of force or fright—is missing. (*See* ELO Ch. 9-VIII(A).)

41. A   The common law crime of mayhem resulted from the need to punish the commission of batteries which resulted in great bodily harm (the common law did not recognize aggravated assault or battery). The crime required both permanent injury to the victim and intent by the accused to cause the injury. (*See* ELO Ch. 8-VII(C).) The statute quoted here conforms to the general requirements at common law. However, a defendant will not be held liable for the injury she causes if the injury occurs through a completely bizarre, unforeseeable chain of events. She is liable, however, if she intends one injury but the actual injury occurs in a slightly different way or is slightly different from the injury she originally intended. In this case, Molly clearly intended to disfigure Samantha and her actions caused Samantha to jump in the pool to wash the acid away. The fact that Samantha was injured in a desperate attempt to escape the acid was not a bizarre or unforeseeable event under the circumstances, and Molly is guilty of mayhem as defined in the statute. (*See* ELO Ch. 2-V.) The correct answer is Choice **A**. Choice **B** is incorrect because a victim's attempt to avoid injury will rarely be a supervening event without the occurence also of some bizarre and unforeseeable event. Samantha's attempt to remove the acid by jumping in the pool was obviously not an abnormal reaction to Molly's action. (*See* ELO Ch. 2-V(C)(4).) Choice **C** is incorrect because Molly's conduct was the proximate cause of Samantha's injuries. Her actions caused Samantha's injuries without the intervention of any other event or conduct and the result was foreseeable. Finally, Choice **D** is incorrect because, as explained above, Molly is still culpable even if the injury is different from the injury intended or is caused in a different manner.

42. C   When the defense of insanity is raised by the accused, the trier of fact
has the burden of accepting or rejecting the evidence, including the
testimony of expert witnesses. The court will instruct the jury that the
state has the burden of proving all the material elements of the crime,
in effect forcing the jury to decide between conviction and acquittal by
reason of insanity. (*See* ELO Ch. 3-I(H)(5).) The jury is free to disregard or disbelieve the witnesses' evaluation of the defendant's mental
condition, even if the witnesses are eminent psychiatrists, all of whom
have found that the defendant has an incurable mental illness. *People
v. Wolff,* 394 P.2d 1959 (Cal. 1964). Under the Insanity Defense Reform
Act of 1984, which constitutes the federal insanity statute, neither side
may offer the testimony of an expert as to the ultimate issue of the
defendant's sanity; this is left to the jury. Thus, despite the substantial
amount of expert testimony to the contrary, the jury could conclude
that David was *not* insane when the sacrificial killings were committed. The correct answer is Choice **C**. Choices **A**, **B**, and **D** are incorrect
because each one depends on substituting the judgment of the appel-
late court for the jury's verdict.

43. B   Rape is usually defined as having unlawful sexual intercourse with a
female without her consent. It is clear on these facts that Debbie did
not consent and that a reasonable man would have understood that
she was not consenting. We are therefore required, under this statute,
to ask whether Donald's intoxication deprived him of the ability to
"know or reasonably believe" that Debbie had not consented and/or
whether Donald "recklessly disregarded the possibility" that she was
not consenting. Traditionally, intoxication by the accused has not been
recognized as a defense to the "general intent" crime of rape. Some
authorities have recognized the defense when the accused is so intoxicated that he lacks the intent to have intercourse. However, if the
accused argues that his intoxication prevented him from realizing that
the victim was not consenting, then his conduct was *reckless,* and
recklessness is enough to constitute the "general intent" required for
the crime of rape.(*See* ELO Ch. 3-IV(B)(4).) On these facts, Donald's
conduct in permitting himself to become so intoxicated as to prevent
him from realizing that Debbie was not consenting was reckless and
satisfies the second arm of this statute. The correct answer is Choice **B**.
Choice **A** is wrong because the word "wrongly" does not adequately
describe the mental state required under this statute. The statute
requires a showing of reckless disregard for the victim's lack of consent. Choice **C** is wrong because Donald's belief was unreasonable on
these facts. His intoxication prevented him from recognizing that Debbie did not consent. Finally, Choice **D** is incorrect because the degree

of intoxication is relevant only in establishing whether or not the accused was so intoxicated as to amount to a "reckless disregard" of the possibility that Debbie was not consenting. A defendant's claim that he was legally drunk does not in and of itself constitute a defense to rape.

44. A The courts have recently been confronted by many cases involving battered wives who claim that they acted in self defense in killing their abusive husbands. Although sympathetic to these wives, the courts have consistently applied the traditional requirements for self-defense. One may use deadly force when she reasonably believes that she is in imminent danger of being killed or is being threatened with serious bodily harm. Although Jenny is clearly a battered woman and legitimately frightened, she must still show that the danger of her death was imminent. The general rule is that when the batterer goes to sleep, and the defendant shoots him while he sleeps, the defendant's self defense claim fails because the danger is not sufficiently imminent. (*See* ELO Ch. 4-IV(J)(4).) The logic behind this rule is that the defendant had ample time to protect herself by other means, such as calling the police or leaving the house. Although Jenny's self-defense claim fails, some jurisdictions allow the intentional homicide to be reduced to voluntary manslaughter when the accused honestly, but unreasonably, believes she is killing in self-defense. (*See* ELO Ch. 4-IV(M).) However, most jurisdictions follow the rule of the jurisdiction in this question and do not permit a claim of imperfect self-defense to reduce murder to voluntary manslaughter. [**Note:** An "imperfect" self-defense is one which does not constitute a complete defense to homicide. It arises when the defendant has killed because of an unreasonable mistake as to the need for force, when she is the initial aggressor, or under other circumstances which do not provide a complete defense against the homicide but mitigate against the crime of murder. (*See* ELO Ch. 4-IV(M))].Therefore, Jenny is guilty of murder and the correct answer is Choice **A**. **B** is incorrect because Jenny did not meet the standards for invoking an "imperfect" self-defense. Choice **C** is incorrect because an intentional killing cannot be involuntary manslaughter. Choice **D** is incorrect because Jenny did commit the crime of murder.

45. D Every person has the right to defend himself against unlawful force. i.e., force used in the commission of a crime or tort. Whether he may use deadly force depends on the nature of the force which threatens him. If the force he faces is either death or serious body harm, then he may use deadly force in reply. (*See* ELO Ch. 4-IV(B)-(E).) His belief that he is facing deadly force must be reasonable. If it is reasonable, he may assert a claim of self-defense and will be acquitted. If it is unreasonable, the claim of self-defense will not be available. (*See* ELO Ch. 4-IV(I)(2).) The cases turn on the facts leading to the homicide. Here, Jeremy had received a series of death threats and would be reasonably apprehensive of any threatened aggression. He was reasonable to believe under the circumstances that his life was at risk. He saw some one running toward him with what appeared to be a loaded gun, shouting what could reasonably be interpreted as a threat. He had no reasonable way of knowing that the teenager was engaged in an initiation, or even that the boy was only twelve. Given these facts Jeremy can successfully assert a claim of self-defense to the homicide charge. The correct answer is Choice **D**. Choice **A** is incorrect because Jeremy's self-defense is considered a perfect, rather than an "imperfect", defense. [**Note:** the claim of self-defense becomes "imperfect" when the accused kills in a mistaken belief about the need for deadly force or when he is the original aggressor. (*See* ELO Ch. 4-IV(M))]. Choice **B** is incorrect because, although Jeremy committed an intentional homicide (voluntary manslaughter is an intentional homicide committed under extenuating circumstances), he has a perfect defense. Finally, Choice **C** is incorrect because the crime of involuntary manslaughter depends on a homicide caused by criminal negligence, not specific intent. Jeremy intended to kill because he pointed and shot the gun at the boy's chest. In any event, he can assert the claim of perfect self-defense.

46. **B**   The crime of involuntary manslaughter occurs when the grossly negligent conduct of the accused results in the death of another human being. The jury must consider and decide two critical questions: 1) how far did the accused deviate from standards of reasonable care; and 2) was the accused aware of the risk of death or bodily harm. (*See* ELO Ch. 8-VI(A).) The Model Penal Code (§ 210.3(1)(b)) requires that the accused act recklessly, with awareness of the risk. On these facts, the jury would almost certainly find Biff guilty. Biff acted with complete disregard of the danger when he ordered Morton to run through the "wall" of fire. There was always the risk that a pledge would be burned seriously and might die. Biff was aware of the danger and his conduct was grossly negligent and, indeed, reckless. The fact that Morton died from a contaminated blood transfusion will not relieve Biff of liability. Although the prosecution must show a causal link between the defendant's acts and the death, intervening medical treatment is not a superseding intervening cause if it results directly from the injuries sustained by the victim. Obviously, when medical treatment is made necessary, there is always the possibility that the treatment will involve

some negligence. That should not operate to benefit the person who caused the injuries in the first place. Accordingly, ordinary negligence in the medical treatment is not considered so "abnormal" as to constitute a superseding event. [*See* ELO Ch. 2-V(C)(3), *State v. Clark*, 248 A.2d 559 (N.J.2d 1968)] The correct answer is Choice **B**. Choice **A** incorrectly states the degree of negligence which is required for involuntary manslaughter. Most jurisdictions require more than a showing of ordinary tort negligence; they require a showing of criminal negligence, i.e., gross negligence or recklessness. Choice **C** is incorrect because the waiver is ineffective. A consent which purports to waive a risk of death or serious bodily harm is effective only in very limited circumstances (i.e., organized sporting events, etc.). Finally, Choice **D** is incorrect under the analysis of negligence in supervening medical treatment, above.

47. A In recent years, the courts have broadened the liability for **attempt crimes**. Traditionally, the prosecution was required to show that the accused had committed acts which brought him close to commission of the crime itself. The modern view is that any overt act which shows a substantial step towards commission of the crime, will be adequate. The modern view also restricts sharply the defense of "legal impossibility." (*See* ELO Ch. 5-IV(C).) The Model Penal Code imposes attempt liability if 1) the accused intends to commit the substantive crime itself, and 2) the accused has taken a substantial step towards completion of the crime. Model Penal Code § 5.01(1). Under the MPC, "lying in wait" constitutes a substantial step towards accomplishment of the target crime. M.P.C. § 5.01(2)(a). The correct answer is Choice **A**. (*See* ELO Ch. 5-III(D)(3)(a).) Because Barney was waiting in the warehouse to assassinate Jordan, gun in hand, his actions come within the MPC standard. Choices **B** and **C** are incorrect because Barney had already committed overt acts which were a substantial step towards commission of the crime—he had positioned himself at the right spot in the building; he was carrying a high-powered gun; and he was "lying in wait". Choice **D** is incorrect. When a defendant argues that it was impossible for him to commit the crime because of some intervening fact, he will almost always lose. This is because we are dealing with the crime of *attempt*, which should be punished if the accused intends to commit the crime even if the crime itself was never factually possible. (*See* ELO Ch. 5-IV(B).)

48. D The question requires us to analyze the essential components of all the homicide crimes. The traditional crime of murder is generally divided into two degrees: murder in the first degree, which requires a showing of premeditation and deliberation; and murder in the second degree, which includes all other murders [felony murders; murders without premeditation; murders which result not from intent to kill, but an intent to do bodily harm; and murders which result from an act that shows a reckless indifference to the value of human life. (*See* ELO Ch. 8-IV(C),(D)]. Because David did not intend to kill anyone and did not act with premeditation or deliberation, he did not commit murder in the first degree. Choice **A** is therefore wrong. It's not so clear, however, that he is not guilty of murder in the second degree. Throwing pebbles from a bridge onto an oncoming car is certainly a reckless act which creates a risk that a driver might, as in this case, lose control of the car. David threw small pebbles, intending only to damage the rooftops of passing cars. However, the stone with which he hit the Toyota was larger and may indicate that he was willing to increase the risks. Neverthleless, David's conduct probably falls just short of the "depraved heart" test for murder in the second degree—an extreme indifference to the value of human life. Choice **B** is therefore not the best answer. The best answer is Choice **D** which identifies involuntary manslaughter. The crime of involuntary manslaughter occurs when an act of gross negligence results in the accidental death of another person. The negligence required is criminal negligence, i.e., an act which risks serious bodily harm, not tort negligence. David's conduct satisfies the requirements of involuntary manslaughter. (*See* ELO Ch. 8-VI(A).) Finally, Choice **C** is incorrect. Voluntary manslaughter requires an intentional killing committed by a man who has reasonably lost his self-control, is acting in the heat of passion, and has not waited so long after the provocation which causes him to kill as to cause us to conclude that his passion is no longer reasonable. (*See* ELO Ch. 8-V(C).) If one of the essential elements of this crime is missing, the accused may be guilty of second degree murder (*see* above).

49. B   The crime of conspiracy requires the agreement of two or more persons who have the culpable intent (*mens rea*) to commit an unlawful act or a lawful act by unlawful means. (*See* ELO Ch. 6-I(A).) Doris and Martin were guilty of the crime of conspiracy because they agreed to burn down the plant. Some states require a showing of some overt act in furtherance of the conspiracy. That requirement is also satisfied on these facts because Martin and Doris bought the gasoline with which they would set the fire. But the question asks whether Doris is guilty of arson, not conspiracy. Because the arson was committed by Martin alone, the key issue is whether Doris's subsequent repudiation of the conspiracy was sufficient to protect her from criminal liability for arson. In order for a defendant to escape liability for the substantive crime committed after her departure from the conspiracy, the defendant must merely show that she took an affirmative act bringing home her withdrawal to the other conspirators. It is not necessary that she actually thwart the conspiracy's criminal objectives. (*See* ELO Ch. 6-VII(B)(2).) Doris is not guilty of arson because she told Martin she did not want to go through with the arson and vigorously urged him to abandon the plan. Doris' withdrawal does not relieve her of the crime of conspiracy. The crime of conspiracy occurs when the agreement is made. The correct answer is Choice **B**. Choice **A** is incorrect because a co-conspirator who has not withdrawn can be found guilty of arson even if she does not set the fire herself. Choice **C** is incorrect because notification to each co-conspirator of the withdrawal is sufficient. Calling the police, therefore, is not required, although it may substitute for notice to the other conspirators. Choice **D** is incorrect because, for the reasons set forth above, Doris's withdrawal from the conspiracy protects her from liability.

50. **B**   The idea to kill the drug dealer originated with Larry and was communicated by him to Francine. Larry also suggested that they hide behind the trash can to fire at the dealer. Clearly, Larry aided, abbetted, encouraged and assisted Francine and is therefore an accomplice to the homicide. The key issue then is whether Larry's decision to withdraw and his departure from the scene give him a defense to the accomplice to murder charge. The answer is "no." It's not enough that a defendant have a change of heart and leave the scene. That would be especially true under these circumstances in which Larry initiated the entire plan. Larry was obliged to tell Francine in no uncertain terms that he was withdrawing from the project. Although he was not required to stop Francine, he certainly had the duty of influencing her act by announcing his own withdrawal. (*See* ELO Ch. 7-VI(A)(1) Since Larry did not convey his withdrawal and disapproval to Francine, his withdrawal defense must fail. The correct answer is Choice **B**. Choice **A** is incorrect because Larry is not required to stop Francine. He is only required to withdraw, so long as he advises Francine clearly that he is withdrawing. Choice **C** is incorrect because an accomplice can be culpable even if he didn't pull the trigger. Finally, Choice **D** is incorrect because a conspirator need not be present at the scene when the crime is committed. [**Note:** the student should consider whether Larry is guilty of the crime of solicitation, as well as conspiracy. (*See* ELO Ch. 7-IX).]

51. A   The common law crime of solicitation is complete when the accused
            requests or encourages another to perform or participate in a criminal
            act, with the intent to cause commission of the crime. Because the
            crime is complete when the request is made, it's irrelevant that the
            solicitee does not agree or that the crime is not in fact committed. Nor
            is it relevant whether the solicitee will commit the crime himself or
            simply be an accomplice. Aaron is guilty of solicitation because he left
            a note requesting that Josh join him in robbing the bank, with the
            intent that the robbery be committed by the two of them. (*See* ELO
            Ch. 7-IX.) The correct answer is Choice **A**. Choice **B** is incorrect
            because the reaction of the solicitee is immaterial to the crime of soli-
            ciation, which depends only on the acts and mental state of the solici-
            tor. Choice **C** is incorrect because Josh's reaction to the note is
            irrelevant. Finally, Choice **D** is incorrect because the crime of solicita-
            tion is complete once the defendant makes his request. The charge
            does not require a "substantial step" toward commission of the target
            crime.

52. D   This question requires an understanding of the elements which make
            up the different categories of homicide. The facts make it clear that
            Carl did not intend to kill Ethan. But he did commit a battery upon
            him by throwing him against the wall and poking him several times in
            the chest. He probably also committed a criminal assault on Ethan by
            putting him in fear of immediate bodily harm. (*See* ELO Ch. 8-
            VII(B)(2).) Because there was no intent to kill, neither murder in the
            first degree nor voluntary manslaughter is applicable (murder in the
            first degree requires a showing of premeditation and deliberation; vol-
            untary manslaughter is essentially an intentional killing committed in
            the heat of reasonable passion). Because Carl's conduct cannot be said
            to exhibit an extreme indifference to human life—the test for murder
            in the second degree—he cannot be found guilty of that crime. Carl is
            guilty of the crime of involuntary manslaughter under the misde-
            meanor-manslaughter rule. This rule invokes the crime of involuntary
            manslaughter when a death occurs accidentally during the commis-
            sion of a misdemeanor or other unlawful act. (*See* ELO Ch. 8-VI(B).)
            Carl committed a simple battery (and probably also, the misdemeanor
            of criminal assault, by frightening Ethan into fearing immediate bodily
            harm) a misdemeanor, by throwing Ethan into the wall and poking
            him in the chest. Since Ethan's death occurred during the commission
            of the battery, Carl is guilty of involuntary manslaughter. The correct
            answer is Choice **D**. Choice **A** is incorrect because Carl did not intend

to cause death. Choice **B** is incorrect because Carl did not act with a reckless indifference to human life. Finally, Choice **C** is incorrect because Carl did not intend the death of Ethan.

53. **D** The accused is guilty of the crime of attempt if he intends to commit a crime and commits some act or acts in furtherance of the crime which go beyond "mere preparation." The majority of courts look to see how close the accused came to committing the target crime. This is called the proximity approach. Obviously, the closer the actual crime becomes, the clearer the attempt. A number of tests have been developed in an effort to define "proximity." (*See* ELO Ch. 5-III((B).) The facts show that Ilya stalked Jim with the intent to kill him and that he ran at Jim with knife at the ready. Clearly, his actions satisfy the proximity test for attempt. The Model Penal Code, and many courts, on the other hand, require that the accused take a "substantial step" towards completion of the crime. Model Penal Code § 5.01(1)(c). This is a less stringent test than the proximity test; and it, too, was satisfied by Ilya's actions in following Jim and running at him with knife in hand. Ilya is guilty of attempted murder; the correct answer is Choice **D**. Choice **C** is incorrect because mere intent is insufficient; some act is required which satisfies one of the tests for conduct beyond mere preparation. Choice **A** is incorrect because Ilya did take a substantial step as defined by the Model Penal Code and the cases. Finally, Choice **B** is incorrect because the decision to abandon the attempt must be voluntary. In this case, Ilya's renunciation is not voluntary because he left out of fear that he would be caught by the police. The courts will not accept the withdrawal under these circumstances. (*See* ELO Ch. 5-V(C).)

54. **A** The crime charged is conspiracy, not solicitation. [Angie is clearly guilty of the common law crime of solicitation for intending to kill her husband and offering Danny $20,000 to commit the homicide. (*See* ELO Ch. 7-IX)]. A conspiracy exists when two or more persons agree to commit an unlawful act, or a lawful act by unlawful means, with culpable intent. (*See* ELO Ch. 6-I(A).) The key issue is whether a conspiracy can exist when one party to a two-party agreement is an undercover police officer. The traditional rule was that a conspiracy occurs only when there is an actual agreement among two or more persons to commit a crime. Under this traditional view, a conspiracy cannot exist when one party, such as an undercover police officer, feigns agreement. The more modern view holds that a defendant can be convicted of conspiracy even if the other party lacks the subjective intent to commit the target crime. This means that a defendant can be

convicted of conspiracy if she and a police officer agree to commit a crime even though the officer has no other intention than to secure an arrest. The Model Penal Code (§ 5.03(1)(a)) also finds that the defendant is guilty of conspiracy in cases where the other party feigns agreement. The Model Penal Code uses a unilateral approach in defining conspiracy, rather than the traditional bilateral approach. Under this approach, conspiracy is not defined as an agreement between two or more parties, but rather, as a crime committed by any one party when he agrees with the other party to commit a crime. This means that if the defendant intended to reach an agreement, he is guilty of conspiracy, even if the other person is in reality not part of the plan. (*See* ELO Ch. 6-II(D).) Since Angie agreed with Danny to have her husband murdered, she is guilty of conspiracy both under the modern view and under the Penal Code. The correct answer is Choice **A**. Choice **B** is incorrect because Angie's mere intention to have her husband killed is an insufficient basis for conspiracy culpability. The crime requires agreement between two or more persons. Choice **C** is incorrect because under the modern view and the Penal Code, the agreement of one of the parties can be feigned. Finally, Choice **D** is incorrect on the law because no "substantial step" towards commission of the target crime is necessary for a conspiracy to occur. On the facts, it may be said that Angie had taken a substantial step by offering Danny the money. (The "substantial step" requirement is a necessary element for attempt crimes.)

55. **A**   Under the English common law, one could be culpable of conspiracy to commit an immoral objective, even if the target deed was *not* a crime. This is the still the view in England. However, virtually all U.S. jurisdictions require that the objective of a conspiracy be an act which has expressly been made criminal. The Model Penal Code (§ 5.03(1)) requires an agreement "to commit a crime". (*See* ELO Ch. 6-IV(1)(a),(2).) The conduct of the soccer players may have been reprehensible and disgusting, and even immoral, but it was probably not criminal. The correct answer is Choice **A**. Choice **B** is incorrect because an accused may be prosecuted for a criminal offense, whether or not the victim actually files a complaint against him. Choice **C** is incorrect because, as explained above, it is does not represent the view typically held in the United States. Finally, Choice **D** is incorrect because the fact that Mindy became physically ill is *not* a basis for imposing criminal culpability for the crime of conspiracy. [**Note:** the student should consider whether the men are guilty of criminal assault.]

56. D   The crime of adultery occurs when a married person intentionally or knowingly engages in sexual relations with someone other than her spouse. Choice **D** is correct because it is the only Choice which depends on a lack of intent or knowledge by Caroline to commit the act which constitutes the crime. Choice **A** is incorrect because condonation by the other spouse is not a defense to adultery. Choices **B** and **C** are incorrect because, in both instances, Carolyn would have known that she was participating in sexual intercourse with someone other than her spouse.

57. D   Choice **D** shares with the *facts*, the use of force by the defendant to commit a homicide in response to a provocation. In Choice **D**, Defendant had just been advised that his wife had committed adultery. His response, while unlawful, was provoked by a situation that frequently engenders such a reaction. The courts will generally regard adultery as sufficient provocation to require the reduction of murder to manslaughter, even when the accused did not himself witness the adultery but was told about it by a third person (*See* ELO Ch. 8-V(D)(2)(c).) The *facts* raise the issue whether a homicide in the course of forcible resistance to an unlawful arrest justifies a finding of voluntary manslaughter instead of murder. Traditionally, a person subjected to an unlawful arrest could act in self defense and resist with reasonable force. The more modern view rejects this position and argues that the arrest process is too complicated to permit forceful reaction by the public and that it's better to insist that the citizen go along with the arrest and resort to his legal remedies later. The Model Penal Code (§ 3.04(2)(a)(i)) forbids the use of force to resist an arrest by a person known to be a police officer. (Some cases permit resistance when the police officer himself uses excessive force.) Under the *facts*, therefor, Fan would probably be guilty of murder. Choices **A, B** and **C** are not correct because none of them raises the issue of what provocation is necessary to reduce the charge of murder to voluntary manslaughter.

58. B   The defense of duress can be asserted when the accused commits a crime because he receives a threat which produces a reasonable fear that he is in imminent danger of suffering death or serious bodily harm. (See ELO Ch. 4-II.) A common rationale for the duress defense is that the defendant should not be forced to suffer a greater harm than the crime itself. Therefore, some courts will not permit the defense if the crime the accused commits is more serious than the harm or injury with which he is threatened. (See ELO Ch. 4-II(C).) The Model Penal Code, however, does not require that the harm threatened be greater than the crime committed. Instead, the MPC's test is whether the threat was sufficiently great that "a person of **reasonable firmness** in [the defendant's] situation would have been unable to resist." M.P.C. § 2.09(1). In addition, the MPC requires only that the defendant face a threat of bodily harm, not serious bodily harm. M.P.C. § 2.09(1). Even under the more stringent test of the courts which do not follow the MPC, Choice **B** is probably the best choice. Given Frederick's reputation for violence, Bruce was reasonably entitled to believe that he was in imminent danger of serious bodily injury which could be prevented by the lesser evil of mailing the letter. However, the defense of duress is not generally available against a charge of intentional homicide. (*See* ELO Ch. 4-II(D).) The facts raise the interesting question (Choice **C**) whether Bruce can assert a defense based on the risk of injury to himself if he believed that Frederick would carry out the threat to harm the president. It may be reasonable to argue that Choice **C** is the better answer on the theory that Bruce should not be permitted to prefer his own safety to that of the president in the face of a threat on the president's life. Choice **A** is incorrect because it does not recognize the defense of duress. Finally, Choice **D** is incorrect because the defense of duress does not require a threat of death; it may be asserted when the threat involves serious bodily injury. The MPC does not even require serious bodily injury; all it requires is a threat of bodily harm.

59. **B**   If Bruce is acquitted on the theory of duress, that defense is obviously not available to Frederick. When a crime is committed by the instrumentality of an innocent or nonresponsible agent, the agent is regarded as a tool of the sponsor of the crime. In these cases, the sponsor is considered the principal and the person who commits the act, his agent. The principle is as responsible as if he had committed the act himself. (*See* ELO Ch. 7-V(B)(5).) Since Bruce was a mere instrument of Frederick, Frederick is deemed to have sent the letter himself. The correct answer is Choice **B**. Frederick had the necessary *mens rea* and the *actus reus* is imputed to him. Choice **A** is incorrect because the doctrine of transferred intent applies when a defendant intends to harm one victim but actually harms another. The intent to harm is transferred from the intended victim to the actual victim.(See ELO Ch. 2-IV(A)(2).) The doctrine does not apply to this case. Frederick did not in fact transfer his intent to Bruce. Bruce would not have acted except for the duress. Choice **C** is incorrect because the fact that Frederick did not actually write or mail the letter is immaterial to his guilt. Frederick is guilty because he forced Bruce to write and mail the letter. Choice **D** is incorrect under the general law of agency, which provides that a principal may be vicariously liable for the torts of his agent.

60. B Under common law principles, a conspiracy occurs when there is an agreement between two or more persons to commit a crime.(See ELO Ch. 6-I(A).) Some jurisdictions also require an overt act by one of the conspirators in furtherance of the conspiracy. The Model Penal Code uses a unilateral approach in defining conspiracy, rather than the traditional bilateral approach. Under this approach, conspiracy does not require an agreement between two or more parties; the crime is satisfied as to any one party so long as he has committed to join others in the commission of the crime. M.P.C. § 5.03(1)(a). In addition to the agreement, the crime of conspiracy also requires that the conspirators have the *mens rea* to commit the target crime. In this case, there was no agreement because Bruce was an unwilling agent of Frederick; and Bruce lacked the *mens rea* required for the crime. Choice **B**, therefore, is the correct answer. Choice **A** is incorrect because the crime of conspiracy is an independent crime which is not normally merged into the completed target crime. Choice **C** is incorrect because Bruce's participation was not done as a consequence of any "agreement" with Frederick; nor did Bruce have the required *mens rea*. Finally, Choice **D** is incorrect because compliance under duress cannot be considered to exhibit either an agreement to commit the target crime or the necessary *mens rea*. (*See* ELO Ch. 6-I(C).)

61. D Common law burglary is the **breaking** and **entering** of the **dwelling** of another **at night** with the **intent to commit a felony.** (See ELO Ch. 9-VII(A).) The crime requires all of the elements emphasized in the first sentence above. Because two of the elements are missing on these facts, there is no burglary. The first missing ingredient is the element of "breaking." At common law, there had to be a "breaking". This meant that the accused had to create the opening which permitted entry into the dwelling. Here, the window through which Len entered was wide open. [**Note:** most American jurisdictions no longer require the element of breaking for most burglaries.] The other missing element is the intent to commit a felony (note that any felony, not only a theft felony, satisfies this element). When Len entered the house, his sole purpose was to retrieve his TV. Since it is not a felony to retrieve your own property, Choice **D** is the correct answer. Choice **A** is incorrect because a mere entry is insufficient; the defendant must also have the intent to commit a felony once inside the house. Choice **B** is incorrect because, even if Bill lawfully obtained possession of the television, Len's repossession is not a felony. Len was entitled to reclaim the set when Bill failed to return it. Choice **C** is incorrect because Len did not have the right to enter Bill's house without invitation, to retrieve his television set. He may be guilty of criminal trespass. This is a misdemeanor recognized under the Medal Penal Code.

62. **A**   Sharp was a private citizen employed by the bank to thwart robberies. A private citizen may use a reasonable degree of non-deadly force to prevent the commission of a felony or of a misdemeanor amounting to a breach of the peace. He may use *deadly force* only to prevent a *dangerous felony*. If the robber is armed and it is likely that serious bodily harm could occur to anyone, then the use of deadly force is permissible. (See ELO Ch. 4-VII(D).) However, the Model Penal Code takes a more restrictive view of the use of deadly force even in situations involving dangerous felonies. Model Penal Code § 3.07(2)(b)(ii). The rationale behind the MPC attitude may not be applicable here, however (the MPC purpose is to discourage rash action by untrained private citzens and Sharp was a trained former police officer). Choice **A** is correct because robbery is a dangerous felony, the robber was armed, and he pointed his gun directly at a cashier (the security officer doesn't have to wait until the robber actually pulls the trigger) [**Note:** there is one troubling aspect about these facts: did the bank and Sharp contribute to the dangerous situation by hiding Sharp in the ceiling outside of Rob's sight; if Sharp had been stationed on the floor in uniform, Rob might have refrained from attempting the robbery.] Choice **B** is incorrect because Sharp was not protecting only property; he was also preventing serious bodily harm to the teller and the bank's customers. [**Note:** deadly force may *not* generally be used in the protection of property.(See ELO Ch. 4-VI(B).)] Choice **C** is incorrect because if the killing was justified, it was justified precisely because a warning would not necessarily have prevented Rob's use of his gun. Finally, Choice **D** is incorrect because Sharp was justified in using deadly force deliberately to prevent the commission of a dangerous felony.

63. **B**   The crime of larceny requires that the accused take and carry away, in a trespassory manner, personal property of another, with the intent to steal (i.e., permanently deprive the owner of the property). The taking is trespassory if the accused is not in lawful possession of the property at the time he appropriates it. (See ELO Ch. 9-II(B).) If Leo's delivery of the clock to Mike conveyed lawful possession to Mike, then he cannot be convicted of larceny. However, the rule is that when a lower-level employee receives property from his employer, he is deemed to have only custody of the property (possession remains with the employer). (See ELO Ch. 9-II(B)(2).) His appropriation of the prop-

erty is therefore a trespass which satisfies the requirements for larcceny (*See* ELO Ch. 9-II(B)(2).) Choice **B** is correct because Mike was merely a salesperson and had only custody of the clock (not lawful possession) when he appropriated it. Choice **A** is factually incorrect (Mike saw his opportunity to keep the clock at the moment Leo handed it to him). Choice **C** is incorrect. The fact that Leo voluntarily gave the clock to Mike does not change Mike's status as a mere employee who is being given temporary custody of property with specific instructions to use it only as dictated by the employer. Finally, Choice **D** is incorrect because a trick or inducement by Mike would be relevant only if the crime charged was larceny by trick, not simple larceny, which does not require the element of fraud or deceit.

64. **D**   If the accused had the intent (*mens rea*) to commit a criminal act against A, but succeeds, instead, of committing the same or a similar crime against B, he is said to have **transferred his intent** from A to B and he is guilty of an intended crime against B. This is called the doctrine of **transferred intent.** However, the doctrine does **not** apply to attempt crimes, because of the difficulty of relating the attempt to the result.(See ELO Ch. 2-IV(A)(2).) Because the question asks whether Deft is guilty of **attempted murder,** his intent with respect to Vic cannot be transferred to Cal. The correct answer is Choice **D**. Choice **A** is incorrect because, as noted above, the doctrine of transferred intent does not apply to attempt crimes. Deft is not guilty of attempted murder of Cal, but he is guilty of attempted murder of Vic and of criminal battery on Cal. Choice **B** is incorrect because, although Deft acted with premeditation and malice towards Vic, two elements of murder which prove that he intended to kill Vic, his intent does not transfer to Cal. Choice **C** is incorrect because the extent of injury to Cal is not material to the issue of Deft's *mens rea* (his intent to kill Vic) or to the crime of attempted murder as it relates to Cal.

65. **A**   The law surrounding the right of an individual to use deadly force against a fleeing suspect has many ramifications. If he is a police officer, he is allowed to use deadly force to stop a fleeing suspect *in cases of dangerous felonies,* if that is the only way to effect an arrest. In cases involving misdemeanors, or non-dangerous felonies, even a police officer may not be free to use deadly force. (*See* ELO Ch. 4-VII(3)(a),(b).) *Tennessee v. Garner,* 471 U.S. 1 (1985). The law for persons who are not police officers is even more strict. The Model Penal Code specifically prohibits private citizens from using deadly force to stop a fleeing felon, even in those cases where the suspect has committed a dangerous felony. M.P.C. § 3.07(2)(b)(ii). Under the MPC,

because Cal was no longer facing a threat to himself, he was not justi-fied in shooting Deft. *People v. Crouch*, 439 N.W.2d 354 (Mich. App. 1989). However, Cal is probably guilty of voluntary manslaughter instead of murder. An individual is guilty of voluntary manslaughter if he kills another intentionally *and*: 1) he acts in response to a provoca-tion that is sufficient to cause a reasonable man to lose self-control; 2) he in fact acts in the heat of passion; 3) the period of time between the provocation and the killing is not enough to cause a reasonable man to cool off; and 4) the defendant has not in fact cooled off. A gun shot fired at you by a fleeing gunman is almost certainly enough provoca-tion to cause a reasonable man to lose his self-control and act in response. (See ELO Ch. 8-V(D)(2)(a).) Thus, Choice **A** is the correct answer. Choice **B** is incorrect because the provocation is sufficient to reduce murder to voluntary manslaughter. Choice **C** is incorrect because Cal intended to kill Deft and involuntary manslaughter does not apply to intentional homicide. Choice **D** is incorrect because, as noted above, Cal's actions satisfy the elements of voluntary man-slaughter.

66. A   The crime of embezzlement involves a ***fraudulent conversion*** of the ***property*** of ***another*** by one who is in ***lawful possession*** of the prop-erty. (*See* ELO Ch. 9-III(A).) Because Ace was authorized by Lender to collect Borrower's debt and received the money initially as Lender's agent, Ace came into possession of the money lawfully. However, Ace's possession was solely as agent for Lender. When Washington fraudu-lently paid the money to Lender not for the account of Borrower but for the joint account of Ace and himself, he converted the money, i.e., he claimed and applied it for his own benefit and not the Borrower's. (Washington's obligation was to deliver the money collected to Lender for application against Borrower's debt.) Because all the elements of embezzlement are satisfied, Choice **A** is the correct answer. Choice **B** is incorrect because the facts do not tell us that the $5,000 was obtained through fraud or other deceptive circumstances (presumably, Little represented to Borrower that he was acting for Ace as collection agent for Lender). Thus, the $5,000 was not obtained by Ace fraudulently, a necessary element of the crime of false pretenses. Choice **C** is incorrect because a necessary element of larceny is a trespassory taking, and Ace came into posession of the money lawfully. (See ELO Ch. 9-II.) Finally, Choice **D** is incorrect because Ace caused Lender to misapply the funds to the account of Ace and Washington instead of to the account of Borrower, thereby creating an unlawful conversion of the funds.

67. A A corporation can act only through its officers, employees and agents. The liability of corporation for crimes committed by these individuals is a matter of debate and flux. Increasingly, the courts are attributing guilt to corporations, especially in strict liability cases and in cases of serious crime. A corporation may be held criminally culpable if a high-level managerial agent, acting for the corporation and within the scope of his employment, has a direct connection with the crime by authorizing, requesting, commanding, performing or recklessly tolerating its commision. Model Penal Code § 2.07(1)(c). (See ELO Ch. 1-II(K)(5).) Washington was president of Ace. As president, he had the authority to hire Little, contract with Lender, collect the funds from Borrower, and remit them to Lender. Since Washington embezzled the money in order to satisfy Ace's (as well as his own) obligation, Ace can be convicted of the same offense. *Commonwealth v. Beneficial Finance Co.*, 275 N.E.2d 33 (Mass. 1979). The correct answer is **A**. However, since a corporation cannot be imprisoned, the only penalty that could be assessed against Ace itself would be a fine. Choice **B** is incorrect because the prosecution would not be required to proceed against Washington before trying Ace. It could charge and convict Ace before proceding against Washington. Note, however, that it might be impossible to convict Ace if Washington is tried first and acquitted, because a corporation is generally only vicariously liable for the torts and crimes of its employees. Choice **C** is incorrect because even though a corporation cannot be imprisoned, it may be convicted and fined. Finally, Choice **D** is incorrect because there is no rule that limits a corporation's culpability to specific intent crimes.

68. C The claim of entrapment can be asserted by the accused as a defense to all but the most violent crimes. Moden Penal Code § 2.13(3). The courts use one of two tests to determine whether entrapment exists. A majority of courts, including the Supreme Court, use the predisposition test. Under this test, the defense of entrapment is available when: 1) a government agent induces the defendant to commit the crime; and 2) the defendant is not predisposed to commit the crime. In this case, Deft responded immediately to the agent's offer to buy drugs "at the going rate", and also immediately acknowledged the correct code-word. This exchange, combined with Deft's prior record, shows a predisposition to sell drugs. Choice **C** is correct. A minority of courts prefers the police conduct test. Under this test, the government's agent must originate the crime and his inducement must be sufficiently strong to lead even an unpredisposed individuals to commit the crime, whether or not the defendant himself is predisposed. (*See* ELO Ch. 4-X(b).) Deft's entrapment defense would fail under the police conduct test because the ordinary, unpredisposed person would not have responded to the agent's offer to buy by agreeing to make the sale, acknowledging the code word and accepting the cash. Choice **A** is incorrect because it doen't help Deft that he was willing to sell only when he thought it was safe. His use of the code word only proves his predisposition to sell. Choice **B** is incorrect because it is too narrow a definition of entrapment. The government agent must not only offer to buy; he must induce the sale. In any event, the defense is not available to a defendant who is predisposed to commit the crime. Finally, Choice **D** is incorrect because a defendant's entrapment defense can succeed even if the defendant commits the crime. But he must prove, at least, that he was induced to commit it and that he was not predisposed to do so.

69. A   The law relating to finders of lost or mislaid property revolves essentially around the intent of the finder at the moment he takes possession of the property. If he intends at that moment to keep the property for himself, he has satisfied the intent necessary for larceny and will be guilty of larceny *if* he knows who the true owner is or has reason to believe that he can learn the name and address of the true owner. If neither of these conditions exists, he is not guilty of larceny even if he intends to keep the property. (*See* ELO Ch. 9-II(C)(5).) The Model Penal Code rejects this traditional view by imposing an obligation on the finder to take **reasonable measures to restore the property** to the rightful owner. Model Penal Code § 223.5. Because Roger never intended to return the wallet though he had the owner's address, Roger is guilty of larceny under both views. The correct answer is Choice **A**. Choice **B** is incorrect because Roger did not have lawful possession. (See ELO Ch. 9-III(A).) Because Roger intended immediately to keep the wallet though he knew the identity of the true owner, his possession was larcenous and unlawful. Choice **C** is incorrect because Roger's taking was trespassory, i.e., he converted the wallet' and its contents though he knew the identity of the rightful owner. Finally, Choice **D** is incorrect because Roger was wrong on the law—the finder of a lost item is not entitled to retain it (or any part of it) if knows the identity of the owner.

70. D   A conspiracy is an agreement by two or more persons with culpable intent, either to commit an unlawful act or to commit a lawful act by unlawful means. Although there must be an agreement, it is not necessary that each conspirator participate equally in the commission of the crime. A conspirator who aids and abets the other participants in the crime is guilty of conspiracy. He is guilty even if he helps only in the

planning stages. (*See* ELO Ch. 6-II(B),(C).) A co-conspirator who actively aids another in committing a substantive crime in furtherance of the conspiracy is liable for that substantive crime on the theory that he intended to further the common criminal objective. Here, Mike knew that he was supplying guns and ammo which would be used to commit a robbery. (*See* ELO Ch. 6-IV(D).) Since Mike agreed to supply the guns for the robbery, he is a co-conspirator and he is guilty of conspiracy. Mike is also guilty as an accessory before the fact. Anyone who provides pre-crime assistance to the perpetrator of the crime but who is not present at the commission of the crime is an accessory before the fact. He may be the brains behind the crime, or even a small contributor.(*See* ELO Ch. 7-I(A)(3).) Since Mike supplied the guns and ammunition with the intent that these items be used for the robbery, he was an accessory before the fact, even though he insisted on not being present at the time of the robbery. An accessory before the fact is liable for the target crime. Choice **D** is the only correct answer because Mike can be held liable for the robbery as a co-conspirator and as an accessory before the fact. The other Choices are wrong because they do not include both I and II.

71. **D**   An accused who is prosecuted for attempt ***must intend*** to commit the target crime and must undertake some act towards the completion of the crime. There are essentially two different views on what kind of act is required to establish intent. The more modern view is exmplified by the Model Penal Code. The Code (and many courts) requires only that the accused take a "substantial step" towards completion of the target crime. M.P.C. § 5.01(1)(c). The more traditional view uses the "proximity test", which requires that the accused come reasonably close to completion of the crime. The critical questions on these facts is whether Art intended the crime of robbery—the target crime. The crime of robbery occurs when the accused, by force (or the threat thereof), takes and carries away from a person (or from his presence) his personal property with the intent to permanently deprive him of the property. Since Art acted under duress, it cannot be said that he had the intent necessary for the crime of robbery. If he does not have the *mens rea* necessary for the target crime, he cannot be guilty of attempting that crime. Duress is a defense when the accused can show that he committed a crime under a threat which put him in reasonable fear of immediate or imminent bodily harm. (*See* ELO Ch. 4-II(B) The defense of duress on these facts negates not only the target crime of robbery, but also the attempt. The correct answer is Choice **D**. Choices **A** and **B** are incorrect because Art committed the acts described under duress and not because he intended them. Choice **C** is incorrect

because Art never had the intent to commit robbery. Although he did carry out some of the steps necessary for robbery, he did so under duress which occurred before any of the steps. His surrender is only one element in proving his lack of intent.

72. D   The facts tell us that Dave did not intend to injure Abel, but only to scare him. However, he did fire a gun at a relatively distant target. We are not told that he was an expert marksman, so it must be said that his conduct was probably so reckless as to constitute criminal negligence. By causing the cup in Abel's hand to shatter, Dave committed a battery on Abel, under the elemental principles that battery consists of either bodily injury or an offensive touching, and that an offenive touching extends to the personal effects of the victim (clothing, jewelry being worn, coffee cup being held, etc.). Because the battery was committed with a deadly weapon, in many jurisdictions Dave's crime will constitute a felony rather than a misdemeanor. Model Penal Code § 211.1(2)(b). (See ELO Ch. 8-VII(A)(4)(b).) Further, Dave committed the felony of assault with a deadly weapon. The crime of assault requires that the defendant's actions instill the fear of imminent injury in the victim. If he uses a deadly weapon in instilling fear, he is guilty of the felony of assault with a deadly weapon. (*See* ELO Ch. 8-VII(B)(4).) The correct answer is Choice **D**. Dave is guilty of aggravated battery and of assault with a deadly weapon. Choice **A** is incorrect it identifies only the crime of battery, and Dave is guilty of both crimes. Choice **B** is incorrect because it also depends on only one of the two crimes. Choice **C** presents some difficult issues. If Dave had killed Abel, he would be guilty of murder even though he did not intend to kill him. This conclusion is based either on the felony-murder rule, which defines any homicide which results during the commission of a felony as murder, or on the theory that Dave acted with reckless indifference to the value of human life by shooting into the kitchen. (*See* ELO Ch. 8-II(E), III(A).) Generally speaking, however, the accused cannot be convicted of an ***attempted crime*** if he does not intend to commit the crime itself. Under this view, Dave would not be guilty of attempted murder because he did not intend to kill Able. Many courts, however, would apply a much more stringent test and convert the recklessness exhibited by Dave into an intent to commit homicide, and therefore, culpability for the attempt. However, Choice **D** is a less controversial answer than Choice **C**.

73. B   First degree murder, a crime now recognized by most states, generally requires premeditation and deliberation by the defendant. These concepts are difficult to define and are usually established at trial by circumstantial evidence as to the accused's motives and degree of planning. Since the facts tell us that Dave did not intend to kill Abel but only to scare him, it may be hard to prove a first-degree murder charge (*See* ELO Ch. 8-IV(C).) However, some states do classify felony-murders as first degree murders. Because Dave committed two intentional felonies—aggravated battery and assault with a deadly weapon—he may be guilty of first degree murder in those states. Second degree murder is a catch-all for all murders which are not murders in the first degree. It includes the following: murders in which the defendant does not intend to kill, but has acted "recklessly under circumstances manifesting an extreme indifference to human life"[M.P.C. § 210.2(1)(b)]; murders in which the accused does not intend to kill but does intend to inflict serious bodily injury; and felony murders. (*See* ELO Ch. 8-IV(D).) In this case, even though Dave did not intend to kill Abel, he did fire a pistol in his direction, displaying an extreme indifference to the value of human life and committing the two felonies of aggravated battery and assault with a deadly weapon. In most jurisdictions, Choice **B** is the most serious crime for which Dave can be convicted. Choice **A** is incorrect because, as noted above, Dave would be guilty of murder in the first degree only in those states which included felony murder among murders in the first degree. Choice **C** is incorrect because Dave is guilty of murder, which is a more serious crime than voluntary manslaughter. Choice **D** is incorrect on the same basis.

74. **A** The crime of solicitation occurs when one requests or encourages another to commit a crime, with the intent that the crime be committed. (See ELO Ch. 7-IX(A).) The crime does not require commission of an overt act furthering the target crime; the solicitation itself is complete when the request is communicated. On these facts, Wimp will argue that she did not solicit Ready to do anything, because her message was communicated only to Rough, who never received it. She will rely on the line of cases which hold that a communication addressed to a large, undefined group cannot be construed as solicitation. However, Wimp did intend to have Vic roughed up and it certainly did not matter to her whether Rough or Ready did the roughing up. Many cases hold that it's immaterial whether the intended solicitee actually receives the communication. This view is shared by Model Penal Code § 5.02(2). (*See* ELO Ch. 7-IX(H).) The correct answer is Choice **A**. Choice **B** is wrong because the solicitation was complete when Wimp requested the act of beating Vic up; it was not necessary that anybody act on the request. (The court is not likely to be sympathetic to Wimp when the consequence of her message was that Vic

died as a result of the beating.) Choice **C** is incorrect because it doesn't matter that Ready was not the person the message was intended for. Choice **D** is incorrect because Ready's interpretation of the message is not material to Wimp's guilt, which is established by her intent to have Vic roughed up and by her request that the act be committed.

75. A   The common law crime of conspiracy occurs when there is an agreement between two or more persons to do either an unlawful act or a lawful act by unlawful means. (See ELO Ch. 6-I(A).) The term "agreement" is not synonomous with that same term in the law of contracts; it's not necessary to find a true "meeting of the minds." What is required is a communication between the parties looking towards a common criminal objective. At common law, there is no need that the parties perform an overt act in furtherance of the conspiracy. (*See* ELO Ch. 6-IV(B).) The Model Penal Code eliminates the need for an overt act in cases of serious crime. M.P.C. § 5.03(5). When Tough agreed during his call from a distant city to carry out Wimp's request to beat Vic, the crime of conspiracy occurred. The fact that the crime was now impossible because of Vic's intervening death is immaterial. (*See* ELO Ch. 6-IV(C).) The correct answer is Choice **A**. Choices **B** and **C** are incorrect because Wimp never communicated with Ready, and some communication is necessary for conspiracy. Choice **D** is incorrect because a conspiracy was formed between Wimp and Tough during their telephone conversation.

76. B   The common law crime of conspiracy occurs when there is an agreement between two or more persons to do either an unlawful act or a lawful act by unlawful means. (*See* ELO Ch. 6-I(A).) The agreement need not be the kind of item-by-item recital of promises and obligations that defines the usual "agreement" in the law of contracts. All that is required is any communication between the parties proving a common criminal purpose. Here, Bob did not need to say a word. His agreement to aid in the burglary was confirmed when he gave the money to Art. The correct answer is Choice **B**. Choice **A** is incorrect because Art's **request** for the money would constitute only the crime of solicitation by Art; until Bob actually gave the money to Art, no conspiracy existed. Choice **C** is incorrect because the accused need not participate in the commission of the target crime; he is guilty if he supplies goods or services to the perpetrator or if he has a stake in the proceeds, both true here. (*See* ELO Ch. 6-III(D).) Finally, Choice **D** is incorrect because a conspiracy exists once there is an agreement to commit the target crime. It is not necessary under common law that any overt act be committed in furtherance of the target crime. Today, some jurisdictions do require an overt act in furtherance of the agreement. The Model Penal Code restricts this requirement to non-serious crimes, of which burglary is certainly not one. M.P.C. § 5.03(5). (*See* ELO Ch. 6-IV(B).) Furthermore, if Art argues that he withdrew from the conspiracy because he never bought the gun and gave the money away, he will be met with the fact that the common law does not generally permit the defense of withdrawal because the crime of conspiracy is complete when the agreement is made. Even under the more liberal Model Penal Code, he must at least inform the police to avoid culpability. M.P.C. § 5.03(6). (*See* ELO Ch. 6-VII(B)(2).)

77. **C**   It's important to note that the question asks, "Did Art commit a crime in using the money for another purpose", not, "can Bob sue Art for the money." In taking Bob's money without returning it, Art is certainly guilty of one or another of the larceny crimes. He is not guilty of the crime of simple larceny (Choice **B**), because he did not take the money by trespass; he was given the money voluntarily by Bob himself for a common purpose. (*See* ELO Ch. 9-II(A),(B).) Nor is he guilty of the crime of False Pretenses (Choice **D**), which requires as an essential element that the accused obtain the money as the result of the false representation of a material fact. Here, Art did not misrepresent his purpose or his motive. The crime of embezzlement occurs when the defendant fraudulently converts the tangible personal property of another, at a time when the item is rightfully in the defendant's possession. (*See* ELO Ch. 9-III(A).) Since Bob had voluntarily delivered the $200 to Art (even though the money was to be used for an unlawful purpose), the money was lawfully in Art's possession because Bob intended to put it there. Choice **C** is the the best answer. Choice **A** is not the right answer only because it is not responsive to the question asked. If the question had instead asked whether Bob could recover the money from Art, then A would be the correct answer because of the doctrine of *pari delicto.* This doctrine prevents a court from enforcing a claim based on an illegal contract by one participant against the other. Some courts construe the doctrine to require weighing the guilt of one party against the guilt of the other. On these facts. it's hard to believe that any court would allow either party to recover anything.

78. **C**   Most crimes are defined so as to require both *actus reus* and *mens rea. Actus reus* requires that the accused have committed the act which constitutes the crime. (*See* ELO Ch. 1-I.) *Mens rea* requires that, in committing the act, the accused have the state of mind which evidences either specific intent or recklesssness. (*See* ELO Ch. 1-II(A).) As defined in this statute, the crime required the sale of Xtol. Since defen-

dant Druggist sold Customer Ytol, not Xtol, an essential element of the crime is missing. The correct answer is Choice **C**. Defendant did, however, manifest the *mens rea* necessary for the crime as defined because he meant to sell the prohibited drug, Xtol. Because he did not intend to make the mistake of substituting Ytol, his mistake does not negate his intent. Choice **A** is therefore incorrect. Choice **B** is incorrect because it addresses only the *mens rea* element of the crime; whether or not *mens rea* exists, the *actus reus* element of the crime (the sale of Xtol) is absent. Finally, Choice **D** is incorrect because even in a jurisdiction which holds that legal impossibility is no defense to the crime of attempt, we are not dealing here with the crime of attempt, but with the defined crime of selling the proscribed drug Xtol. (*See* ELO Ch. 6-IV(C),(D).)

79. **C**   The best answer is offered by Choice **C**, but even that answer may be subject to question itself. In general, conduct which violates a rule or law is not excused because the accused was ignorant of the law. (*See* ELO Ch. 1-II(L)(4).) The modern view has eased this principle somewhat. Many states now permit the defense of ignorance of the law when there is reasonable reliance by the accused upon a judicial decision that the conduct involved was not illegal. (See ELO Ch. 1-II(L)(10)(b).) If the defendant's belief was based upon her attorney's reasonable interpretation of an outstanding court decision, most jurisdictions would absolve the defendant of culpability. This principle makes **C** the best choice. However, it is certainly arguable that defendant on these facts probably should not have relied on the decisions of the lower courts, but waited instead until the issue was resolved by the jurisdiction's highest court. His interest in selling a drug prohibited by statute would not seem to outweigh the public interest of enjoining sales of Xtol. Choice **A** is incorrect because it is too broad. An attorney's opinion may not always be relied on, but it is not necessarily irrelevant on the issue of *mens rea;* and misunderstanding of the law is sometimes a defense, as we have seen. Choice **B** is incorrect because a defendant's mistake or ignorance of law, alone, will not negate *mens rea* in most instances. Finally, Choice **D** is incorrect because Defendant relied on his misinterpretation of the law, not on a mistake in fact.

80. **B**   The question carefully calls for the ***best*** defense, not necessarily the one that will actually result in acquittal. This is an important distinction because Jimmy is probably guilty under all the possible answers. The crime of involuntary manslaughter requires 1) that the defendant's gross negligence result in the accidental death of another (or, under the Model Penal Code, that the defendant act recklessly); or 2)

that the death occur unintentionally during the commission of a misdemeanor or other unlawful act. (*See* ELO Ch. 8-VI(A),(B).) Under
both tests, it's necessary for the prosecution to show that the defendant's actions were the proximate cause of the victim's death. The
defendant here will try to show that his conduct was not the proximate
cause of Mrs. Jones's death because the drug was not an ordinarily
dangerous drug and because the offense was *malum prohibitum*, i.e.,
prohibited by a public-welfare statute, and not *malum in se*, i.e., inherently dangerous or reckless. This makes Choice **B** the **best** defense.
(However, it is unlikely that Jimmy will prevail on this defense
because, as a druggist, he was held to a higher standard than the ordinary citizen. When Doctor X told him that the drug was mispre-
scribed, he had an affirmative duty to notify the authorities and to find
Mrs. Jones to keep her from taking the drug. His conduct displayed
criminal negligence.) Choice **A** is not as good an answer as **B** because
Jimmy did commit a misdemeanor by violating the statute. Choice **C**
is incorrect because Dr. X was not exclusively culpable for Mrs. Jones's
death. First of all, she notified Jimmy that the presription was wrong
and Jimmy had the opportunity to avoid the death, and secondly,
Jimmy contributed to the death by violating the statute. Finally,
Choice **D** is incorrect because the statute required notice to the
authorities, not only a search for the patient; if Defendant had
reported the violation to the authorities, they would have had the
opportunity to locate Mrs. Jones in time to prevent her death.

81. **D**   The law recognizes several defenses which either negate the *mens rea*
necessary for a guilty intent, or excuse the act which constitutes the
crime. Among these defenses are insanity, duress, and reasonable
defense of others. All three are **affirmative defenses**, i.e., the defendant
is required to produce the evidence supporting them. (*See* ELO Ch. 3-
I(H)(1), also ELO Ch. 4-Introductory Note.) In the jurisdiction
described in this question, all three must be proved by a preponderance of the evidence or they will not be submitted to the jury. It is not
necessary that the prosecution **disprove** these defenses because the
burden is on the defendant. However, if the accused raises the claim
that his actions were **reflexive** and, therefore, **involuntary**, the element
of *actus reus*, which requires that the criminal act be voluntary, is put
at issue. On this issue, many courts merely require that the defendant
produce some evidence of the involuntary nature of his actions and
then shift to the prosecution the burden of showing beyond a reasonable doubt that the defendant was acting voluntarily. (*See* ELO Ch. 1-
I(C)(3)(ii).) Choice **D** is the correct answer because it is the only one
which identifies a defense which the prosecution must disprove.

Choices **A**, **B** and **C** are all incorrect because insanity, duress and the defense-of-others privilege are affirmative defenses which must be proved by a preponderance of evidence by the defendant.

82. **A**   The crime of involuntary manslaughter requires either (1) that the defendant's gross negligence (or, under the Model Penal Code, his recklessness) result in the accidental death of another, or (2) that the death occur unintentionally during the commission of a misdemeanor or other unlawful act. Under the misdemeanor-manslaughter rule, the defendant is guilty if his actions are the proximate cause of death. They will be deemed the probable cause if his actions are *malum in se,* i.e., they are inherently wrong, even if he did not intend or desire the victim's death.(*See* ELO Ch. 8-VI(B)(2).) Simple battery, a misdemeanor, occurs when the accused intentionally causes either: 1) bodily injury; or 2) offensive touching of a person or of property held by or near the person. (*See* ELO Ch. 8-VII(A).) Since Dan committed a battery (a *malum in se* misdemeanor) when he pushed Arthur, he is guilty of involuntary manslaughter. The correct answer is Choice **A**. Choice **B** is incorrect because one may be guilty of involuntary manslaughter under the misdemeanor-manslaughter rule even though he did *not* intend the victim's death. Choice **C** is incorrect because, as discussed above, Dan is criminally responsible for Dan's death under the misdemeanor-manslaughter rule. Finally, Choice **D** is incorrect because voluntary manslaughter requires the same *mens rea* as murder. It involves an intentional homicide which is reduced from murder only by virtue of a provocation which would cause a reasonable man to lose his self control or to act in the heat of passion. Dan's insult was not the kind of provocation (e.g., battery, assault, combat, adultery by spouse) which the law requires. (*See* ELO Ch. 8-V(D)(2).)

83. **D**   The crime of rape is defined as having unlawful sexual intercourse with a female without her consent. The critical question, therefore, is whether the woman gave her voluntary consent. The requisite lack of consent will be found if the woman indicates by reasonable word or action that she is not giving her consent. (*See* ELO Ch. 8-VIII(A).) Consent obtained by "fraud in the inducement", i.e., fraud which results in consent to the act of intercourse itself, is consent neverthe-less. (*See* ELO Ch. 8-VIII(A)(3)(b).) However, consent obtained by representing to the victim that she is committing some act which is not intercourse, is consent obtained by "fraud in the essence", and is not consent because the victim does not know that she is having inter-course. Choice **D** is the correct answer, because, even though John lied to obtain her consent, Mary knew that she was having sexual inter-

course with him. Choice **A** is incorrect because most jurisdictions would hold that a woman is incapable of giving her consent if she is too intoxicated to realize what's happening. (*See* ELO Ch. 8-VII(A)(3)(a).) Choice **B** is incorrect because this representation would constitute fraud in the essence, and would thereby negate Mary's apparent consent. Finally, Choice **C** is incorrect because consent obtained by the threat of physical violence is not consent to intercourse.

84. **D**   The common law crime of conspiracy occurs when there is an agreement between two or more persons to commit either an unlawful act or a lawful act by unlawful means. (*See* ELO Ch. 6-I(A).) John and Dick formed a conspiracy to rob the bank. A conspirator is liable for the criminal acts which occur in the course of the conspiracy or which are a reasonably foreseeable outgrowth of it. The objective of the conspiracy was robbery and the murder occurred during the commission of the robbery. While John and Dick agreed to use toy guns, it was reasonably foreseeable that a guard would mistake the toy for a real gun and respond by shooting at Dick. Thus, the death of an innocent bystander was a reasonably foreseeable outgrowth of the conspiracy. The felony-murder rule holds a defendant guilty of murder when a homicide is committed during the felony, even if the defendant lacks the intent to kill. Since this murder occurred during the commission of a dangerous felony, it was not necessary that John or Dick have an intent to kill. (*See* ELO Ch. 8-III(A)(B).) Therefore, Choice **D** is the correct answer. John can be convicted of murder under the felony-murder rule because he was a co-conspirator involved in a dangerous felony. Choice **A** is incorrect because a conspirator does not have to participate in the target crime in order to be found culpable; he doen't even have to be present when the homicide is committed. Choice **B** is incorrect because John did not effectively withdraw from the conspiracy. Most jurisdictions require that the party attempting to withdraw communicate the fact of his withdrawal to the other conspirators or to the police. (*See* ELO Ch. 6-VII(B)(2).) Choice **C** is incorrect because John should have realized that robbery is a dangerous felony and that it was reasonably foreseeable that a guard might mistake the toy gun for a real gun and respond by shooting at Dick.

85. **D**   We are being asked to consider the essential elements of three separate crimes. The crime of solicitation occurs when the defendant requests, incites, induces or encourages another to commit a crime with the intent that the crime be committed. (See ELO Ch. 7-IX((D).) Because Bill was not very concerned about getting his money and did not know

that Frank had previously robbed a bank, Bill probably lacked the *mens rea* necessary for solicitation, i.e., he did not really intend to have Frank rob the bank. Choice **A** is therefore incorrect. If Bill is not guilty of solicitation, there was no conspiracy because Bill and Frank did not agree to commit a crime, and the crime of conspiracy requires an agreement by two or more persons to commit an unlawful act. (*See* ELO Ch. 6-I(A).) Choice **B** is therefore incorrect. Choice **C** is also incorrect. Bill is not guilty of the robbery because he did not solicit Frank to commit the robbery, did not conspire with Frank to commit the robbery, did not intend the robbery, and did not participate in the robbery. Thus, Choice **D** is the correct answer.

86. **A** There has been a continuing conflict in the cases over the misappropriation of funds by a lower-level employee who receives the funds from a third person rather than from his employer. Misappropriation by a bank teller, as in this question, furnishes a perfect example of this dilemma. Some cases hold that the teller receives funds from the bank's customers as custodian for the bank, which is said to have **constructive possession.** In these cases, the teller is found guilty of larceny rather than embezzlement because he comes into **possession** of the money only when he converts it for his own use. (In other words, when he takes it, we first have the elements of larceny—a trespassory taking and carry away.) The more widely accepted view is that since the teller is taking the money from a third person (the customer) rather than his employer (the bank), he has lawful possession, not custody, immediately and is therefore guilty of embezzlement when he keeps the money. The broad embezzlement statutes of many states make it embezzlement rather than larceny when an employee steals property which comes into his possession or "under his care." Under these statutes, even a lower-level employee would be guilty of embezzlement rather than larceny if he kept property which came into his posession. (*See* ELO Ch. 9-III(E)(2).) The best answer is Choice **A.** Choice **B** is incorrect for the reasons we have stated. Choice **D** is incorrect because the crime of larceny by trick requires that the accused acquire posession of the property by fraud or deceit. Choice **C** is incorrect because Bill's actions do not satisfy the elements of the crime of false pretenses. These require the passage of title to property as a result of a false representation of a material fact by a person who knows that the fact is false. (*See* ELO Ch. 9-IV(A).)

87. **D** The common-law crime of conspiracy requires an **agreement** between two or more persons to commit a crime. The components of the crime are the agreement, a criminal objective, and a culpable intent (*mens*

rea). (*See* ELO Ch. 6-I(A).) Knowledge is not agreement. The mere fact that Maud was informed by Mick of his intent to rob Jim, does not amount to an agreement by her to join in the crime. On the contrary, Maud specifically stated she could not participate because her license had been revoked. The correct answer is Choice **D**. Choice **A** is incorrect. In the absence of a statute making it a crime not to inform the police when a person acquires knowledge that a crime is about to be committed, there is no requirement that the police be informed. A co-conspirator may have an obligation to inform the police if she wishes to withdraw from the conspiracy, but Maud was not a conspirator. Choice **B** is incorrect because the receipt of stolen property does not make the recipient guilty of conspiracy in the crime which produced the property. Maud would, however, be guilty of the crime of stolen property. The elements of this crime are the *receipt of stolen property* with *knowledge* that the *property is stolen* and with *the intent to deprive* the owner of his property. (*See* ELO Ch. 9-VI(B).) All these elements are satisfied by Maud's actions in taking some of the stolen funds. Finally, Choice **C** is incorrect because the crime of conspiracy is complete when the agreement is made. It does not require that the accused participate in the commission of the target crime, or even that she be present.

88. D Anyone who aids or abets in the commission of a crime becomes an *accomplice* to the crime and is guilty of the commission of that crime. (*See* ELO Ch. 7-II(A).) The facts of each case will determine whether the accused has actually aided and abetted in the commission of the crime. Even words of encouragement may be enough. The failure to intervene when the accused is told of the ensuing crime, or to speak out against the crime, is generally not enough. The question before us presents a close call. Sue was not only told by Mick that he was about to rob Jim, but did actively encourage him by disparaging Jim and announcing that she would gladly participate in the crime if she could. Except that she was not present at the crime, she is not very different from the mother who is judged guilty of aiding and abetting her husband when she stands by and watches him abuse their child. (*See* ELO Ch. 7-II(4)(a).) Nevertheless, she is probably not guilty because she did not evidence the intent *to bring about the robbery*, i.e., to associate herself with the robbery, to help bring it about, or to make it succeed. *U.S. v. Peoni,* 100 F.2d 401 (2d Cir. 1938). (*See* ELO Ch. 7-III(C)(1).) On this analysis, Choice **D** is the correct answer. Choice **A** is incorrect because an accused does not become an accomplice simply because he has knowledge that a crime is to be committed or because he fails to notify the intended victim. Choice **B** is incorrect because a person does

not become an accomplice simply because he fails to inform the police
of an impending crime which he has not aided or abetted. Finally,
Choice **C** is incorrect for the reasons stated in our analysis of the
knowledge and intent required for accomplice liability.

89. C   The crime of conspiracy requires an agreement between two or more
persons to commit either an unlawful act or a lawful act by unlawful
means. (*See* ELO Ch. 6-I(A).) Since the essence of a conspiracy is an
agreement between two or more parties, the acquittal of one defendant in a conspiracy involving only two people would appear to man-
date acquittal of the other defendant. The courts do, therefore, grant
automatic acquittal when the two are tried together and one is found
innocent. The rationale is that the jury cannot legally find "agreement" if one of the two is found not to have agreed.This rationale does
not apply when the conspirators are tried separately, which happens
often. If they are tried separately, one accused may be convicted of
conspiracy even if the other is acquitted. In separate trials, there are
different juries who have heard different evidence and are entitled to
reach different conclusions. (*See* ELO Ch. 6-VIII(E).) Under the unilateral view of the Model Penal Code, which makes each conspirator
separately culpable for his own agreement, it is an open question
whether one conspirator might be acquitted and the other convicted
even in the same trial. M.P.C. § 5.03, Comment 2(b). (*See* ELO Ch. 6-
VIII(E)(5).) Mick can be convicted of conspiracy even after Bill's
acquittal. With respect to the crime of robbery, because the crime can
be committed by one person acting alone and we do not know the
facts and circumstances which the jury considered in acquitting Bill,
the acquittal would not preclude Mick's trial or conviction. The correct answer is Choice **C**, because it includes both crimes. Choices **A, B,**
and **D** are incorrect because they do not rely on both crimes.

90. C   The crime of common law burglary requires the **breaking and entering** of the **dwelling house** of **another** at **night** with the **intent** to commit a felony**. (*See* ELO Ch. 9-VII(A).) For purposes of this question,
the key elements are **breaking** and **felony**. A breaking occurs when the
accused creates the opening which permits entry. If the owner leaves
his door wide open, as in this case, there can be no breaking and no
burglary. The correct answer is therefore Choice **C**. (*See* ELO Ch. 9-
VII(B).) (Note, however, that many states have eliminated the **breaking** requirement for burglary). At first impression, it may appear that
Choice **D** is the correct answer because John did not intend a larceny.
However, it is not necessary for the crime of burglary that **larceny** be
the intended crime; any **felony** will do. Because John intended to strike

Michael with a hammer, a dangerous instrument, he certainly intended a criminal battery. Choices **A** and **B** are incorrect because even though the facts stated are true and both Choices identify elements of burglary, it is also true that another element essential to common law buglary—the **breaking** element—is still missing.

91. **C** The question tests the various elements which divide homicides into different crimes. The homicide characterized as murder occurs when it is the **killing** of one human being **caused** by another with the **intent** (**mens rea**) to **kill** or **cause** the victim **serious bodily harm**. (*See* ELO Ch. 8-II(B).) The facts clearly establish that John intended to use the hammer on Michael, did in fact hit Michael repeatedly with the hammer, and did in fact cause his death. Since all the elements of murder are satisfied, Choice **C** is the correct answer. Choice **A** is incorrect. Although voluntary manslaughter requires all the elements of murder, it is a homicide which is reduced from murder to manslaughter upon proof by the accused that he acted in the heat of passion, or was otherwise reasonably provoked. (*See* ELO Ch. 8-V(B),(C).) Here, John did not even know for certain that Michael had indeed taken the tools and power saw. And a reasonable person would not be likely to kill with a hammer in response to a theft of tools. (*See* ELO Ch. 9-V(D).) Choice **B** is incorrect because an intentional killing (one committed with intent to kill or to inflict serious bodily harm) cannot be **involuntary** manslaughter, which is based instead on a homicide resulting from criminal negligence or recklessness (*See* ELO Ch. 8-VI(A).) Finally, Choice **D** is incorrect because there was no legally sufficient excuse for John to kill Michael. (*See* ELO Ch. 4-III, IV) for an extended discussion of the rules relating to homicides committed out of necessity or in self-defense.)

92. **A** The common law crime of arson consists of the malicious (i.e. intentional or reckless) burning of the dwelling of another. A person acts recklessly if he consciously disregards a substantial and unjustifiable risk of harm or injury. (*See* ELO Ch. 1-II(H).) The burning of any part of the house is sufficient for arson. "Charring" constitutes "burning". It was reasonable to assume that setting fire to the sofa would result in the spread of fire to other parts of the contents and structure, especially because John intended that the fire consume both the sofa and the bodies of Anne and Michael. John is guilty of a fire maliciously set with reckless disregard for the dwelling. The correct answer is Choice **A**. Choice **B** is incorrect because the crime of arson is an independent crime which does not have to be supported or accompanied by another felony; besides, John was not involved in the commission of a

burglary because there was no breaking. Choice **C** is incorrect because it's not necessary that "substantial" damage result to the dwelling for an arson to occur; charring is usually sufficient to satisfy the burning requirement. Finally, Choice **D** is incorrect because the requsite malicious intent (*mens rea*) is supplied by John's reckless and unreasonable indifference to the reasonably foreseeable consequences of setting fire to the sofa.

93. **C**   The crime of murder can result from the commission of a felony when the felony results in a killing, even if the killing is accidental. Here, John had just committed two felonies—criminal battery upon Michael and the murder of Michael. The homicide which results during the commission of another felony is called felony-murder. Because Anne was present during the attack on Michael and saw him fall, her death constitutes felony-murder. This is true especially because John's actions were ***inherently dangerous***. (*See* ELO Ch. 8-III(B)(2)(a).) The correct answer is Choice **C**. Choice **A** is incorrect because voluntary manslaughter is appropriate only in situations in which a crime which has all the elements of murder is deemed justified by some external factor (e.g., adequate provocation). Because there was no reasonable provocation on these facts for John's attack on Michael, voluntary manslaughter is inapplicable. Choice **B** is incorrect because a charge of involuntary manslaughter is appropriate in the case of a homicide resulting from the commission of a misdemeanor, not a felony. This is called misdemeanor-manslaughter. (*See* ELO Ch. 8-VI(B).) Choice **D** is wrong because the victim's death may be accidental or fortuitous; if it results during the commission of an inherently dangerous felony, it is felony-murder.

94. **B**   *See* Answer 93 above for a discussion of the elements constituting felony murder. Because the felony of arson is an inherently dangerous felony, any death resulting from its commission would be classified as felony murder. (*See* ELO Ch. 8-III(B)(2)(a).) John is guilty of the felony murder of Ellwood, the first firefighter to arrive on the scene. An accused who commits arson can expect that injury or death will occur to any resident of the building as well as to firefighters who arrive to fight the fire. This is because these deaths are the natural and probable consequences of the act of setting fire to an occupied building. (*See* ELO Ch. 8-III(C)(3).) Deaths involving firefighters have been deemed to satisfy the elements of probable cause in setting a fire. *State v. Glover*, 50 S.W.2d 1049 (Mo. 1932). Choice **B** is the correct answer. Choice **A** is incorrect because John's suspicions that Michael had stolen his tools are irrelevant to the crimes committed by John. His suspi-

cions were not sufficient justification for the crimes of murder and arson. Choice **C** is incorrect because under the felony-murder rule, the intent (*mens rea*) necessary to commit the felony is **deemed sufficient to meet the mens rea requirement for murder.** *(See* ELO Ch. 8-III(A).) Finally, Choice **D** is incorrect because the missing power saw could not be construed by any reasonable person as sufficient provocation for a severe beating resulting in death.

95. **C**   Agnes married Clyde while she was still legally married to Fred. Unless she comes within one of the exceptions listed in Section II of the law, she is guilty of bigamy. Because Fred left only four years prior to Agnes's marriage to Clyde, the five-year period required by Section II(b) of the statute is not satisfied. Because Clyde was an unmarried individual, he can escape liability under Section III of the statute if he did not have actual knowledge of the circumstances constituting the departure of Fred and the length of his absence. Clyde was entitled to rely on Agnes's assurances to him, and he was not required to conduct his own independent investigation into Fred's departure. Choice **C** is the correct answer because Agnes is guilty of bigamy and Clyde is innocent. Choice **A, B** and **D** are incorrect because they are inconsistent with the facts.

96. **B**   John relied on his attorney's incorrect advice and married Lois while he was still legally married to Betty under the laws of North Dakona. What liability does a person have for actions committed in ignorance of the law, especially when he has relied on incorrect advice from his attorney? In general terms, "ignorance of the law is no excuse." However, the modern cases sometimes allow the defense if the ignorance negates the mental state required for a material element of the crime. Because the mental state required for marriage is a sincere belief that one is not then already married, it would appear that John's reliance on his attorney's advice was justified and that he is not guilty of bigamy. This would probably be the result under the Model Penal Code. M.P.C. § 2.04(1). But society has a special interest in preventing adultery and bigamy, and most courts would find John guilty. *State v Woods*, 179 A. 1 (Vt. 1935). (*See* ELO Ch. 1-II(L)(4).) [But, see for the contrary view ELO, Ch. 1-II(L)(8)(a); *People v. Vogel*, 299 P.2d 850 (Cal. 1956); *Long v. State*, 65 A.2d 489 (Del. 1949).] On the facts, John would be guilty of bigamy in most jurisdictions, although he could argue that the same "knowingly" test contained in Section III of the statute should also be applied to him. Lois is clearly guilty of bigamy because she proceed "knowingly", despite the advice of her lawyer that John was still legally married to Betty. She does not come within

the exception provided by Section II of the statute. The correct answer is Choice **B**—both John and Lois are guilty. The other Choices — **A, C,** and **D** — are all incorrect on the facts and the law in most jurisdictions.

97. B The facts of this question may be misconstrued as raising the simple issue of ignorance of the law, which is not normally a defense to a complaint of bigamy. However, on analysis, they do not really involve ignorance of the law. Roger knew the law—he knew that he was required to wait for a final decree of divorce before he could remarry. His mistake related not to the law, but to a collateral fact—was the document he received a final decree or something else? When there is a mistake as to a collateral fact, the courts are more willing to hold that the mistake negates the mental state required for a material element of the crime. (*See* ELO Ch. 1-II(L)(8).) *People v. Weiss,* 12 N.E.2d 514 (N.Y. 1938). This view would be especially applicable under this statute, which shows the intent of the legislature to require "knowledge" in the case of unmarried persons who married in ignorance of circumstances suggesting bigamy. Because Roger did not have the mental state required for bigamy, he is not guilty. The correct answer is Choice **B**, which recognizes that Roger is relying on a mistake of collateral fact. Choice **A** is wrong because Roger was not really ignorant of the law. Choice **C** is wrong because it relies in part on the defense of ignorance of the law. Choice **D** is wrong because Roger is not guilty for the reasons cited.

98. C The question deals with the effect of intoxication on the mental state required for the commission of a criminal act such as bigamy. If the intoxication is involuntary, a strong argument can be made that the accused cannot possibly have the required intent. The issue is more difficult when the intoxication is voluntary. However, increasingly, courts are holding that intoxication, voluntary or involuntary— although clearly not an excuse for crime—is a valid defense because it negates the intent necessary for the crime (*See* ELO Ch. 3-IV(B).) Section III of the statute states that an unmarried person can be convicted only if she **knowingly** marries another under circumstances that would make the other individual guilty of bigamy. Peggy believed that Susan had died. Her intoxication prevented her from knowing that she might be alive. Therefore, she did not have the knowledge required by the statute. The excuse of intoxication—even voluntary intoxication— has been recognized even in crimes of violence (rape, murder) and should be recognized on these facts which show only that Peggy had no recollection of being told of Susan's letter. Choice **C** is correct because Peggy did not have the knowledge necessary under the statute. Choice **A** is incorrect because Peggy would have an even better excuse if her intoxication were involuntary. Choice **B** is incorrect because even her voluntary intoxication nullifies knowledge. Choice **D** is wrong because Peggy's intoxication negates the required element of knowledge.

Table of References to the Model Penal Code

Index

References are to the number of the question raising the issue.
"E" indicates an Essay Question; "M" indicates a Multiple-Choice Question